How to Practice Dharma

FPMT LINEAGE is a series of books of Lama Zopa Rinpoche's teachings on the graduated path to enlightenment (*lam-rim*) drawn from his four decades of discourses on the topic based on his own textbook, *The Wish-fulfilling Golden Sun,* and several traditional lam-rim texts and in general arranged according to the outline of *Liberation in the Palm of Your Hand*. This series will be the most extensive contemporary lam-rim commentary available and comprises the essence of the FPMT's education program.

The FPMT LINEAGE SERIES is dedicated to the long life and perfect health of Lama Zopa Rinpoche, to his continuous teaching activity and to the fulfilment of all his holy wishes.

May whoever sees, touches, reads, remembers, or talks or thinks about these
books never be reborn in unfortunate circumstances, receive only rebirths
in situations conducive to the perfect practice of Dharma,
meet only perfectly qualified spiritual guides, quickly develop
bodhicitta and immediately attain enlightenment
for the sake of all sentient beings.

FPMT LINEAGE SERIES

Lama Zopa Rinpoche

How to Practice Dharma
Teachings on the Eight Worldly Dharmas

Edited by Gordon McDougall
Series editor Nicholas Ribush

LAMA YESHE WISDOM ARCHIVE • BOSTON
www.LamaYeshe.com

A non-profit charitable organization for the benefit of all
sentient beings and an affiliate of the Foundation for
the Preservation of the Mahayana Tradition
www.fpmt.org

First published 2012

Lama Yeshe Wisdom Archive
PO Box 636
Lincoln
MA 01773, USA

Library of Congress Cataloging-in-Publication Data

Thubten Zopa, Rinpoche, 1945-
How to practice dharma : teachings on the eight worldly dharmas / Thubten Zopa ;
edited by Gordon McDougall; series editor, Nicholas Ribush.
pages cm. — (FPMT lineage series)
Includes bibliographical references and index.
Summary: "This book is drawn from Lama Zopa Rinpoche's graduated path to
enlightenment teachings given over a four-decade period, starting from the early 1970s,
and deals with the eight worldly dharmas, essentially how craving desire and attachment
cause us to create problems and suffering and how to abandon these negative minds in
order to find perfect peace and happiness" —Provided by publisher.
ISBN 978-1-891868-28-3
1. Dharma (Buddhism) 2. Religious life—Buddhism. 3. Thubten Zopa,
Rinpoche, 1945- I. McDougall, Gordon, 1948- II. Title.
BQ4190.T58 2012
294.5'48—dc23
2012020805

ISBN 978-1-891868-28-3

10 9 8 7 6 5 4 3 2 1

Cover and interior photographs by Carol Royce-Wilder:
Lama Zopa Rinpoche at Lake Arrowhead, California, 1975
Line drawing by Lama Zopa Rinpoche
Designed by Gopa & Ted2 Inc.

♻ Printed in the USA with environmental mindfulness on 30% PCW recycled paper.
The following resources have been saved: 21 trees, 618 lbs. of solid waste, 9,742 gallons of
water, 2,160 lbs. of greenhouse gases and 9 million BTUs of energy. (papercalculator.org)

Contents

Publisher's Acknowledgments

─────────── ⚜ ───────────

I WOULD LIKE to say a little about how the FPMT Lineage Series has come about.

My first Kopan course was the third, October-November, 1972. When we arrived we were given a text book, Lama Zopa Rinpoche's *The Wish-Fulfilling Golden Sun of the Mahayana Thought Training*, and Rinpoche's month-long teachings were essentially a commentary on this book. I took fairly sketchy notes but at the end of the course realized that the *Golden Sun* and Rinpoche's teachings had changed my life. However, the book was pretty rough, so after the course I asked Rinpoche if I could edit it into better shape. He said that what we had been given was basically a compilation of the students' notes from the previous course and that what he really wanted to do was to rewrite the whole thing from beginning to end and asked me if I would like to help him do that.

For six weeks my friend Yeshe Khadro and I spent several hours a day with Rinpoche as he painstakingly revised the entire book. In the evenings she would type up what we had written down and I would then try to edit the manuscript into publishable form. By the time the fourth course arrived in March 1973 the first official edition was ready and Rinpoche taught from that. This time I took better notes than the first time and Brian Beresford's notes were even better than mine.

That summer a few of us went up to Lawudo and while I was there I edited Brian's notes and mine into a commentary to the *Golden Sun*. In doing so I realized how much of Rinpoche's precious teachings we had missed and determined to get more of them down next time. In those days we had no electricity or tape recorders at Kopan, so at the fifth Kopan course, November 1973, I plopped myself down right in front of Rinpoche's throne and basically wrote down every word he said. My notes were a horrible scrawl and I made up abbreviations as I went along, and by the end of the course I'd filled several Indian notebooks with fairly illegible hieroglyphics. Miraculously, however, Yeshe Khadro could read it perfectly and dutifully typed it all up. I edited this as well and in early 1974 we printed two volumes of *Meditation Course Notes,* Rinpoche's teachings on the *Golden Sun* from the third, fourth and fifth courses. Looking back, this was the beginning of not only the Lama Yeshe Wisdom Archive but Wisdom Publications as well.

By the time the sixth course arrived in March 1974 we had a primitive little Panasonic tape recorder and unreliable Indian batteries, but this just served as a backup to Sally Barraud, who took the whole course down in shorthand. She typed it up, I edited it, and back in the USA, Pam Cowan typed the stencils. In 1975 we published *Meditation Course Notes, Volume 3.* All this, and most of the subsequent Kopan courses are now available on the LYWA website, LamaYeshe.com.

Lama Yeshe and Lama Zopa Rinpoche started traveling the world in 1974 and their students began recording and transcribing their teachings wherever they went. By the time the Lamas got back to Kopan for the seventh course in November, we had electricity. Thus we began building up our collection of tape recordings and transcripts of our Lamas' precious teachings. Between courses, I did more work with Rinpoche refining the *Golden Sun.* The last time we worked on it was during the Lamas' world tour of 1975. Rinpoche stopped using it at Kopan in the late '70s. The book as it then stood is also available on line.

Still, it was always my dream that one day we would publish a series of Rinpoche's complete teachings on the *lam-rim.* At first I thought we would base it on the *Golden Sun,* but when in 1991 *Liberation in the Palm of Your Hand* was published, its excellent outline became the natural choice, not just because it was available but because Rinpoche based many of his teachings on that text. However, the idea languished as there was never enough money to support the transcribers and editors we needed to do the work.

In 1996, Rinpoche asked me to establish the LYWA as a stand-alone FPMT entity and the idea of a series of his commentaries on the main lam-rim topics again became a possibility. After a couple of failed attempts to finance plans that would allow this to happen, in 2007 we came up with one that worked, thanks to an inexpressibly kind benefactor who offered us a $500,000 matching grant. That allowed us to hire the staff we needed to finally go ahead, especially Gordon McDougall, who has taken the lead in combing through nearly four decades of Rinpoche's teachings to compile his lam-rim commentaries, building on the previous "basketing" work done by Ven Trisha Donnelly and Tenzin Namdrol (Miranda Adams). He describes the process in his preface. You can see details of our "Publishing the FPMT Lineage" program on the LYWA website under "Current Projects."

In retrospect, the masterpiece *Heart of the Path*, Ven. Ailsa Cameron's wonderful editing of Rinpoche's guru devotion teachings published in 2009, can be seen as the first in this series. This book—Rinpoche's teachings on the eight worldly dharmas, a topic that doesn't actually fall into any classical lam-rim outline—is the second. It is to be followed by books on the perfect human rebirth, impermanence and death, the three lower realms, refuge, karma and beyond. The dream is a reality.

In our previous books and on our website we have mentioned in detail all the people who have made the ARCHIVE possible and continue to do so, so I won't repeat all that here. I would, however, like to thank those who directly supported the editing and printing of *How to Practice Dharma*— the Hao Ran Foundation, Taiwan, and Edwin Lau and Tan Cheng Guan of Singapore—our kind Publishing the FPMT Lineage benefactor again, and all the people who have made matching grants to this program. We still have a ways to go to match the entire grant, so if you would like to support the preparation of more of Lama Zopa Rinpoche's peerless lam-rim commentaries, please do so at LamaYeshe.com. Thank you so much.

Dr. Nicholas Ribush

Editor's Preface

ONE OF THE FIRST times I met Lama Zopa Rinpoche was when he visited Hong Kong in 1985. He was scheduled to teach lam-rim for five evenings but the group there asked him to also do a Highest Yoga Tantra initiation, which he agreed to do after the first evening. As a beginner, I left when the initiation was about to begin. The next day I was told that there had been no initiation, only more lam-rim teachings. And so it went, all week, with the initiates leaving the center in time to grab a quick breakfast and get to work, only to return in the evening for more of the same. On the final day, at the very end, he gave the initiation. Before he did, he apologized. "Your job is initiations," he said. "My job is lam-rim."

Lam-rim, the Tibetan term meaning the graduated path to enlightenment, is the very foundation of Buddhism. It is the systematic assembling of the Buddha's teachings and those of later great masters into a coherent and easily followed whole. The beauty of the lam-rim is its logic. We all want to be completely and perfectly happy, whether we label that enlightenment or not, but we are blocked. The lam-rim shows us exactly what we must do, laying out a step-by-step guide for taking us from where we are now to where we want to be.

In the eleventh century, King Jangchub Oe invited the renowned Indian scholar and yogi Atisha from the great monastic university of Vikramashila to Tibet to help revive Buddhism there. When he arrived the king explained that in Tibet the teachings had completely degenerated and begged Atisha not to give advanced teachings but basic ones instead; teachings that encompassed the entire path to enlightenment and would be easy for "uncivilized" Tibetans to practice. Consequently Atisha wrote *Lamp for the Path*, a short text that summarized all the Buddha's teachings on the steps to be taken to achieve buddhahood.

From that, the many other important lam-rim texts grew, in particular the fourteenth-century master Lama Tsongkhapa's *Lam-rim Chen-mo (The Great Treatise on the Stages of the Path to Enlightenment)*, which remains the seminal work on the lam-rim. In 1921, Pabongka Rinpoche taught what was to become *Liberation in the Palm of Your Hand*, another important lam-rim text. When these two great texts were finally translated into English, I was struck with just how familiar they seemed. I then realized that I had been listening to them for years, in the teachings of Lama Zopa Rinpoche.

The vastness and the depth of his knowledge is staggering. Recently, while editing this book, I watched a live streaming of Rinpoche from Paris, where he talked briefly about the eight worldly dharmas. What he was saying was word for word with what I had been just editing from a Kopan course he had taught thirty years before. That he never tires of telling us what we need to hear suggests to me that this is something we *really* need to hear.

Within the lam-rim structure, however, the teachings on the eight worldly dharmas barely rate, which is surprising, considering how important the subject is. Lama Tsongkhapa hardly mentions it and Pabongka Rinpoche gives it just three pages. My feeling is that it is a given, something so basic and known that it can just be glossed over in traditional teachings. (We can see this, too, with the four noble truths, the first and most fundamental discourse of the Buddha, which is just there in the background of traditional Tibetan Buddhist texts.)

When Lama Zopa Rinpoche started teaching Westerners he saw that this was a subject that we needed. Badly. He says that teaching the eight worldly dharmas was his "main hobby" during the early one-month Kopan meditation courses. That he is still teaching it today seems to show that we need it as much today as we did then.

Whereas Pabongka Rinpoche mentions the eight worldly dharmas in the context of his teachings on death, Lama Zopa Rinpoche usually talks about them in his teachings on the perfect human rebirth, specifically in the subsection of how this precious rebirth is useful and how following these worldly dharmas is such an incredible waste of our life.

Quite early in the piece the students at Kopan recognized the importance of recording Lama Yeshe's and Lama Zopa Rinpoche's teachings in full, and over the decades we have collected almost 2,000 teachings—ranging from a single evening's discourse to a full three-month teaching retreat. This collection was formalized in 1996, when Lama Zopa Rinpoche established the

LAMA YESHE WISDOM ARCHIVE. In 2007, *Publishing the FPMT Lineage* commenced, a project to make all Lama Zopa's lam-rim teachings available. The aim is to extract the individual lam-rim topics from all the teachings recorded, assemble, edit and publish them in a series of books. Until now the ARCHIVE has generally published edited teachings of one course, but with *Heart of the Path*, this book and the ones to follow, we will offer a comprehensive presentation of everything Rinpoche has said on each lam-rim topic.

How to Practice Dharma was created in this fashion. Having collected as many of Rinpoche's teachings on the eight worldly dharmas as possible, I assembled them into topics. While most of the FPMT Lineage Series books will follow the outline in *Liberation in the Palm of Your Hand*, an outline Rinpoche himself used in the very first Kopan courses, since Pabongka Rinpoche said very little about the eight worldly dharmas, I had to devise a logical structure to the book without it.

Because Rinpoche gave his most extensive teachings on the eight worldly dharmas at the sixth Kopan course in the spring of 1974, I made that the template and added to it teachings from the other Kopan courses. I then "trawled" the entire ARCHIVE to find whatever else Rinpoche had said on the topic and built that into the template course, like a sculptor adding layer and layer of clay to make a well-shaped statue.

The whole text was then edited. I have tried to maintain the informal, experiential style that Rinpoche uses and have included many of the anecdotal and almost parable-like stories that often pepper his discourses.

The edited text comes from verbatim transcripts that have been checked for accuracy, so we can be confident that what is here is exactly what Rinpoche taught. Mistakes and confusions belong one hundred per cent to the editor. When Rinpoche offers textual quotations, however, they should be regarded more as paraphrases than word-for-word translations. When he cites a text, I have listed its title in English only, the one exception being *Lam-rim Chen-mo*, which is better known to many people than the much longer English title. For the Sanskrit or Tibetan title, please see the bibliography.

When I first started working on this project I familiarized myself with the ARCHIVE's vast collection of teachings by going on a virtual tour around it. It looked a little bit like the Matrix at first, but there is a way to translate it and when accessed we find file after file after file, both audio and transcript, stacked up like skyscrapers, each one representing many hours of painstaking time by a transcriber and a checker, not to mention the time and effort put in by the center hosting the teaching and the people recording it. The work done by the LYWA team and its supporters over the decades is truly staggering.

I worked from over two hundred ARCHIVE documents, using excerpts from about sixty for the final edit.[1] How many hours of labor does that represent for all the many people involved? And how many people have actually been involved in the creation of this book? I can't start to name names; there are just too many. All I can do is offer each and every one of you who have given so much a huge thank you.

But most of all, I wish to thank from the bottom of my heart Lama Zopa Rinpoche, the inspiration for all this, the source of all this incredible knowledge. To me he is a living example of how one person can make a huge difference and how everything is possible when one's mind has compassion and wisdom. May whatever small merit gained from the creation of this book be dedicated to his continued long life, health and the attainment of all his holy wishes.

Bath, England
September 2010

---

[1] From the 1972 second Kopan course to the 2009 Mani retreat at Institut Vajra Yogini, the ARCHIVE numbers used for the final edit are: 005, 017, 022, 027, 028, 029, 081, 091, 092, 107, 111, 144, 158, 163, 170, 181, 266, 280, 328, 333, 335, 350, 394, 395, 436, 476, 488, 511, 513, 514, 576, 582, 634, 758 , 823, 855, 856, 872, 946, 1047, 1055, 1061, 1067, 1159, 1227, 1229, 1240, 1331, 1344, 1372, 1379, 1391, 1420, 1443, 1472, 1580, 1604, 1605, 1606, 1700, 1783. (Get more information about the teachings these numbers denote by using the "Search the Archive Database" function on the LamaYeshe.com homepage.)

1. Discovering the Meaning of Dharma

A̲ttachment to the happiness of this life is the cause of all our problems. It is the cause of every individual person's problems, every family's problems, every country's problems; it's the cause of all the global problems. The basic problems facing young people, teenagers, middle-aged people, elderly people—every problem we can think of—can be traced to this root, attachment to the happiness of this life. If we could read our own life story and remember all the pain we have gone through so many times in this life alone, it would be like a commentary on the shortcomings of desire, our attachment to sense pleasure.

The basic message of Buddhism is renunciation of the thought of the *eight worldly dharmas*, the mind grasping at the four desirable objects and rejecting the four undesirable objects. The thought of the eight worldly dharmas is a mind solely concerned with the happiness of this life, and any action done with this motivation, even if it is meditating or praying, becomes nonvirtue, the cause of suffering. This is the very first thing we need to understand when we study Dharma, the very first thing we need to wake up to. Even in Tibetan monasteries, where monks and nuns gain so much Dharma knowledge through debating and memorizing thousands of root texts and commentaries on very profound subjects, they can still fail to discover this fundamental and crucial point.

Knowing what is Dharma and what is not Dharma—knowing the difference between holy Dharma and worldly action—is the most important understanding for us to have at the beginning of our spiritual journey, otherwise we can live in ignorance and cheat ourselves for our entire life.

I used to spend a lot of time teaching on the evil thought of the eight worldly dharmas during many of the early Kopan courses.[2] I'd spend weeks talking about it, finishing off with the hells, like ice cream with a cherry on top—the eight worldly dharmas were the ice cream and the hells were the cherry on top! Talking about the eight worldly dharmas used to be my main hobby in those early courses. I think I was a little bit selfish spending so much time on a subject in which I was so interested.

Now, of course, it's not like before. I've totally degenerated. Compared to how I was back then I've become absolutely lazy, but at that time I was able to do many things. One thing I did for a while was go to Lawudo to supervise the building of the Lawudo Retreat Center.

The person who lived there previously, the "Lawudo Lama,"[3] must have had a lot of energy—he received the initiations of many practices and teachings on the methods to achieve deities. He was a *ngagpa*, not a monk, and Tibetan, not Sherpa like me and the people of the area. He lived above Namche Bazaar in the cave behind Khumjung, on the other side of the mountain from the cave where a footprint of Padmasambhava—the great being who helped bring Buddhism to Tibet—and the syllable AH spontaneously appeared.

Before I left for Tibet,[4] the Lawudo Lama's son told me he would return all the Nyingma texts that had belonged to the Lawudo Lama, so when I arrived at Lawudo from Kathmandu in 1969 they were there in the cave. Most of the scriptures had been written by hand with much effort because in the past it was very difficult to get printed texts in that area. During a later visit I found a very special text called *Opening the Door of Dharma: The Initial Stage of Training the Mind in the Graduated Path to Enlightenment*.[5] A text on the fundamental practice of all four Tibetan traditions, it was composed by Lodrö Gyaltsen, a disciple of both Lama Tsongkhapa and Khedrub Rinpoche, one of Lama Tsongkhapa's two spiritual sons.

Opening the Door of Dharma is a collection of the Kadampa geshes' life

[2] The annual fall meditation courses held at the main monastery of the FPMT, Kopan Monastery in Kathmandu, Nepal, now usually taught by Lama Zopa Rinpoche and a Western teacher. The first one was in 1971.

[3] Lama Zopa Rinpoche is recognized as the reincarnation of the Lawudo Lama. See *The Lawudo Lama*.

[4] In 1957. Chapters 18 and 19 of *The Lawudo Lama* detail Rinpoche's journey and time in Tibet.

[5] This text is the basis of the book *The Door to Satisfaction*. In the prologue, Rinpoche says he discovered it during his 1974 visit to Lawudo. *The Lawudo Lama* (p. 237) has Rinpoche discovering *Opening the Door of Dharma* during his second visit in 1970.

stories and advice on how to practice Dharma based on their experiences and describes the initial stages of thought transformation, or mind training. Its main focus is on the distinction between worldly and spiritual activities and it shows clearly what should be practiced and what should be abandoned. The main emphasis is cutting off the thought of the eight worldly dharmas. I hadn't seen this text before that visit to Lawudo.

Not following desire is practicing Dharma; following desire is not practicing Dharma. It is as simple as that. Because the mind is a dependent arising, which means that it exists in dependence upon causes and conditions, our mind can be transformed in any way we choose; it's possible to gain realizations but that had not been my experience at all.

Up at Lawudo I was supposed to be watching the workers, checking whether they were cutting the stones to build the temple or just wasting time chatting. But since I couldn't read texts and supervise the workers at the same time, I finished up spending most of my time in the cave reading and they went mostly unsupervised. The only time I would see them was when I went for pipi, and most of the time they'd just be standing around chatting. But what could I say? I found it difficult to scold them. Somebody else might have been able to do that but to me, scolding seemed very strange.

Paying their wages also felt very strange because I was more accustomed to receiving money as offerings, not handing it out. I paid the workers every day at sunset, knowing that some of them had done very little or no work that day. I was the secretary, the bookkeeper—everything. I kept the money in a little plastic suitcase and it would go down, down, down, and when it had almost run out somebody would show up with more money and it would go up again. I did that job for a short while.

Anyway, later, reading *Opening the Door of Dharma* caused me to look back on my life. I was born in 1945 in Thangme, a village near Lawudo. When my father was alive my family might have had a bit of wealth but he died while I was in my mother's womb, so all I can remember is how terribly poor our family was. There was only my mother and my bigger sister to look after my brother, my other sister and me. It was very cold in the winter and I remember how the whole family would be wrapped in my father's old coat, as we did not have any blankets. My mother had debts and was hassled by tax collectors, so she made potato alcohol to sell.

When I was very small I had a natural interest in becoming a monk. I would sit on a rock pretending to be a lama. Because I was virtually alone

I was often rather bored, but I had one mute friend who was my everyday playmate. He was very good hearted and would pretend to be my disciple, taking initiations, doing *pujas*, sitting on the ground, serving food by mixing earth and stones with water. Maybe we were serving food to the thousands of Sera Je monks, a preparation for what came later.[6] It's possibly that children's games have some meaning, that the games they play reflect their interests and are somehow a preparation for the later life.

When I was four or five my uncle used to take me up to Thangme monastery, not far from my home, where I played and attended some of the prayers and initiations, although most of the time I just slept. This was still before I became a monk. I remember sitting in somebody's lap watching the lama's holy face, not understanding a word. He had a long white beard, like the long-life man in long-life pujas, and a very kind and loving nature. Sitting there dozing in a lap, I had a very good, deep feeling.

Because I was naughty I had two alphabet teachers, who were also my gurus, Ngawang Lekshe and Ngawang Gendun. Ngawang Lekshe had a beard. He used to carve really beautiful OM MANI PADME HUM mantras[7] on rocks by the side of the road for people to circumambulate, taking months to carve just one mantra on one rock.

He tried to teach me the alphabet, but when he'd go inside to make food the thought of escaping would come to me and I'd run home, I think because there I could play and there was nothing special I was expected to do. After two or three days my mother would send me back up to the monastery, carried up on somebody's shoulders.

Because I kept running away, my uncle sent me to Rolwaling, very close to the snow mountains and a very dangerous three-day journey. The area is very beautiful and is regarded as one of the hidden places of Padmasambhava as it contains many of his caves and his throne as well.

I stayed there for seven years, returning home only once. I took the eight Mahayana precepts every morning, memorized Padmasambhava prayers and read long scriptures such as the *Diamond Cutter Sutra* all day long. I read that one many times. Besides mealtimes, I would distract myself whenever I could. When I went out for pipi or kaka, I would play a little bit and

[6] One of Rinpoche's many current projects is offering three vegetarian meals a day to the 2,600 monks of Sera Je Monastery in south India. In the past twenty years over fifteen million meals have been served.
[7] The mantra of Chenrezig, the Buddha of Compassion.

stay out as long as possible. When my teachers would go out to cut trees for firewood in the forest, I would collect twigs, take them back to the monastery, line them up as if they were my lamas and play music to them with two round things representing cymbals. I wasn't actually reciting prayers from memory, just imitating the chanting.

When I had to read all the volumes of the *Prajnaparamita* and other texts people asked me to read for pujas, such as the *Kangyur*, I was also very naughty. The many big texts belonged to the monastery, but because I was often left alone I would sometimes draw black circles on them with charcoal. I can't remember whether my teacher beat me for that or not.

When I was about ten years old I went to Tibet, to Domo Geshe Rinpoche's monastery in Phagri,[8] where I was ordained. In the mornings I memorized texts or the prayers that had to be recited at the monastery; in the afternoons I went to puja in the monastery or did pujas at the houses of benefactors. There were two volumes of texts to be memorized; I memorized one but not the other. Nevertheless, I did well in my memorization examination.

By the time I did my exam, Tibet had already been overtaken by the Communist Chinese. Lhasa had already been taken and they were coming to our area, so it was decided we should escape. Many of the monks were very frightened by the danger ahead but I was very happy. I couldn't see any reason to be afraid. We escaped in the middle of the night. There was a little bit of snow and a lot of mud, which sometimes sucked our legs down. It felt like there were nomads and Chinese spies everywhere, dogs barked as we passed by, but nobody in our party spoke. Perhaps they were all meditating. The next day we crossed the Bhutanese border and the following day the thirty or forty of us arrived in India.

I was in Buxa Duar[9] for eight years, and during all that time I didn't really study Dharma. I wasted a lot of time painting and learning English in my own way, like memorizing the words of Tibetan texts. Once I tried to memorize a whole dictionary; I started but couldn't finish.

I spent most of the time playing or washing in the river. At night the monks washed under a tap, but during the day we went to the river, mainly because it was unbelievably hot. All the monks put their red and yellow

[8] See *The Lawudo Lama*, p. 168 ff. for the detailed story.
[9] The refugee camp in West Bengal where many Tibetan monks and nuns stayed when they fled Tibet after the Chinese takeover of 1959.

robes on the bushes and swam in just their shorts. When you looked down on the river from the mountain above, the robes on the bushes looked like flowers. During those years I took teachings, memorized texts and did some debating, but it was like a child playing. Later, just as my debating skills were starting to develop, I became sick with TB and was sent to a school in Darjeeling, where I stayed for a long time for my health and learned a lot of different subjects.

Reviewing my whole life like this in the light of reading *Opening the Door of Dharma*, I could not find one single thing that had become Dharma.

In Tibet, my teacher had given me a commentary on the *Lama Tsongkhapa Guru Yoga*. He put it on the table and I read few pages, but of course there was no way I could understand it at the time as I had never read a complete lam-rim text or ever received teachings on one.

Now, all those years later in Lawudo reading *Opening the Door of Dharma,* I could see very clearly that in all my years as a monk I had never had any real understanding of what Dharma was. More than that, I could see that there was nothing I'd done before that wasn't a worldly dharma. It was a huge shock.

Just reading that text made an enormous difference. The next time I did a retreat there was a big difference in my mind. I felt much quieter, much calmer, more peaceful and had no expectations—just by understanding what Dharma was. In that way my retreat became a perfect retreat. Because I understood from this text how to practice Dharma, even the very first day of retreat was unbelievably peaceful and joyful. Because of a slight weakening of the eight worldly dharmas, there were fewer obstacles in my mind, like having fewer rocks blocking a road, which meant less interference to my practice. This is what makes a retreat successful. I hadn't studied the commentaries of the tantric practice I was doing, but somehow, because there were fewer problems in my mind, I was able to receive the blessings of the deity.

Now my mind has completely degenerated, but at that time, having thought a little about the meaning of *Opening the Door of Dharma*, I felt really uncomfortable when people came to make offerings. In Solu Khumbu the Sherpas would often bring offerings to the cave, filling the brass containers they usually use for eating or drinking *chang*[10] with corn (or whatever else they had). That text really made me afraid of receiving offerings!

[10] Tibetan beer.

In retreat after reading *Opening the Door of Dharma* I saw that, like molding dough in our hands, we can definitely turn our mind whichever way we want; we can train it to turn this way or that. By habituating our mind to the Dharma we can definitely gain realizations. Even the immediate small change of mind that happened during my retreat was logical proof that it's possible to achieve enlightenment.

As Kirti Tsenshab Rinpoche, holder of the entire holy Buddhadharma, said, the *Kangyur*, the teachings of the Buddha, and the *Tengyur*, the commentaries by the Indian pandits, are solely to subdue the mind. The evil thought of the eight worldly dharmas, the desire clinging to this life, is what interferes with our practice of listening to teachings, reflecting on their meaning and meditating on the path they reveal. This evil thought is what makes our Dharma practice so ineffectual. The purpose of *Opening the Door of Dharma* and other texts like it is to completely reverse that way of thinking. These texts are therefore considered thought transformation, or mind training, texts.

In fact, the whole lam-rim, the graduated path to enlightenment, is thought transformation. Its main purpose is to subdue the mind. This is why, when other teachings have little effect, hearing or reading the lam-rim can subdue our mind.

What prevents us from generating the graduated path to enlightenment in our mind? What keeps us from having realizations? From morning to night, what stops our actions from becoming holy Dharma? It's the thought of the eight worldly dharmas, the desire that clings to the happiness of this life alone. This is what stops us from achieving lam-rim realizations, from the fundamental realizations of guru devotion and the perfect human rebirth[11] up to enlightenment.

We need to train our mind by reflecting on the shortcomings of worldly concern and the infinite benefits of renouncing it. In particular, we need to train our mind by meditating on impermanence and death. If we do this initial thought training we'll open the door of Dharma. Then, without difficulty, we'll be able to practice Dharma and succeed at whatever we wish, whether it's a retreat or any other Dharma practice. All our actions will become Dharma.

---

[11] The first two lam-rim topics and therefore the first ones we need to realize.

2. The Eight Worldly Dharmas

THE DISSATISFIED MIND OF DESIRE

WHETHER WE ARE a Dharma practitioner or not, every problem in life comes from our own mind, as does every happiness. The cause of suffering is not external; the cause of happiness is not external. The cause of what we experience is within us, in our mind.

And what is that particular thing that creates every problem we experience in life? It is the dissatisfied mind of desire, the mind clinging to this life. We try to obtain the immediate happiness of this life through what are called the eight worldly dharmas: desire for comfort, material things (such as gifts, friends and so forth), a good reputation and praise, and aversion to lack of comfort and material things, a bad reputation and criticism, or blame.

Wealth is not a problem; the problem is having desire for wealth. Friends are not a problem; attachment to our friends is. Objects become a problem for us because of the emotional mind of desire. When desire, the thought of the eight worldly dharmas, is there, not only does a lack of wealth cause us problems but so too does having wealth. When we are controlled by the thought of the eight worldly dharmas, we're miserable and lonely without friends but having friends does not give us complete satisfaction either. When our mind is controlled by desire, neither having nor not having an object can bring anything but dissatisfaction.

It might seem that we know the distinction between happiness and suffering but in fact, when we see how we so constantly and diligently work toward bringing ourselves suffering, it is very clear that we really don't know at all.

Because of our attachment, we feel elated when we meet the four desirable objects and mistake this excitation for happiness. We fail to see that meeting these objects brings no calmness or peace in our heart. Instead, because we have not eradicated the dissatisfied mind of desire, we subject ourselves to constant mood swings and instability. Clinging is an uptight mind where we're painfully stuck to an object, unable to separate ourselves from it.

When our mind is overcome with desire, not only is the reality of the object obscured but we're also unable to see the shortcomings of desire itself. Seeing a friend in the distance, we're immediately lifted up by attachment as our mind labels and exaggerates the good qualities of the object: "How wonderful he[12] is! How gorgeous! How lucky I am to meet him on the street like this!" We grasp at objects of attachment as if they truly exist, adorning them and blocking our understanding of their true nature. We project all these exaggerated qualities onto that object walking toward us and hold the unrealistic expectation that he can make us truly happy.

When we first see our friend in the distance we see the body alone. Only after that do we recognize and then label that body "my friend." First we see the base; then we apply the label "friend" to that base; then we see the friend. But this is not how it appears. To us, the "friend" and the body walking toward us are inseparable, but in fact, "friend" is just a projection of our mind. Although it was our own mind that imputed the label "friend" onto the object, we believe what's merely a label to be reality and see the object as being more than an imputed friend; it seems to us to be a *real* friend. Then we say, "This is my friend."

To us that friend, rather than being a mere imputation of our mind, is something totally the opposite, totally contradictory. Walking toward us is a friend who intrinsically exists, completely independent of our mind. There *is* someone there, but that truly-existing friend is nothing more than a decoration, a projection, labeled on the base, the aggregates of the merely-imputed friend, caused by the negative imprint left on the mental continuum by past ignorance.

This is our fundamental confusion, and all the delusions that plague us

---

[12] Or she. A design fault with the English language is the third person singular indefinite. Historically, "he" has been taken as the default gender, and more recently "they" (with the ensuing confusion of plural verb for singular subject) has become fashionable. We, the editors, will simply swap the pronouns back and forth between genders.

and rob us of happiness—minds such as anger, jealousy and pride—grow from that. Misreading the object, we get stuck. As if intoxicated by a drug, we hallucinate a real, independent object where there is none. Under the control of the thought of the eight worldly dharmas, we see that merely-imputed friend as permanent and unchanging, as the true cause of our true happiness. This is our friend and he will never change. But change is natural and inevitable, and when something happens and he does change, we get shocked.

Confused about the nature of reality, we see impermanent things as permanent and so we suffer. Nobody gives us trouble but ourselves. We torture ourselves by not having realized reality, by not seeing things the way they really are. We perceive them in a way that is completely contradictory to reality and grasp onto these false appearances. In this way we become the creator of our own suffering.

Something that is only suffering in nature appears to us as happiness; something that is impermanent appears as permanent; something that is impure appears as pure; something that is not truly existent appears as truly existent. While we're clinging to these appearances, enjoying these objects with desire, they look good, but sooner or later they will cheat us. The final result of our relationship with them is only suffering. This is samsara. It seems good to have samsaric perfections, but since we have not renounced clinging to this life, we're bound to be deceived. Even after we've found our object of desire, it's never perfect; there's always something missing in our heart. The dissatisfied mind of desire robs us of our happiness.[13]

For most of us, success in life means success in obtaining the four desirable objects, but actually this is only success in achieving suffering, because desire by its very nature disturbs our mental continuum and causes dissatisfaction. Whether we're born as a human being or even a *deva*, whose sensual enjoyments are millions of times greater than those of the human realm, in reality there's only dissatisfaction.

When we're told that we have to give up desire, we feel as if we're being asked to sacrifice our happiness, that without desire there's no possibility of happiness and we're left with nothing, just ourselves, completely empty, like a deflated balloon. We feel as if we no longer have a heart in our body, as if we've lost our life.

---

[13] See Rinpoche's teachings on "Four Wrong Concepts" in *Bodhisattva Attitude* for more details on all this.

This is because we have not realized the shortcomings of desire. We have not recognized that the nature of desire is suffering. Desire itself is a suffering, unhealthy mind. Because of desire, our mind hallucinates and we're unable to see that there is another kind of happiness, a real happiness.

If obtaining an object of desire were real happiness, the more we had of it the happier we'd be, whereas in fact the opposite happens. Our pleasure in the object decreases until it becomes discernable suffering, such when we eat something: at first we enjoy it but if we just keep on eating, it soon turns to discomfort and then outright suffering.

The conditions come together and we encounter favorable objects, so we call it happiness, but under the surface there's a pain in our heart, a tightness in our chest. This mind is bound up tight, like a prisoner with his hands and legs tied with rope. There's no real peace even when we manage to meet an object of desire—our mind is still in the nature of suffering.

That's why it is vital that we understand the eight worldly dharmas. The more we recognize what's really going on in our mind, the more we understand the source of our problems. When we go to the East, there are problems; when we go back to the West, there are problems. Wherever we go there are problems and dissatisfaction. When we see this, we see the root of life's problems, the core delusion that creates them—for the individual, for society, for countries, for the world. Thinking that happiness comes from sense objects, worldly people are robbed of real happiness and satisfaction. The great pandit Aryadeva said,

> Worldly beings find it very difficult to see that happiness comes from renouncing this life. In that, they are extremely deceived.

We might achieve all the things that people commonly regard as signs of a successful life. We might have hundreds of thousands, millions or billions of dollars, which we consider success. We might receive praise, which we consider success. We might have comfort, food, clothing, shelter and so forth, which we consider success. We may have everything that people commonly call success. However, even achieving all these things is *still* suffering because we're clinging to them.

All the negative actions we do through pride, attachment and so forth, harming and even killing others, all the suffering and worry we have, is caused by the evil thought of the eight worldly dharmas. If we check up—like watching a movie—checking back and back to really find the cause of our problems, we'll find that they all stem from the attachment concerned with only the happiness of this life. This is a revelation, because we can at last see that all suffering (and happiness) comes from the mind, not from external phenomena.

In his *Lam-rim Chen-mo,* Lama Tsongkhapa said,

> We follow desire in the hope of getting satisfaction, but follow-ing desire leads only to dissatisfaction.

In reality, the result of following desire is only dissatisfaction. We try again and again and again, but true satisfaction is impossible.

Following desire is the major problem of samsara. It ties us to the cycle of death and rebirth continuously, causing us to experience the sufferings of the six realms over and over again, endlessly, never finding real satisfaction or peace. Having cancer or AIDS is nothing compared to being trapped forever in samsara by desire. The suffering caused by disease will end, but if, while we have this perfect human rebirth, we don't overcome desire, the suffering it causes will continue forever.

We should be terrified of the future rebirths that desire will bring, such as rebirth in the unbearable suffering of the lower realms or the endless dis-satisfaction of the upper realms. But instead of that, most of us only worry about the small transient sufferings of our present life and put all our effort into stopping them alone. However, working to obtain the happiness and avoid the suffering of just this life is negative, because the methods we use are negative. Whatever we do for just this life is done with the self-cher-ishing thought, the wish for samsaric pleasure, for the comfort of this life.

Because we're attached to pleasure, when we get sick we treat our sickness motivated only by the wish for the relief of our discomfort, nothing higher, so taking medicine becomes a negative action. When we feel hungry, we eat with self-cherishing, so that too becomes a negative action. If we get hot or cold, we turn on a fan or a heater with the same negative mind.

From morning to night we do everything with the self-cherishing mind. Inside the house, outside the house, getting dressed, walking around, talk-ing to people, working, eating, seeing things, shopping, going to bed—we do everything with self-cherishing.

Even though everything we do is motivated by the wish to obtain tem-poral happiness and avoid temporal problems, in fact, everything we do creates the cause of greater, continual suffering in the future. For countless previous lifetimes we've been carrying on like this, perpetuating the cycle of suffering, living fulltime with the thought of the eight worldly dharmas.

Unless we can break this cycle we will continue like this, doing the same thing on and on endlessly, because we're using entirely the wrong methods to deal with our immediate worldly problems. We're forever creating the causes for much greater suffering for ourselves. Really, we are crazy; completely crazy.

When lam-rim practitioners—those who have renounced the thought of the eight worldly dharmas and live in pure practice—look at us clinging to samsaric happiness, they see us as children playing, as completely hallucinated.

Look at children playing in the sand. They make piles of sand and give them labels, calling one pile "my house" and another "my car." They believe in their labels and grasp on to them, and when challenged, they argue and fight, as attachment, hatred and anger arise. Clinging to the eight worldly dharmas, we're just like children. In fact, we're completely childish. We cling to actions as if they have meaning, whereas they don't at all. We chase the meaningless in search of happiness; we believe the essenceless to have essence.

Perhaps we might think that even though it's not real happiness, as long as we're enjoying ourselves it doesn't matter; we're causing no harm. That's like seeing poison and labeling it medicine. We take it and get sick, mentally and physically. The result of clinging to temporary pleasures is agitation and lack of peace, lack of freedom. That's the nature of negative mind.

When we truly understand that all of life's problems are caused by the evil thought of the worldly dharmas, then, as we're all looking for happiness, it's only natural to renounce this one main cause of all our suffering. Doing so really brings peace into our mind and life. If we check, this becomes utterly apparent.

When we step on a thorn we recognize that the pain we feel comes from the thorn and that removing it will stop the pain. Similarly, as the eight worldly dharmas are the source of all our problems, renouncing them is the essential method, the root from which both this life's happiness and real peace come.

Any action we do is either Dharma, the cause of true happiness, or non-Dharma, the cause of suffering, and the distinction between the two is based solely on whether that action is motivated by the thought of the eight worldly dharmas or not. Thus, if we want to be happy, renouncing the evil thought of the eight worldly dharmas is the very first step we need to take.

THE DEFINITION OF THE EIGHT WORLDLY DHARMAS

"Dharma" is not just a name, it has great meaning. It is not a term owned by a religion such as Buddhism, Christianity, Hinduism and so forth. The pure practice of Dharma belongs to us all—it is created by the mind. It is the method shown to us by the enlightened being, the Buddha. It is the method he followed, practiced and experienced completely.

The Sanskrit term *Dharma* means "holding" or "guiding," so Dharma is that which leads us from the suffering of the three lower realms to the state of enlightenment. Each of us has to create our own essential practice of Dharma and become our own positive guide instead of an enemy to ourselves.

With the eight worldly dharmas the word "dharma" is used differently. Here *dharma* refers to an existent phenomenon. Specifically, it means "anything that holds its own nature," in other words, an inherently-existent phenomenon. To the ignorant mind each object holds its own nature. It sees a flower as truly existing without causes or conditions and hence holding its own nature; therefore, a "worldly" dharma is whatever the ignorant mind grasps on to as existing from its own side.

Thus there are two meanings for *dharma*. One is the method that leads to enlightenment, and one—this *dharma* of the eight worldly dharmas—is the dharma that keeps ordinary beings trapped in samsara.[14] These two are opposites.

A worldly dharma is an object of the thought of either attachment or aversion. It is either an object of worldly pleasure that we cling to and desire to have or an object of suffering that we dislike and desire to be free of or not experience. Having and not having comfort and pleasure, having and not having material things, having and not having a good reputation and hearing praise and hearing criticism—these are the four desirable and the four undesirable objects.

Because we cling to the four desirable objects and feel aversion for the

---

[14] LYWA's convention is to capitalize the Dharma that is the former and use a small d for the dharma that means existent phenomenon.

four undesirable ones, we are "worldly" beings, the opposite of somebody who lives within the holy Dharma and is a pure Dharma practitioner.

THE EIGHT WORLDLY DHARMAS

In *Letter to a Friend*[15] Nagarjuna describes the eight worldly dharmas:

> Gain, loss, happiness, unhappiness, fame, notoriety, praise and criticism: these eight worldly dharmas are not objects of my mind. They are all the same to me.

The eight worldly dharmas[16] are:

1. Craving for material possessions
2. Craving to be free from a lack of material possessions
3. Craving for happiness and comfort
4. Craving to be free from unhappiness and discomfort
5. Craving for a good reputation
6. Craving to be free from a bad reputation
7. Craving for praise
8. Craving to be free from criticism

These eight worldly dharmas (also called the eight worldly concerns) are the four desirable objects that we crave to have and the four undesirable objects that we crave to be free from.

Our usual mental confusion is this. We feel happy when we're in a pleasant, comfortable situation, we feel unhappy when we're in an unpleasant situation; we feel happy when we have the material possessions we desire, we feel unhappy when we don't have them; we feel happy when we have a good reputation, we feel unhappy when we have a bad reputation; we feel happy when we're praised, we feel unhappy when we're criticized.

---

[15] V. 29

[16] Over the many years that Rinpoche has taught the eight worldly dharmas he has used many terms to describe them. For instance, for material possessions he has also used material things, comfort, getting what you want. For happiness and unhappiness he has also used pleasure, interesting things, comfort; and suffering, uninteresting things, discomfort. For good and bad reputation he has also used fame, hearing sweet or interesting sounds; and being unknown, notoriety, hearing unsweet or uninteresting sounds. For praise and blame he has also used admiration and abuse, slander, criticism, puts you down (and its opposite "puts you up").

Loss of possessions, unhappiness and discomfort, a bad reputation and criticism are commonly recognized as problems but most people don't recognize that their opposites are also suffering: receiving material things, having comfort and happiness, having a good reputation and being praised. Without checking up, we meet a desirable object and call that pleasure; we say we're happy. We don't see that our mind is actually uptight.

Kadampa Geshe Gönpawa, who had clairvoyance and many other realizations, said,

> Receiving the four desirable results of comfort, material things, good reputation and praise due to actions motivated by the thought of the eight worldly dharmas is only for the transient pleasure of this life and has no benefit at all in future lives. Furthermore, such actions can also bring the four undesirable results and in that way be of no benefit even in this life as well.

We *believe* meeting any of the four desirable objects is happiness. We feel we are happy because we receive a present or meet a friend or a very flattering article has been written about us in a newspaper saying how educated or compassionate we are. Something pleasant happens and suddenly our mind gets lifted up and sticks tight to that object.

Here's an experiment. Watch your mind when you meet any of the four desirable objects. How does it feel at that time? When you look below the surface of the excitement and sense pleasure you'll see that it's never peaceful or relaxed but confused, agitated, disturbed. It's lifted up but also uptight, as if gripped by an iron glove. When there's attachment, concentration is impossible because the mind is not free, as it has sunk into the object. We call that tight, agitated mind "happiness" but it's just a different degree of suffering. By understanding its nature, we can understand clearly how, although we have received what we want, there's still something missing.

That is the nature of attachment. We're in pain, but it's different from the pain of sickness; it's the pain of attachment. This is hard to see or control because strong attachment is mixed with our experience of the object; it obscures us from seeing the object's real nature and what is happening in our mind. Wrapped as we are in desire for the object, we're unable to see that all the worry, aggression, unhappiness and fear we have in this life come from that desire, which is excessively concerned with the happiness of this life.

Clouded by desire, we fail to see that real happiness comes only when we're free from desire. Like an addict never thinks she can be happy without her drugs, we feel we need external objects to be happy and cannot see that there's another way. But if we read the biographies of lamas such as Milarepa, we can see how they attained great peace, stability and happiness by renouncing the eight worldly dharmas and that these qualities only increased; they never decreased. This is real peace. Even the root of the great inner peace, *nirvana*, starts from this fundamental first step of renouncing the eight worldly dharmas.

Gain and loss

To like something doesn't always mean being attached to it, but if we think of the material possessions we most treasure—money, cars, jewels and so forth—we'll probably see the strong attachment we have for them. And this is true of not just objects but friends as well. When we meet friends we feel a kind of pleasure and completely believe that it's real, true pleasure and don't recognize that there's attachment there as well.

We think that we receive real happiness from our friends or our precious objects but that mind of attachment is confused. The temporal happiness we get from attachment is not true happiness; it does not arise by diminishing desire but by following it, by making friends with desire.

Furthermore, whenever there's attachment there's fear of losing the object of attachment, and the stronger the attachment, the stronger the fear. If it's a material object, we always have to keep it in safe place and lock all the doors. Even if it never gets stolen or lost, we're constantly afraid it will be. If it's a friend, the greater our attachment the more worried we are that he or she might leave us.

With strong attachment, even if we live in a very luxurious house, wear very expensive clothes and eat delicious food, life has little taste. Our body is there but our mind is not happy. The greater our attachment to the four desirable objects, the greater our worry about meeting the four undesirable objects. And when we meet those undesirable objects we don't know what to do. Our life gets completely confused and we go crazy; perhaps we even see suicide as the only escape from our suffering.

We have the constant, nagging worry that the four undesirable objects are waiting for us just around the corner. They might not exist for us now— we haven't met the object of dislike yet and might in fact never meet it—but in our mind it's as if the problem were already there. And when something *really* happens to an object we cherish—it gets lost or destroyed or our friend leaves us—then the greater our attachment, the greater our suffering. We get incredibly upset, our mood plummets into depression and our whole face completely changes.

Think about some precious object to which you're attached. Do you have any anxiety about its being lost, stolen or destroyed? Even though you have that object and are never separated from it, even though that hasn't happened yet, are you still afraid that it will? Visualize that precious object or that precious friend. Visualize the object being destroyed or your friend dying and imagine how you'd feel, how it would affect your mind.

Let's say that we have a bowl to which we are very attached, whether it's a valuable antique or just an old cracked Tibetan one. One day we break it. Our mind gets incredibly upset; we become inconsolably unhappy. If we'd been less attached to the bowl, we'd suffer much less at its loss. On the other hand, if somebody steals our garbage, we're not worried at all; it doesn't shake our mind. Since we're not attached to it, losing our garbage doesn't cause our mood to plummet. Of course, it's always possible that there *are* people who are attached to their garbage and would be upset if it were stolen.

If we compare our lack of attachment to garbage to our attachment to a precious object and compare our lack of suffering at the loss of one to our intense suffering at the loss of the other, we can easily see that our suffering comes from attachment, not the loss of the object.

Whenever there's the thought of the worldly dharmas—clinging to shelter, food, clothing and so forth—there's worry and fear about losing them. Whenever there's attachment to comfort, there's fear of losing it; whenever there's attachment to receiving material things, there's fear of not receiving them; whenever there's attachment to praise, there's fear of being criticized; whenever there's attachment to a good reputation, there's fear of receiving a bad one. That's the fundamental suffering. Not having the four desirable objects is suffering, but so is having them and, because of attachment, being afraid of losing them.

We're in samsara, so of course we can't always get the objects we desire. We're constantly looking for the four desirable objects but more often meeting the four undesirable ones. This is not a new experience; in fact, it has been going on forever. The antiquities in a museum are absolutely nothing compared to this—no matter how old they might be, they originated after this world system started and we can still count their age in centuries or millennia. Our experience of meeting undesirable objects, on the other hand, started long before our current rebirth, even long before this world was created, and as long as we're not free from samsara we'll continue to encounter undesirable things and situations. That's the nature of our samsaric life.

As long as we rely on external objects such as consumer goods and praise for our happiness, we'll never find stability. The external world is always changing, so our reaction to it always changes too, up and down all the time—the sun shines, happy; the rain comes, unhappy; praise, happy; criticism, unhappy; good program on television, happy; boring program, unhappy. Whenever the conditions change our mind changes along with them, up and down, up and down, constantly.

Say it's Christmas and there's somebody who's usually very generous and always gives us a nice present. We come to expect presents from her, so when we see her our mind suddenly gets lifted up. That's a sign that we're attached to receiving material things. Then, one Christmas, for some reason she doesn't give us a present. We get confused. We make up all sorts of reasons for why she has neglected us and strong dislike for her arises in our mind. We complain to her face that she loves everybody but us. We shout at and criticize her. Perhaps we even spit in her face. If we're sitting at the table having dinner, even before we've finished eating, we hurl our plate to the floor, stamp our feet, run from the room to our bedroom and slam the door shut so loudly that everybody can hear. Then we throw ourselves onto our bed crying and complaining, criticizing her over and over, like a mantra. For hours and hours we recite the criticizing mantra. Thinking how she loves everybody else so much more, we get completely depressed and generate incredible anger toward this friend and jealousy toward everybody else. This is the work of the thought of the eight worldly dharmas.

With clinging, it seems that when we're in the middle of bad times they'll never end, but when there's no clinging we can see that it's not like that. If something unpleasant is happening, it doesn't bother us so much. If we cut off the desire clinging to this life through such basic techniques as meditating on impermanence and death, then even if the four undesirable things happen, it's no big deal.

We might have huge problems in our life—nobody in our family loves us, everybody hates us, we have to go to court and it looks as if we might have to spend the rest of our life in prison, we have a very bad reputation and everybody gossips about us, wherever we go in the street or at home everybody criticizes and refuses to help us—and in our mind it might appear that this is going to last forever, as if it's permanent, but in reality this life is over in a flash. It's like lightning; it happens, then it's gone.

While the lightning is flashing we can see the objects around us vividly, then suddenly that appearance disappears. The appearance of this life is the same; it happens, then suddenly it's gone. Compared to our beginningless past lives, this life lasts just a second, like lightning.

Lama Tsongkhapa says that this life is as impermanent as a water bubble, gone in a second. Seeing this, we should strive to extract the essence from this perfect human rebirth and let go of clinging completely.

Happiness and unhappiness

Normally we feel unhappy only when dislike arises, when the happiness of this life has been disturbed in some way—usually when we've encountered something undesirable. And we feel happy when there's no such dislike arising but rather we've encountered one of the four desirable objects. In fact, our definition of happiness is meeting an object of attachment.

That's why most people in the world equate attachment with happiness. They fail to see that this is completely mistaken because they have no experience at all that real happiness, great happiness, can arise only *without* attachment. They've never even heard of the peace and happiness that the Dharma can bring, even though it's the experience of the great meditators. Recognizing only temporary pleasure as happiness, they fail to understand how anyone can have happiness without attachment. The way the mind works is such that the dislike of meeting the four undesirable objects is directly related to the wish to meet the four desirable objects, so the more we need objects of attachment, the more likely we are to be disappointed.

Why are we so obsessed with comfort? For example, many of us are extremely attached to food. Milarepa warned about attachment to food, calling it a "spy of Mara"[17] in that enjoyment of good food tricks us into generating more and more attachment. If we check, we'll find that this unhappy mind definitely comes from craving for transient pleasures, the thought of the worldly dharmas. Simple nutritional food is not enough; we want something delicious every time, and if we don't get it we get upset and disappointed. Not getting exactly the food we want or getting something that's

[17] Mara is the manifestation of internal interferences. For the quote and explanation of why food is a "spy" see p. 181.

not quite right becomes a huge problem in our mind. We're agitated the entire day, from morning till night; our whole house is filled with the experience: "Lunch was awful today; I didn't get anything I wanted." It becomes a major tragedy.

The amount of disturbance we experience depends on how much clinging we have. When we're full of needy desire, nothing can ever satisfy us. We've all seen people like this. There's always something missing in their lives, always something wrong. Wherever they stay there's something wrong; whatever clothes they have or food they eat, nothing ever satisfies them. To a lesser extent, perhaps, this is us; this is samsara. This is the psychology of how mind and object relate to each other. Investigating this is the best way of studying the mind.

If we were less attached to objects, even receiving tasteless food wouldn't be much of a problem. There'd be no reason to feel upset, no problem of the mind being down. As much as we can lessen our attachment to receiving the four desirable objects, that much can we lessen our unhappiness at not receiving them. By cutting through our attachment, Dharma practice brings peace into our life, frees us from confusion and makes us happy. Whatever happens—comfort, discomfort, praise, criticism or whatever— our mind is always happy, stable and at peace.

From his deep experience, the Kadampa geshe Shawo Gangpa, a great yogi who practiced Lama Atisha's teachings on *bodhicitta,* said,

> When we do not renounce attachment—seeking happiness in this life—negative karma, suffering and bad reputation all afflict us at the same time. When we renounce this worldly thought, the sun of real happiness arises in our mind.[18]

Harboring strong attachment is like having a sharp shard of glass stuck in our mind. It's not a happy mind; it's suffering. For us, there's a big difference between receiving a dollar and not receiving one. For the meditator who has renounced the eight worldly dharmas, however, there's no difference between receiving even a million dollars or not; it doesn't change his mind. It's not like receiving is happiness and not receiving is unhappiness. Neither temporal happiness nor temporal suffering mean that much to him.

---

[18] See also *The Book of Kadam,* p. 597 ff.

If we're free from clinging we have no problem when we meet the four undesirable objects. Whatever situation arises, we're stable. If the house we rent is not well furnished, if the food we eat is not well cooked, there's no real problem. Even if the food we've been served is spoiled, we can just stop eating it without getting upset—our friend accidentally serving us bad food is the situation; the anger, fighting and court cases that come next are what our dissatisfied mind adds to it.

When we're obsessed with our own comfort and pleasure, we're easily disturbed. Everything distracts and annoys us—any little noise outside, any tiny insect flying around. Every unwanted thing becomes a huge disturbance to our mind, the cause of great unhappiness. For example, you might have seen certain old people shouting and screaming whenever there's even a little bit of noise, making themselves and everybody around them unhappy.

Things happen. We're woken up by somebody in the apartment above dancing or playing loud music. That's the situation. The additional thing is our getting angry, calling the police, creating a big problem for the other person. All that extra stuff isn't necessary and doesn't get us back to sleep. How big a problem the noise creates for us depends on how much we're clinging to comfort.

If we don't renounce desire, our mind will always be unhappy. To make our mind happy, we need to have patience. When somebody criticizes us, we should have patience. When somebody blames us or treats us badly by stealing from us or not giving us the things we expect, we should have patience. In that way our mind doesn't get disturbed and we don't get angry. Psychologically, too, with less clinging there's less anxiety that things *might* go wrong in future.

If we expect everything to be perfect, we inevitably get disappointed and our mind gets disturbed. For instance, some Western tourists are shocked when they go to primitive countries like Nepal, where material conditions are terrible compared to their own country. Even though they stay in the best hotel in Kathmandu, which Nepalese people consider unbelievably luxurious and completely perfect, they always find many things missing, not having this, not having that. As they remember more and more things that they're missing they get increasingly dissatisfied and unhappy and want to go home right away.

Even somebody who's planned to live in Nepal for years ends up leaving very quickly. No hot showers, no supermarkets…so many things are missing. The Nepalese, on the other hand, live there very happily. Living in the mountains in primitive places with almost nothing, there's not much suffering, not much fear.

The thought of the eight worldly dharmas prevents tourists from having the same happy, relaxed mind as the primitive villagers. The unhappiness doesn't lie in the bedbugs or the noise but in the thought that longs for worldly pleasures.

It's quite possible to be completely happy no matter what the external conditions, no matter how much noise there is or how unfavorable the conditions are. Nothing becomes a distraction for the person whose mind is free from the thought of the eight worldly dharmas. Her mind is unworried, happy and stable all the time.

Good reputation and bad

One of the worst problems that we ordinary beings have is attachment to a good reputation. Renouncing attachment to food and clothing is comparatively easy but renouncing attachment to reputation is much more difficult. Whereas praise and criticism are given us directly, reputation is what others say about us. It's more general knowledge, such as articles in newspapers about what we've done or others' gossip about us.

Desperately wanting to be admired brings us many worries and problems and they're all created by ourselves. Gaining a good reputation requires great effort and expense, and then, when we have it, no matter how successful we are, we're always worried that we might lose it. There are many examples of people working ceaselessly and spending incredible amounts of money—millions of dollars—for a good reputation but they never get rid of the pain in their heart that they might lose it all.

Everybody knows of Elvis Presley. After he won the Nobel Peace Prize, His Holiness the Dalai Lama became much better known than before, but Elvis Presley is still much more famous, especially among young people. He's like an object of prayer for them, a role model, a god.

At least the religious people of the world who believe in God always remember to pray to him but young people just want to emulate Elvis or other famous actors and singers and always practice just to become famous and have a good reputation. But then even if they succeed, there's still no real satisfaction and many finish up killing themselves.

In his day, Elvis Presley was the most successful entertainer in the world, but the year he was going to die, maybe while he was singing his last song, he was crying, tears flowing down his cheeks. It was very sad, very sad. People in the audience were crying too. Even though he'd become as famous as anybody can get, had countless friends and was immensely wealthy, there was still such sadness and depression in his heart when he saw he was going to die and still hadn't achieved satisfaction. All this is due to attachment, clinging to this life, and not having reflected on impermanence and death.

Even when we try to create good karma by giving clothes or money to beggars, if we do it out of a need for admiration, that thought of the eight worldly dharmas stops our action from becoming positive. We might think we're doing something good but our real motivation is for others to hear about it and think how generous and good we are, or we do it with the thought that at some later time, when we ourselves need help, we'll be able to get it from those we've assisted. That's not true charity. As long as our motivation is possessed by attachment to reputation, the action doesn't become pure generosity, pure Dharma.

The bodhisattva Thogme Zangpo, a great Tibetan meditator, said,

> Even if you give much material as charity, if you do it seeking a good reputation it has very little result because the merit is destroyed by the evil thought.

If we're rich and generous, people will flock to us thinking that they might receive our charity, making it very easy for us to exploit them. We can see how people, attracted by the possessions and great wealth of the very rich, always want to work for them.

Sometimes a heavy dew very early in the morning can harm the crops it covers; moisture that is vital for crops to grow can also kill them. Similarly, the merit of an act of giving can be destroyed by the need for a good reputation, which can turn a pure act of charity into a deed done for one's own mundane happiness.

Attachment to a good reputation can even disturb us when we try to meditate, like when we sit in a perfect meditation posture with a mind puffed up by the thought that others must be jealous of how wonderfully we're meditating. Such a mind is not Dharma. If we're not careful to always check our motivation whenever we're trying to practice Dharma, mundane concerns will almost certainly come to disturb us.

The other side of craving a good reputation is craving to be free from a bad one. When people complain about us, criticize us, tell others about our faults and mistakes (even though we may not have the actual faults that they say we have), this can bring a lot of pain into our mind and make us very unhappy. This is caused by aversion to a bad reputation.

The more we crave a good reputation, the stronger our aversion to a bad one becomes. Our mind becomes depressed and aggressive. When people suddenly lose their job, even if it's because of redundancy and not because they've done something wrong, they often feel that they've failed in some way. They suffer from low self-esteem and think that others consider them failures. Feeling that their bad reputation is unjustified, they can even have a nervous breakdown. People have even gone completely crazy because of this.

If, on the other hand, we don't crave the admiration of others, we don't care when they speak badly of us. Whether they admire us or not, whether we have a good reputation or not, our mind remains undisturbed. Whatever the external conditions, our mind remains equal, tranquil; we lead a life of equanimity. When we cut attachment to having a good reputation, fear of a bad one disappears automatically. Whatever people say, we have no fear. This brings peace into our life, into our heart, and we're able to practice purely.

Unhappiness at not having a good reputation and having a bad one can be alleviated by reflecting on impermanence and death. Try to remember that all phenomena, including good and bad reputation, are in the nature of impermanence. Nothing lasts; everything changes, hour by hour, minute by minute, second by second and even within a second. These things can stop any time. It's not as if by meditating on impermanence we're making something that's permanent impermanent or by meditating on death we're immediately going to die. We're just trying to remember that impermanence is the very nature of this life.

Praise and criticism

When people praise us by telling us how good, generous or wise we are, our mind creates problems; our attachment immediately blows up like balloon. Since there is this danger, we need to be very careful when being praised; in order to protect ourselves we have to be keenly aware of what's happening in our mind and use one of the many useful techniques that exist.[19]

Expecting praise or compliments makes us susceptible to disappointment. Say we give somebody a cup of coffee or a piece of chocolate and she doesn't even say thank you but just takes it without a word. This can become

---

[19] See the meditation at the end of this and later chapters.

a great source of suffering in our mind, a huge problem! It's so very important! For days after that we scowl at that person and feel completely alone. We go around with a red-hot needle in our heart.

If we're brave enough we might even criticize her to her face for not thanking us, otherwise we just complain to others behind her back: "She asked me for a piece of chocolate, I gave her what I had and she *didn't even thank me!*" Then we gossip. Criticizing her, we all create negative karma together.

Logically, there's no point at all in getting worried, angry or such, but logic doesn't stop us from suffering. Problems arise because we have failed to destroy our attachment to admiration—suffering, anger and the resultant negative karmic actions of body and speech arise from attachment to the happiness of this life. Desire for praise, good reputation and so forth are poisonous minds that always cause suffering and the creation of more negative karma and lead to an endless cycle.

When we practice the most essential Dharma—avoiding the eight worldly dharmas, not following attachment to this life—there's no reason for attachment or anger to arise at the sound of praise or blame. We see praise and blame as the sound of the wind; meaningless and of no interest. Such a mind free of anger and attachment is a really strong mind and brings much happiness and freedom.

If we get angry when somebody calls us a dumb animal, why don't we get angry when we say the same words to ourselves? We would if the words themselves caused the anger, so it's completely illogical to get angry simply because they were said by another person. If a tape recorder complains that we're a terrible person, breaking it won't help. That's a useless, childish thing to do. We might think that we have a right to get angry at the person who recorded it rather than the tape recorder itself, but again, we should investigate the person. He's like a tape recorder too. There's nothing to get angry at in his body; it, too, is just like a machine, a box, a tape recorder.

Just as the tape recorder has no choice not to complain—the complaint was taped by the person—so the person has no choice because his mind is controlled by ignorance. Even though he abuses us, he has no more control than the tape recorder does and we have no reason for him to be the object of our anger. Neither beating him, killing him nor cutting him to pieces will stop his ignorance. Burning his body until there's nothing left won't help either. Nothing we ordinary people do in retaliation becomes a method to stop the problem.

We can't stop his ignorance for him; we can't make it nonexistent. He's under the control of his negative mind and if we retaliate with anger and harsh words, we will not just make him more unhappy but will make ourselves unhappy as well. Seeing this, we can free ourselves from any sense of personal harm that we might feel from his abuse and, furthermore, actually develop compassion for him.

In fact, criticism is very useful. Unlike praise, which causes us to puff up with pride and is therefore an obstacle to happiness and enlightenment, criticism enables us to see our own mistakes and gives us the opportunity to correct them, to make our practice pure and perfect.

The Kadampa geshes who practiced thought training used criticism on the path to enlightenment. Their reasoning was, if we like praise, we should like criticism as well, because both are just words—sound waves hitting our ears, nothing more. For the Kadampa geshes, blame was very good; they liked to receive as much criticism as possible. The more they received, the more opportunity they had to practice thought training. Therefore they were delighted to be abused because they could train their minds in bodhicitta. Instead of getting angry at those who criticized them, they saw them as extremely kind and felt strong love for them.

MEDITATION

Unless we're constantly aware of what's happening in our mind there's a real danger that everything becomes a service to the thought of the eight worldly dharmas. Therefore, we should try to meditate on the eight worldly dharmas and other lam-rim subjects as much as possible.

There are many ways to meditate on the eight worldly dharmas. Before you do, it is always good to start with the preliminaries. Start with some breathing meditation, then visualize Guru Shakyamuni in front of you and say the preliminary prayers such as the refuge and bodhicitta prayers. Then do the purification practice and purify the sentient beings you visualize around you.

From the Guru Shakyamuni that you have visualized, a similar one comes forth and absorbs into you, the original Guru Shakyamuni remaining in front of you. Then you become one with Guru Shakyamuni and then purify sentient beings with wisdom rays from you who are Guru Shakyamuni Buddha. Then all sentient beings become Guru Shakyamuni and absorb into you.[20]

[20] For an extensive preliminary practice and a visualization of Shakyamuni Buddha, see "A

After that, you can begin the main part of the meditation, doing one of the meditations on the eight worldly dharmas.

Meditation on the sound of praise and criticism

You can learn much about your mind by being aware of how it reacts to praise and criticism. How pleased are you when somebody praises you? How depressed are you when you're criticized? Even if you logically know that neither the praise nor the criticism is justified, it's very difficult to separate your mind from the situation and have a more realistic attitude to these two worldly dharmas. Here is a meditation that will help.

Think of a compliment or some praise that you've recently received. Don't worry whether you feel you deserved it or not, just concentrate on the way your mind reacted to it. Were you genuinely pleased to receive that praise without any exaggeration of the mind or did your mind immediately become attached to it? Explore how much you need praise.

Perhaps somebody has praised your wisdom—"How wise you are." Immediately your mind wraps itself around this sentence and you feel very happy. But really, where is the real happiness in those four words? They are just sounds hitting your ears. If they were a true source of happiness then every time you heard them you'd be as happy. If there were some absolute existence in that sentence, then just saying "How wise you are" to yourself would have exactly the same effect. Does it?

It could be your mantra. You could repeat it to yourself over and over, counting your mala—how wise you are, how wise you are, how wise you are. If it were real happiness, the more you repeated it the happier you'd become. You could record it and play it back to yourself all day every day and you'd be the happiest person in the world. But of course it is not like that.

Take each word and see whether there is happiness there. Is there some intrinsic happiness in "how" or in "wise," in "you" or in "are." Of course not. The individual words themselves are no reason for attachment, so why is the whole sentence?

Experiment like this and see how the happiness you feel when praised does not come from the side of the words themselves. The words themselves are empty sounds; the meaning comes from your own mind.

In the same way, if you check whether "You are so terrible" really exists, you'll find that what you believe to exist is utterly nonexistent. You get angry and upset when somebody says that, the actual sentence brings pain to your heart, but really it's only a group of sounds hitting your ear. How can it have that effect? You believe the sentence, but examine each word. Do you get angry with the "you" of "you are so terrible?" There's no point in getting angry at a "you." And there's no point in getting angry at the word "terrible." Does just hearing the sound "terrible" make you angry?

If you add a "no" to "you are good" you get a negative sentence, "You are no good." Those two letters "n" and "o" change the sentence around. The first sentence doesn't have "no"; the second one does. You don't get angry when you hear the word "no" alone, so why get angry at the whole sentence? Is it because the combination of words is related to you? If this is so, then when you tell yourself you are no good, it should cause you to get angry in exactly the same way.

The moment you discover the emptiness of the object that you believed in before, your feeling changes. There's no problem in your mind, no confusion. All of a sudden, by checking like this, your attachment or aversion diminishes and your mind becomes much more relaxed and happier than before. The wrong conception that held the truth to be in that group of sounds simply vanishes, and with it the attachment or aversion you felt because of those words. You can't find the truly-existing object of your negative emotion, so it is naturally dispelled. This way you keep your mind peaceful. You become your own doctor, psychologist and psychiatrist and bring peace to your own life.

3. The Nature of Samsara

The cow on the precipice

THE GREAT PANDIT Chandragomin uses a very effective example to explain the nature of worldly beings who work only for this life. A cow sees a small tuft of grass growing at the edge of a precipice and runs toward it thinking that if she can eat it she will be happy. Because of her attachment to the grass, she finishes up falling over the precipice, killing herself. Her attachment brings her suffering instead of the happiness she expected. Chandragomin said that worldly beings seeking only the happiness of this life are just like the cow. Without seeing the danger that their attachment to pleasure conceals, they run toward it and fall down and die.

This example is incredible. Since we seek solely the happiness of this life and are attached only to that, everything we do becomes nonvirtue. Like the cow that falls over the precipice trying to get the happiness of the grass, we're totally cheated by attachment. Even though we're looking for happiness, our actions only result in rebirth in the lower realms.

Lama Atisha, the great yogi and scholar, was invited to come from India to reestablish Buddhadharma in Tibet. The bodhisattva Dromtönpa, an emanation of Avalokiteshvara, the Buddha of Compassion, was Lama Atisha's translator and offered service to him in Tibet. Once he asked Atisha, "What are the results of actions done with ignorance, attachment and anger and those done without ignorance, attachment and anger?" Lama Atisha replied,

> Actions done with ignorance, attachment and anger bring rebirth in the lower realms as a suffering transmigratory being.

Ignorance causes rebirth as an animal, greed causes rebirth as a hungry ghost and hatred causes rebirth as a hell being. Actions not possessed by the three poisonous minds bring rebirth in the upper realms as a happy transmigratory being.

To understand Lama Atisha's answer, look at human beings who have not the slightest understanding of Dharma, who have no faith in refuge or karma, such as people from your own city or town. Day and night they think of nothing more than this life. They're concerned about nothing more than the happiness of the next few years, or even the next few months. They constantly keep themselves busy with this motivation of worldly concern. It's easy to see that this is all nonvirtue. Lama Atisha explains that all actions of body, speech and mind done with an attitude of worldly concern result in rebirth in the lower realms as a suffering transmigratory being.

Because they have no faith in refuge and no understanding of karma, such people have no opportunity to practice holy Dharma, no opportunity to purify their previously accumulated obscurations and negative karma. We can see this very clearly in the example of the cow, who is so determined to get the grass that she is blind to the danger of the precipice and kills herself trying to get it. Like this, since the method is nonvirtue, the result of everything done for the happiness of this life is rebirth in the lower realms. Even if worldly people are shown the teachings on refuge and karma or given purification methods such as Vajrasattva, they cannot understand or accept them and therefore have no opportunity to practice Dharma.

We should feel extremely fortunate that we have met the holy Dharma. Even though we might still create negative karma, at least we have the opportunity to purify it. With an understanding of karma and refuge we have the opportunity to practice Dharma and know there is a solution. This is Dharma wisdom: it opens our eyes to the precipice before us and gives us the tools to avoid it.

One of Atisha's followers, the great meditator and Kadampa master Sharawa, makes it clear that no matter who we are, all our problems are created by the thought of the eight worldly dharmas. This is just as true for somebody on a spiritual path trying practice Dharma as it is for somebody who doesn't follow any religion. If we don't renounce the thought of the eight worldly dharmas we'll always experience many problems and be unable to develop our mind.

All the problems we experience—from not sleeping to thoughts of suicide—arise from attachment. This is simple Buddhist psychology; it clearly shows the source of both all our problems and all our happiness. This science of the mind is so logical; studying it brings us peace as we come to understand how all our problems are rooted in the mind.

We will see this clearly if we bring to mind all the problems we've recently experienced—last year, the year before and so forth, back as far as we can remember, and analyze the cause of all those problems. If we investigate honestly, we won't find even one problem that was not caused by the thought of the worldly dharmas.

We can also take our investigation beyond our own problems to those that others face—our family and friends, the people we work with and so forth—checking whether their problems also stem from the thought of the eight worldly dharmas. By doing this we'll become very much more aware of the nature of the mind.[21]

Humans, animals: the only difference is the shape

Ultimately, there's very little difference in the lives of those beings ruled by the thought of the eight worldly dharmas. To a beggar, a businessman looks rich, but even though superficially they lead different lives, below the surface, they're the same—both are simply working for the happiness of just this life; both ways of living are negative; both are worldly work. There's no real difference.

In some ways, the beggar's life is preferable. Many businessmen take care of their lives by cheating others, and cheating others means cheating themselves, because cheating others takes cunning, treachery and telling lies. In general, beggars don't cheat others, therefore their lives are not as negative.

Students aren't much better. They study hard from childhood until they graduate with a degree from a top university, but it's all just to take care of this life. They might think that they are working for the good of their country or for world peace, but in the depths of their heart their main goal is only the comfort of this life. So even if it takes thirty, forty or fifty years for them to get their degree, they remain servants of the eight worldly dharmas.

Then, no matter how high up the career ladder they climb, since everything they do is for the comfort of this life, they never become anything more than servants of the eight worldly dharmas. And what if they die three or four years after graduation? Having studied so much and worked so hard,

---

[21] See the meditation at the end of this chapter.

what do they have to carry with them? Nothing! They can't take their fat bank accounts along. All they can take with them to their next life are the imprints on their mindstream of all the actions they've done from the time they were born and beginningless lives, and those are all negative due to their attachment to mundane comfort. They worked all their life to create the cause of suffering, and this is how their lives finish. If we really check up, this is the huge tragedy of life.

In this way, a student is no different from an animal. A cow stays near her home, eating grass and sleeping. She can't talk and knows nothing the student knows—she hasn't even studied her ABCs. She certainly hasn't gained a degree. Her whole life of ten or twenty years is spent trying to find the best grass and water she can. From birth until death, her whole life is dedicated to the comfort of this life, exactly the same as that of the student.

We can easily see that everything that animals do—going to the fields, coming back, eating, drinking—is motivated by attachment, clinging to this life. I haven't heard whether they watch television or go to the movies, but it's possible. I've heard that in the United States there are schools where animals are trained how to live in a house—where to sleep, where to eat, which chairs to sit on, where not to make smells. In the East, people teach dogs to make prostrations but that doesn't make their minds understand Dharma; it's only a physical action. They make prostrations when there's meat, when they're hungry. At night, they go to sleep with no virtuous thought or pure motivation.

If we analyze the lives of the student and the cow, they're basically the same. Just as the cow's life is negative, so is the student's. The cow's life is no higher than the student's; the student's life is no higher than the cow's. When death comes, the student will have done nothing higher than the cow, even though he was born as a human being.

However smart he is, however great his reputation, whether he dives down to the depths of the Pacific or flies up to the moon, since his life is motivated solely by attachment to the comfort of this life, it's all negative, all the cause of suffering. His way of looking for happiness might seem a little bit different from that of the cow, but it's certainly no higher. Everything both of them do is motivated by the impure thoughts of greed, hatred and ignorance and keeps them trapped in the prison of samsara. One might have no possessions and lead a miserable life while the other has every possible material possession and great pleasure, but ultimately there really is not much difference. The only difference is the shape.

If a being has one shape we call it a human; if it has another we call it an animal. The actions are basically the same; the mind is the same. We might proudly think that we're infinitely more competent than animals and that animals are low and uneducated, but if we really check whether our life is in any way more meaningful than that of an animal, we might get a bit of a shock.

How many animals are there in this world? How many people? Check up on the numbers and think about how every one of them is creating the causes of suffering because they're controlled by the thought of the eight worldly dharmas.

First of all, think about all the billions of creatures in the ocean and what their minds are doing. If we could see into the minds of all those different types of fish, all those different creatures busily swimming back and forth, round and round, looking for food, seeking a safe comfortable place, all we'd find in the depths of their heart is the thought seeking only the pleasure of this life.

All the other creatures, too—the birds flying around in the air, the animals on the surface of the earth, the beings underground—what they have in the very depths of their heart is exactly the same thing, only the comfort of this life.

Now think about human beings. Take one city, like New York, and observe. Watch every person in that city; watch their minds. With the exception of only a few, they're all doing the same thing with the same motivation as the creatures that fly, walk and burrow. They're concerned with only the comfort of this life. Those flying in spaceships or airplanes, traveling in cars or floating on the water are all doing the same thing, all thinking in the same way. Their only concern is the comfort of this life, the pleasures of this life. Look closely at all the people and all the animals—you won't find any difference.

Look at the people shopping, the people driving their cars, up and down, back and forth, always busy, day and night, night and day. What are they all doing? Why are they all working so hard? What's in their heart? It's the same thing, desire for the happiness of just this life.

Observe them. Everybody everywhere, so busy doing worldly work, is under the control of attachment, seeking the pleasure of just this life. Everybody's too busy to think about Dharma but never too busy to do all this nonvirtuous work. Such an incredible number of suffering transmigratory beings.

We worldly people look down on animals, thinking that they're stupid and low, but somebody who understands Dharma and knows about karma sees that we're no different. The meditator sees us as totally obsessed by worldly concern and everything we do as suffering. We live in complete darkness, totally devoid of Dharma wisdom and completely unconscious of our actions.

We would probably argue that we're not unconscious; we're very conscious of what we're doing. We know where to eat good food, how to make lots of money, how to work, how to do business, how to turn a profit, how to bargain, what the best consumer items are. Many people who pride themselves on their intelligence even think that animals don't have a mind. To the meditator, however, human or animal, we lead our lives stumbling unconsciously into suffering, completely under the control of delusion. Seeing this, we worldly beings become the objects of the meditator's compassion.

Slaves of the eight worldly dharmas

When we follow the thought of the eight worldly dharmas we're just like a dog following its master. The man can be planning to harm the dog or even kill it, but the dog will always follow him because it expects to get some food, something for its happiness, no matter how uncertain that is. When we're following the mind of worldly concern, then we too will chase the stick whenever our master throws it. So we must be careful.

For most of our life we give freedom to desire, the evil thought of the eight worldly dharmas, and happily become its slave. In return, it constantly abuses and tortures us and brings us many problems, one after another. As slaves to attachment, we're never satisfied with what we have; we're always looking for better and more. This endless quest creates much unhappiness in our life and in those of others. It causes us to create vast amounts of negative karma with our body, such as fighting with others, and our speech, such as saying hurtful words and so forth. We can even become suicidal when our desire doesn't get what it wants—desire tells us to kill ourselves and we do what it says.

Relationships are common examples of how attachment enslaves us. They can be like addictions. Relationship problems can go on and on and on uncontrollably, making our life hell. Before being reborn in an actual hell, we experience hell in a human body. We feel completely trapped, suffocated; we can't even breathe.

It can happen that when we first get involved with a desirable person, we're extremely happy, completely attached and almost become one with that person, but then after a few days we're not even talking to him and see him as a monster, an enemy. The whole situation—first the attachment, then the aversion—is created by the thought of the eight worldly dharmas. If you check up, it's true, very true. I'm not making it up. I'm talking about what happens to all of us. The second situation, the aversion, is clearly confusion, but so is the initial attachment, even though we don't see it as such.

Addictions come about because we're slaves to desire. Think of alcoholics and drug addicts. Their lives become so unhappy and out of control that they can't even do their jobs. The more drugs they take, the more they damage their lives, destroying their awareness and memory. Alcoholics find it so hard to stop drinking—it's mainly a disease of the mind. They can see everything that's happening, all the danger, but don't pay much attention.

An alcoholic spends all his money on drink, then fights, shouts and becomes insensible. Returning home penniless and in a wretched state, he has a huge scene with his family, accusing his wife of things she didn't do. He throws things around, smashing their possessions, then runs out of the house and backs his car out recklessly and drives off very fast, breaking all the rules of the road. Then he has a crash and damages his brain or gets killed, or the police throw him in prison. This whole disastrous situation comes from the mind controlled by the thought of the eight worldly dharmas.

This evil mind makes it impossible for him to stop drinking, even if he sees how dangerous it is. He thinks maybe two or three sips won't hurt, but somehow he needs more. Then it's the same as before and again his mind becomes more and more uncontrolled. He wants to kick the habit but his mind is weak, his mind of desire is too strong.

Addiction to cigarettes is no different. Smoking causes your nails to turn yellow, your lungs to turn black and your face to get wrinkled. And it pollutes your mind as well as your body. Smoking can also cause heart attacks, cancer and many other diseases from which it's difficult to recover. All this is caused by the dissatisfied mind, the thought of the eight worldly dharmas.

It is said in the teachings that the evolution of things like *ganja*[22] and tobacco is due to the wrong prayers of the maras, the evildoers who want to stop the Dharma from developing in the world, disturb its practitioners and destroy any peace and happiness that there might be in the world. Smoking disturbs the mind by polluting the vehicle, the body. It blocks the *chakras*,

---

[22] What marijuana is commonly called in India.

preventing virtuous thoughts from arising, hinders the quick development of realizations and is a huge disturbance for practitioners of tantra.

Besides making the smoker unhealthy, the smoke also sickens surrounding sentient beings and pollutes their minds. There are many sentient beings we don't see, such as the white protectors who protect meditators. If a place is polluted by smoke, they leave. Sentient beings such as *nagas* also usually need a very clean place. The smell of tobacco smoke completely destroys the whole environment, like vast clouds of poison spread by a crop-duster.

The first time I went to America on Pan Am, the plane was full of smoke. I felt like I was asleep the whole journey. Also, when somebody was smoking down the road from Kopan, the wind would bring the smell up into my room. When you breathe, the smell goes into your heart and causes pain. What's so special about smoking? You put a fire in your mouth and the smoke comes out your nose.

As long as we're under the control of the thought of the eight worldly dharmas we're suffering, even if at present it doesn't seem like that. Allowing ourselves to remain under their control is infinitely worse than a parent dying or losing billions of dollars, neither of which can cause us to be continuously reborn in samsara. Being a slave to the evil thought of the eight worldly dharmas is *the* most dangerous thing, the one thing that will keep us dying and being reborn, always circling through the six realms.

We never recognize this internal enemy, this devil inside. Not only that, we serve our attachment as much as we can. When attachment is hungry, we feed it delicious food; when it gets cold, we give it warm clothes; when it gets hot, we give it air-conditioned comfort. We obediently follow whatever orders attachment gives. It's like a king.

Pabongka Dechen Nyingpo compares the eight worldly dharmas to a female cannibal. At first a female cannibal is very sweet. She speaks very nicely, tells us she loves us and wants to take care of us, but if we trust her, she will control and then eat us. This is exactly what samsaric perfections do to us.

We worldly people keep a very close eye on our external enemies, but watching this mental enemy is many million times more important. When this inner enemy arises, we should constantly be conscious of it and not follow it or allow it to control or enslave us. Then we should use all our understanding to destroy it. Unless we do this, no matter how much we try to practice Dharma, we'll just continue creating negative karma. The thought of the eight worldly dharmas is our most dangerous enemy, not just because it brings us confusion and suffering in this life, but more because it is the main cause for rebirth in the lower realms and makes us suffer there for many eons.

SAMSARA IS SUFFERING

All suffering comes from the mind

To have a peaceful, happy life free from problems, we must first find the cause of our suffering and then do whatever is needed to eliminate that cause. As the cause of all our problems is the thought of the eight worldly dharmas, the only way to develop true happiness is to destroy this evil thought. We need to flush it from our minds. We need to be brain washed! Once it's washed out, then there's true freedom, true peace. As long as it sits there in our mind there can never be freedom.

We normally think of desire as good, but if we really examine the nature of desire we'll see that its nature is suffering. We can sometimes recognize this when attachment is so strong it overpowers us. At that time we can actually feel it as physical pain, and because we're unable to let go, that makes the emotional pain associated with it even worse.

If we can actually see that the thought of the eight worldly dharmas that lives in our own mind is the real culprit, we can learn how to control our mind, to disengage ourselves from the influence of worldly concern. Then we're really studying the best psychology. Without understanding the cause of life's problems, how can we find practical solutions that really benefit and bring peace and happiness in this life?

The Kadampa geshes were great meditators who actualized the graduated path to enlightenment and completely freed themselves from this emotional mind, from all thought of the worldly dharmas, the dissatisfied mind of desire. In their texts, when they explain real happiness, real peace, they're talking from their own experience. They explain that whether we experience happiness or suffering is entirely determined by our motivation and nothing else. Everything depends on what type of motivation we have. If our motivation is virtuous, our action becomes virtuous and we experience happiness; if our motivation is nonvirtuous, our action becomes nonvirtuous and we experience suffering.

Both samsara—these circling aggregates, the association of body and mind that is in the nature of suffering—and nirvana—the ultimate happiness of liberation—come from our motivation. That which we call hell and that which we call enlightenment also come from our motivation. Everything comes from our motivation.

Therefore, the mind is the creator of everything. From our positive or negative motivations come the actions that cause all the happiness and suffering that we experience. If we do all of our actions out of desire, clinging to this life, since our motivation is nonvirtuous, our actions become nonvirtuous—they become only the cause of suffering, not the cause of happiness. Actions we do with a motivation unstained by desire clinging to this life become the cause of happiness.

In this way, all problems are created by the mind. Of the four desirable objects and the four undesirable ones, from the objects' side there is no difference: the first four good, the second four bad. It is our attachment to worldly pleasure that labels them as such. We like comfort, gifts, friends, praise, reputation and so forth, so we interpret those objects as good; we don't like discomfort, enemies, blame and so forth, so we interpret those objects as bad. Problems arise from the way that we judge situations. The same person is sometimes a friend, sometimes an enemy.

Not only that, but, as Dharmakirti explains in his commentary on Dignaga's *Compendium of Valid Cognition*, the mind controlled by the thought of the eight worldly dharmas is obscured and unable to get to the point, to see things as they actually are. Calm water is very clean and totally transparent, but we can't see through dirty, disturbed water at all. Similarly, the attached mind can't stay still; it's always disturbed and obscured, like a sky filled with dust from a strong wind—everything is indistinct and blurred.

And because of that, even if we do something for somebody else, it interferes with the sincere attitude to benefit others without any expectation of getting something in return. When our mind is occupied by attachment, there's no space for unconditional loving kindness and compassion for that sentient being.

Love mixed with desire is love created by ignorance. It's not the same as real unconditional love; it brings no peace because the principal cause is the unsubdued, untamed mind. If we have dirt on our face we can't expect to see a clean face when we look in the mirror. In the same way, a state of mind such as desirous love caused by confusion cannot bring happiness and peace.

Overwhelmed by desire, there's no time to think about impermanence and death. In fact, understanding impermanence and death is the complete opposite to attachment, because when we think of impermanence and death, it's impossible to see any point in being attached. So it's the antidote to attachment.

When our mind is possessed by attachment we can't see emptiness either. Attachment obscures the ultimate nature of the I, the aggregates and phenomena. And it interferes with renunciation as well. In this way, the thought of the eight worldly dharmas interferes with our wish to achieve liberation, even for just ourselves.

On the other hand, if we have a renounced mind, neither the four desirable objects nor the four undesirable ones are a problem. The renounced mind is a very healthy mind. It is unstained by attachment to this life and is free from such labeling. When our mind is not ruled by attachment, when it's peaceful and calm and there are no obstacles, we can easily meditate on things like impermanence and death and the sufferings of others. And when we meditate on emptiness, it's easy to get to the point.

Therefore, if we want to escape from the cycle of suffering quickly, it's necessary to make a radical change. We need to come to understand that the future suffering brought about by our current delusions is far, far worse and far more dangerous than whatever immediate problems we're facing at the moment. With such understanding, even if we work to eliminate our current immediate problems, we'll use the right methods.

Real peace comes when we develop our devotion, compassion, renunciation, contentment, loving kindness, bodhicitta and wisdom understanding emptiness. Those minds don't disturb our mental continuum at all but purify our obscurations and negative karma and lead us to the peace of liberation and to enlightenment. This peace starts when we abandon desire—we begin to develop true peace in our mental continuum the moment we free ourselves from the thought of the eight worldly dharmas and eventually experience it forever.

The nature of fire is burning, the nature of samsara is suffering

Seeking the happiness of this life is more harmful than having a poisonous snake coiled in our lap. At worst, a snake bite can kill us, but desire has the power to propel our next life into the lower realms. The thought of the eight worldly dharmas is a million times worse than AIDS or cancer. Having the disease alone, even having all 424 diseases[23] together, without the mind of desire doesn't make us unhappy or cause us to be reborn in the hell, hungry ghost or animal realms.

We may feel a degree of excitement when we obtain one of the four desirable objects but that excitement is in fact only agitation. We're like a fish hooked on a line, an ant mired in honey or a fly trapped in a spider web—completely enveloped and utterly unable to break free. Like a cow eating grass at the edge of a precipice or a person licking honey from a razor's blade, enjoying such pleasure is extremely dangerous.

When a moth flies into melted candle wax, it gets completely trapped. Its body and wings are so fragile that it's extremely difficult to separate them from the wax. The texts say that it might be that the moth sees something beautiful, like a celestial mansion, right inside the flame, so it flies right into it and gets burned and trapped. It doesn't think the flame will burn its body, otherwise it wouldn't fly in, yet the more we try to stop it, the harder it tries get into the flame.

This tells us something about the nature of the animal mind. The moth has only expectations of peace and happiness; it has no desire to suffer. It doesn't plan to fly into the flame in order to suffer. It flies in because it's unafraid, and it's unafraid because it doesn't understand the danger. The moth wants happiness but the result is the complete opposite; it gets burned and dies. It's very important to try to discover why it does this. This is real scientific enquiry, the essential study of natural science.

Just as beings of the animal realm—moths, flies, ants—bring suffering on themselves while seeking happiness, we also do many actions that create only suffering. That is the nature of the mind of desire. We get stuck to the object, so we have no freedom. In the same way that a bird with a stone tied to its leg is unable to fly, we're tied by attachment to our objects of desire.

Among poisons, desire is the worst. Like poison, sometimes it causes terrible pain, sometimes a bit less, but nonetheless, pain is always there. Because of desire we have continued to circle in samsara since beginningless time. From the smallest animal to the biggest, from the poorest human to the richest, all of us who are only concerned with overcoming temporary problems fail to see that in doing so we're actually creating the cause of more and greater problems in the future.

---

[23] The number of diseases categorized by Tibetan medicine, hence covering all diseases that exist.

The nature of fire is burning; the nature of samsara is suffering. Just as it's better not to put our finger in a fire and get burned, it's better not to be in samsara and suffer. It's no use keeping our finger in the flame hoping that the fire will get cooler. That will never happen. In the same way, there's no use wanting to stay in samsara and not suffer. The whole point is to try to get out of samsara. Until we do, we're going to have to accept that we're going to suffer, and when something unpleasant happens we should think, "Of course this has happened. I'm in samsara. Whatever happens to me is going to be in the nature of suffering because this is where I live." So there's no point in worrying.

Whenever we encounter a miserable situation and reject it, thinking how unfair it is and how "this shouldn't be happening to me," we only double our suffering and exaggerate the problem. How much we suffer depends on how we think. If we're able to accept unpleasant experiences we don't get such a shock when they occur; because we're expecting suffering we handle it much better when it arises. It's like jumping into cold water: if we think it's going to be warm we get a shock, but if we know it's going to be cold there's no great surprise. We know we're living in samsara, so we're bound to experience suffering because that's its nature.

This awareness also helps us accept responsibility for our own suffering as we see it as the karmic result of previous negative actions we ourselves have done; we take responsibility for our own suffering and don't point the finger of blame at somebody else. Instead of planning revenge on the person who stole our money, we understand that the theft was the result of our having stolen from that person in the past and that the suffering we're experiencing is entirely our own fault, not the other person's. Realizing that we're the only one to blame and not wanting to experience the result again, we resolve not to create the cause of that suffering any more.

We can also see that having experienced it this time, the result of that negative action we created in the past has now finished and we won't have to experience it again. Therefore, although it's unpleasant, it's also something we can feel happy about. In this way suffering also makes us more conscious, more careful of our actions.

Better not to itch than to scratch

In his *Precious Garland,* the highly realized pandit and Madhyamaka philosopher Nagarjuna, who restored the sutra and tantra teachings in India when they had degenerated, said,

> There is pleasure when a sore is scratched,
> But to be without sores is more pleasurable still.
> Just so, there are pleasures in worldly desires,
> But to be without desires is more pleasurable still.[24]

We're probably afraid that if we sacrifice our desire we'll sacrifice our happiness and be left with nothing. Not understanding that the nature of desire is suffering, we can't see that there is a better happiness independent of any external sense object; a deep peace developed within our own mind. We can't see that feeding desire is like scratching dermatitis.

Because scratching stops the itch for a short time it feels good, so we label it "pleasure." There's some relief but it's still suffering, just a lesser degree of it. Worldly pleasures, such as eating, drinking alcohol, sexual intercourse and so forth are all the same in nature; they're actually suffering but are called "pleasure" by our superstitious mind.

The second or third time we scratch an itchy sore the relief we first felt turns to suffering; then that suffering is doubled. In the same way, the harder we work at worldly pleasures, instead of giving us increasing happiness they always turn into suffering.

Eating relieves the suffering of hunger, so we think it's happiness, but if we keep on eating it becomes very uncomfortable. When we move into the shade of a tree to escape the suffering of the sun's heat we feel pleasure at the coolness for a while, but when we've cooled down we start to feel cold and our pleasure turns into suffering. Soon we have to go back into the sun again to get relief from the cold. There are thousands of examples like this.

Rather than labeling the relief of scratching an itch as pleasure, wouldn't it be better to be free from itchy sores completely? In the same way, it's far better not to have the desire for worldly objects than to have the objects of worldly desire. Conflict arises because desire exists in our mind, the creator; if we're free from desire there's no way for problems to arise when we encounter objects. Therefore, giving up the eight worldly dharmas does not mean making these eight objects non-existent; it means making attachment to them non-existent.

Without desire, the problems that come from desire could not arise and there'd be no samsara. Without this body caused by delusion and karma and contaminated by the seed of disturbing thoughts we wouldn't have to expe-

[24] V. 169.

rience hot and cold, hunger and thirst and all the other problems that fill our lives. We wouldn't have to worry about survival or spend so much time and money looking after our body. Think of how much time we spend just keeping this body looking good, how much work we put into decorating it, from our hair down to our feet. When we get sick, however, even medicine cannot always help, so wouldn't it be better to be free from all these problems and not have this body, this samsara, at all?

Blame delusions, not others

There's desire we should avoid and desire we need and many people don't understand the difference. Negative desire, the desire we should avoid, is the desire for the pleasures of this life. We should avoid it because, as we have seen, this desire is the creator of all suffering. On the other hand, we *need* the desire for enlightenment. That's what makes us follow the path and eliminate the cause of suffering and thereby achieve the goal of ultimate peace and enlightenment. Without that desire we'd have no energy to follow the path and achieve enlightenment.

Similarly, while aversion in general is negative, we need aversion to suffering in order to have the energy to strongly follow the path. Say we're strongly disgusted with living in the West and really want to go to the East. The stronger our aversion to the West, the more avidly we'll try to get to the East. In order to get there quickly, we take an airplane, not a bus. Just as aversion to the West and desire for the East is what we need to get us to where we want to go, aversion to suffering and the desire for enlightenment are vital to get us out of suffering.

Since, as Buddhist practitioners, we're supposed to get rid of desire, we might think that all desire, including the desire to meditate, is somehow wrong; that even that is just another desire to be eliminated. In fact, the Buddha himself said, "If you desire all happiness, abandon all desire." We should realize, however, that whatever Dharma activity we do motivated by the desire to achieve enlightenment is not attachment but is, in fact, very positive. If that kind of desire were a problem I wish that everybody had it. When that desire is there day and night and we can't stop it, when it's there while we're eating, talking, sleeping—every moment—we have incredible energy to be quickly released from suffering.

We all have aversion to suffering, but generally our aversion is only to the gross worldly suffering perceived by our limited mind—the suffering of suffering—and not to *all* suffering or, in particular, the cause of suffering.

We've had aversion to temporary, worldly suffering for countless lifetimes but we're still not out of samsara, so this proves that aversion in general doesn't help. What's missing is aversion to the very cause of suffering, without which we don't have the energy to develop the mind that renounces all of samsara. *That* aversion is the rocket fuel that gives us the energy to practice.

Without seeing the thought of the eight worldly dharmas as the enemy we won't develop the desire to be free of it. From beginningless lifetimes it has played at being our best friend and we've blindly followed it assuming that it will bring us happiness, but now we need to wake up and see that its real intention is to harm us. When we truly understand that this evil thought is the actual cause of all our suffering we'll naturally want to destroy it. To hate and wish to destroy another being is wrong, but to hate and wish to destroy the cause of all our suffering is the wisest thing we can do. Destroying the enemy in our mind is the way to achieve perfect happiness without giving even one atom of harm to other sentient beings; this is the most beneficial way to gain ultimate peace.

Trying to achieve happiness by following the thought of the eight worldly dharmas almost always involves harming others and because of that the path to peace is blocked. It is like being a businessman who trades in pearls from Asia but sends his ships to the West instead. No matter how many eons he looks, he won't find any pearls; he only gets exhausted and never finds success.

We have only one enemy and that's the deluded mind of attachment clinging to this life. It has constantly robbed us of happiness and caused us great suffering in the past. It's the cause of all our current suffering and it will continue to make us suffer in the future. If we find ourselves angry at another person, fighting and hitting him, we should stop and think that in fact he isn't the one who should suffer. The one who should suffer is the actual creator of the situation, the real enemy—the evil thought of the eight worldly dharmas we harbor in our mind. The person we're beating is innocent, having been pushed into the situation by his delusions, but it's our own deluded mind that's the root cause.

Normally when somebody does something really bad to us, the more we think about that person, the angrier we become. Our hatred gets stronger and stronger and we really want to kill her. Now, instead of hating the external enemy and trying to harm her, we turn on the internal enemy, the only true enemy, the one who makes us suffer all our problems and difficulties. The more deeply we think about the countless different problems the thought of the eight worldly dharmas has given us throughout infinite time, the stronger our aversion to it becomes and the easier it is for us to stop creating negative karma and experiencing the suffering result. This is the way we guide ourselves.

This also means that instead of suffering becoming an obstacle to our Dharma practice, it becomes a support for it. We can even use our suffering to cut problems altogether, depending on how well we understand the shortcomings of following the thought of the eight worldly dharmas.

Whenever there's a physical or mental problem such as headache, hunger, depression and so forth—any problem that causes us to suffer—we can turn our suffering into Dharma by thinking that we're suffering because of our negative mind, not because of the external conditions. In the past this negative mind has prevented us from achieving both ordinary samsaric happiness and true Dharma happiness—such as the cessation of samsara, bodhicitta, the realization of emptiness and enlightenment—it's preventing us from achieving all this now, and it will continue to prevent us from doing so in the future. We need to really feel that this is so and not just say the words; words alone are ineffectual. The deeper our understanding, the greater the effect on our mind and the more clearly we see the negative mind as the real enemy.

For instance, hunger and thirst can disturb our meditation but by giving that suffering back to the delusions we can realize that that feeling is not "ours" as such. If we can do that, the suffering feeling weakens and can, in fact, disappear completely. Afterwards we won't even know how it disappeared. Instead of disturbing our Dharma practice, our suffering becomes useful. There's no need to interrupt our meditation to get a drink of water. Our mind created the problem but has cured itself. This is such a nice method.

MEDITATION

Meditation on the nature of attachment

A very useful meditation on the eight worldly dharmas is to check the root of your problems. In your meditation session you should investigate whether or not your life has lived up to your expectations. At the beginning you expected your life to be happy—either by always having whatever material possessions you desired or by always being with one particular person or something like that—but did that happen? If you've had any problems, trace them back to their root to see why they happened. What was the cause of this problem or that? Not just the immediate conditions that triggered it but the real, main cause? Investigate. Go back further and further in time and you'll find out. You'll see that you've been expecting a kind of happiness that's just not realistic. And if you trace the evolution of this problem back as far as you can you'll discover that the root of this and all your other problems is one thing: the thought of the eight worldly dharmas.

When attachment arises, check to see whether you feel happiness arising with it. Compare real happiness with the "happiness" your mind feels when it comes into contact with an object of attachment. Is it real happiness or does your mind just label that feeling happiness? Try to see that the nature of that mind is tight, not free.

Watch how your mind wants to run to an object of attachment and wrap itself up in it. Try to be as conscious as possible of exactly what's going on and to keep an objective distance between you and the object so that you can see the games your mind plays. By investigating the nature of the attachment you can really discover how such a mind is both confused and unhappy.

You can also meditate on other problems you've recently had or look back on your life and explore the cause of all the major problems you've had since you were born. Again, look beyond the immediate conditions to the main cause and try to see how the thought of the eight worldly dharmas is there each time.

It's possible that you might feel angry when you recall your past problems and the people who've harmed you. If you do, remember the antidotes and use them at that time.[25] If you practice like this during the meditation session you'll train your mind so that afterwards, when you're actually with that person, actually involved in a similar situation, you'll be better able to handle the problem; you'll start to become skillful and wise.

From exploring the cause of your own problems in this way, you can then expand your meditation to understand the problems of other people: couples, families, societies and so forth. When you do you'll begin to understand why there are so many problems in all parts of society, from arguments between friends up to wars between countries.

[25] See Rinpoche's advice on this at LamaYeshe.com by searching his teachings for the keyword anger.

First of all, start from your friends and see how they all experience different problems in their lives. Use the same technique of taking a situation back to its main cause to see the role that the thought of the eight worldly dharmas has played. Then, in the same way, check the lives of your parents and then other people you know who are suffering.

Meditating on attachment—what it is, how it arises, what it does to your mind and so forth—is something you can do all the time, not just in meditation sessions. Whenever you feel attachment arise, immediately investigate the state of your mind and see whether the excitation you're experiencing is the true happiness you instinctively think it is. In this way you can start to break the age-old habit that's chaining you to suffering.

4. Seeking Happiness, Getting Suffering

SAMSARIC METHODS DON'T WORK

NO MATTER HOW wise we ordinary people think we are, no matter how much we know, whether we're psychologists or teachers, since we're not aware of how our mind works, we'll always make mistakes in our actions. A meditator living in the pure Dharma sees us as completely foolish. We lead our lives unconsciously. It's as though we're running through a pitch-dark forest where there are rocks and tree roots we can trip over at any moment.

Following the thought of the eight worldly dharmas is like purposely keeping ourselves ignorant; doing so traps us in the cycle of death and rebirth and brings rebirth in the lower suffering realms again and again. It's completely crazy, but this fact isn't recognized by worldly people simply because the ignorant mind never sees ignorance as crazy but rather thinks that its own actions are always positive and good. This kind of thinking is far worse than what a psychiatrist would diagnose as insanity.

The principal cause of samsaric suffering is ignorance—not realizing the absolute true nature of reality—and all actions done without this realization. Seeing all things as self-existent, we grasp onto them as if the happiness we derive thereby were self-existent. The wish to acquire an object of desire follows the desire for that object like a servant follows his master and, in that way, binds us to suffering. The happiness that arises from Dharma practice, on the other hand, is free and loose; its nature is release.

Even if we're physically handicapped, injured or paralyzed—even if we have leprosy—our mind can still be extremely happy; it can even be in a pure realm. But if we're mentally handicapped by the mind of desire, even if we're physically extremely fit, strong and healthy, we can never be happy.

Temporary methods never help in the long term. This is an essential Dharma point. Methods that come from worldly concern only create the cause for the continuous arising of future suffering. When we try to solve our problems in this way, we're working for the thought of the eight worldly dharmas, not our own happiness, like a servant cooking for his master.

We usually think that solving our immediate temporary problems is more important than stopping the greater suffering we're going to face in the future, not to mention stopping the very cause of that suffering—greed, hatred and ignorance. Even if we try to meditate and practice Dharma, we still harbor the assumption that our immediate problems are the most important thing. This is due to the ignorance of not deeply recognizing the difference between negative and positive actions. Instead of following a method that will completely eliminate both immediate and long-term problems, we do things that just become the cause of future suffering. Thus our problems continue to multiply.

The problems we're experiencing now were created in previous lives by the actions we did trying to stop similar problems back then, so even if we manage to get born human a billion times, using the same methods to eliminate our problems is pointless and only causes us to continue to experience the same problems in future.

Attached to pleasure and comfort, we want all problems and discomfort to cease, but the methods we use to try to stop them are based on our deluded mind. We can't stop attachment by generating attachment; we can't get rid of anger by getting angry; we can't eradicate ignorance by perpetuating ignorance. Wrong methods only create more suffering.

We think that *this* cause will create *that* effect, whereas in fact it does the opposite. So our very first mistake is being ignorant of karma, the actual cause of happiness and suffering. Not seeing the link between an effect and what has caused it, we act unskillfully. Even if we have listened to eons of explanations of karma, because we haven't meditated on it continuously, our understanding remains superficial and intellectual. Therefore we don't act on it and continue to make mistakes.

Not only in the West but throughout the whole world, there are so many organizations—social welfare groups, counseling and psychology organizations and so forth—all established with the intent of dealing with people's problems. They're very good at recognizing the problems we all have— aggression, depression, schizophrenia, all the confusion of our modern life—and try their best to do something about them by forming more and more organizations, but they fail to see that the whole reason for all these problems is just one thing: the attachment that clings tightly to the happiness of this life.

If a person who is himself confused doesn't recognize the source of his problems and use that understanding to change, no organization will be able to help him. He will continue to keep the thought of the eight worldly dharma in his heart like a treasure without disturbing it. He will continue to serve it as much as possible and obediently follow whatever orders it gives, as if it were his king. And none of the millions or billions of organizations can help, because the problem is inside. Wherever we are—on earth, in space, in the mountains, in the jungle, in a cage with the birds!—the problem is there with us.

We seem to think naturally that external conditions determine happiness or suffering, but if that were true then all the millionaires and billionaires in the rich countries would be extremely happy. The richer they were, the happier they'd be and the greater the peace they'd feel in their heart. As their wealth grew they'd have greater enjoyment, satisfaction and fulfillment. But in fact, the opposite is true. They feel greater loneliness and depression because they don't understand the cause of happiness and how to alleviate suffering.

We think that the only reason that we're unhappy is because we can't get what we want. We want to sleep, dance, shout and have sex but somehow these are all denied us. We believe that immediately doing whatever we want to do, whatever attachment bids us to do, is the door to happiness and peace in life. And when for some reason we can't get what we want, there's a kind of block in our mind and depression or anger arise.

A monk who did a course in Germany told me that there's a center there that helps people relieve their depression, aggression and other negative minds. Their method is to line everybody up and make them scream for hours and hours. After some time they get tired—you can't shout nonstop from morning to night. So after a while they're totally exhausted and think that their depression has gone away. That exhaustion, which they see as cleaning away their negative minds, is in fact nothing more than the relief we feel when we rest after intense physical labor or put down a heavy load that we've been carrying for a long time.

This same group also has a technique where they take off all their clothes and put kaka all over their body. These are their methods for cutting the root of problems in their mind, of preventing the thought of the eight

worldly dharmas from arising—covering themselves with kaka and screaming for hours. Besides not being the way to recognize the root of problems,
such external changes do not become a remedy and can have little benefit
as long as the eight worldly dharmas are not renounced.

Methods like this are supposed to free us from aggression but in fact all
that happens is that we forget our problems for a short time while torturing
ourselves in another way. As long as we have strong attachment to the happiness of this life we have no peace. There's something missing in our mind,
something missing in our life.

Samsaric methods can never satisfy

The Buddha explained in a sutra that we can never achieve satisfaction as
long as we follow desire. Furthermore, Lama Tsongkhapa said in the *Lam-
rim Chen-mo* that following desire opens the door to many problems. Just as
many branches grow from the root of a plant, most of the disturbing emotions and problems we face in life grow out of desire.

The great yogi Sharawa said that with clinging comes dissatisfaction.
Even though we might have more than enough material possessions, clothes,
money and so forth to last our whole life, we still feel we don't have enough,
we still crave more. Following desire doesn't fill the empty heart. No matter
how many objects of desire we manage to obtain, we still don't experience
satisfaction and *that* is our major suffering. There's never an end. Whether
we experience a little pleasure or a lot, we never find real satisfaction so we
just want it again and again and again and again and again. We're always
craving for better and more but it just doesn't happen. Desire is by nature
hungry; it can never be satiated.

Desire is like a chronic disease. There are chronic diseases of the body;
this is a chronic disease of the mind. Following the dissatisfied mind is like
drinking salt water...or eating Indian popcorn. The popcorn in India is
very salty. Because of that you have to drink tea with it. After a glass of tea
you crave more popcorn, which makes you thirsty, which makes you drink
more tea, which makes you want more popcorn, and so forth, on and on.
Until you actively determine to stop, you just keep on eating and drinking
endlessly.

What the Rolling Stones' Mick Jagger sang is very true: "I can't get no satisfaction." In his heart, no matter how many friends he has, no matter how
many people say they love him, no matter how famous he has become, no
matter how much wealth he has, he's still not satisfied. The song expresses

what's in his heart—he has all these external things but his heart, his inner life, is empty. In singing this he shows us the shortcomings of desire and proves what the Buddha said: samsaric pleasure never gives satisfaction. No matter how much we get, no matter how much we experience, we're never satisfied.

The hunger of dissatisfaction leads to countless problems. Life becomes very expensive. We need this, we need that, we need this, we need that—so many things, billions of things. And because of that we run up many debts. Then we can't pay them back and the court cases start. We try to start a business, but the business fails.

And talking of business, even if it works and we make a thousand dollars, we want one hundred thousand; after one hundred thousand, we want a million; then a million's not enough, we want a billion. After we make a billion, we want a trillion, then a zillion. It never ends. Satisfaction always eludes us. It's always just around the corner; it tells us it's in the next purchase or the next salary increase. Life continues with the same worry, the same fear of losing our wealth, the same fear of being unable to do better than others.

We can travel around the world for months or even years trying to find a desirable object, trying to find a friend. Our mind is so upset, so lonely, so worried we won't get what we want. One country doesn't give us what we need and so we go to another. Maybe we spend some time hanging around in Greece, but not finding the object to satisfy our desires there, we go to California.

We spend all our money like this. We cling to the dream of finding the perfect partner but, unable to meet him or her in one place, our attachment takes us to another part of the world. We experience a difficult life, full of problems, all caused by the evil thought of eight worldly dharmas.

There are many people like this, totally out of control, blindly following attachment. Some end up going crazy or killing themselves because they can't control their lives. They're always searching for happiness but finding only suffering.

There's no end to the wanting; there's no end to the work. Like hundreds of branches spreading from one single trunk, countless problems start from the fundamental dissatisfaction that the thought of the eight worldly dharmas brings us. Problems come like ripples on a lake; they never finish—one comes, then another, then another, without end. Forever. From beginningless rebirths we've been following desire and still it hasn't ended.

Life becomes so heavy and difficult, bringing depression, worry, fear. Chasing satisfaction in things, we have no chance to enjoy what life can offer. Even if we're living in a jeweled palace full of luxuries, even if we have billions of cars—Bentleys, Lamborghinis, Ferraris, Rolls—even if we have billions of swimming pools, we still can't really enjoy life. We might have an army of servants working for us but we're still completely miserable. Look at the very rich beyond their glossy exteriors and ask yourself whether they're truly happy. Many of them look thoroughly worn down and miserable.

When we don't get what our attachment wants, we feel hopeless. This is one of the fundamental sufferings in our life. This is what makes people crazy. Whatever we're attached to that we lose—our business, our friend, whatever—makes us think that our life has no meaning. Then, due to anger, jealousy and so forth, we create negative actions such as killing or stealing. We cause so much harm to ourselves and others. It brings much unhappiness not only to ourselves but also to many others and is the cause of rebirth in the lower realms.

We need to let go by practicing mindfulness, by watching the mind. Then, when attachment to the eight worldly dharmas arises, like the missiles that America used on Iraq that pinpointed their target even after traveling hundreds of miles, we need to see attachment for what it is and launch our nuclear missile of mindfulness right at it to destroy it.

The highly realized Tibetan yogi Drogön Tsangpa Gyare said,

> In the door of the house of the practitioner, a happy person is peacefully lying down, but the person who seeks delicious food can't feel this.
> In the door of the house of one who practices the remedy, the eight worldly dharmas are lying down, but those who have attachment can't feel this.
> In the door of the house of one who has cut off the root, there is a happy mind lying there, but those who have doubts can't feel this.
> In the door of the house of the person who has satisfaction, there is a really rich person lying there, but the desirous, the dissatisfied ones can't feel this.

"Door," of course, refers to the mind. This is where we can find real peace and happiness but the person who still clings to external sense pleasures can never know this. If we still crave delicious food, beautiful clothes and comfortable places, we can never know the peace and happiness that a renounced person does. Drogön Tsangpa Gyare says that only by subduing the thought of the eight worldly dharmas can there be peace. Those who follow this evil thought will never know it.

He goes on to say that if a practitioner completely cuts off the root of delusion, the evil thought of the eight worldly dharmas and the ignorance that grasps a truly-existent I, real happiness can be found. Finally, he says that whether a person has possessions or not—he might be materially poor without enough food for even one meal—if that person is satisfied, he has great wealth, whereas somebody who is full of desire and feels he never has enough is poorer than the poorest beggar, even though he might have untold riches.

As we have seen, satisfaction is not the product of material objects but is a state of mind, an experience of the mind. Not understanding where real satisfaction comes from, people trapped by desire are frightened by the thought of giving up the external things that they wrongly see as the source of their happiness. They can't see that there can be satisfaction without material possessions. They can't see that the greatest wealth, the real gift that brings happiness and freedom from an uptight mind, is freedom from desire.

Living in the confusion of desire, no amount of possessions can cure the problem. But the simplest person, without material possessions but also without the thought of the eight worldly dharmas, has the most valuable possession, the most valuable method of making life happy. Even trillions of dollars cannot bring this gift.

I remember when I first went to the West I found it a bit strange how people always asked dinner guests what they wanted to eat. In the East the food is just served and everybody accepts what is there, but it seems that Westerners have to have a choice. Lama Tsongkhapa advises us to train by not letting attraction to samsaric perfections—samsaric happiness, reputation, power, wealth, all these things—arise for even one second, so accepting what is given is part of our practice. If we can hold this thought in our mental continuum continuously, then we have generated the realization of renunciation, the determination to be free from samsara.

Samsaric happiness never lasts

As long as we're attached to samsaric happiness we'll remain in samsara. Samsaric happiness never lasts; it invariably ends. We can discover this from our own daily life. No happiness based on the eight worldly dharmas lasts:

relationships, places, food, possessions and so forth. Because worldly happiness doesn't last we have to try to renew it endlessly. Like waves in the ocean coming one after the other, such work never ceases. That's the meaning of being a consumer.

Food and clothes are a simple example. Simply buying some food once or one set of clothes doesn't work—the food won't last until we die and the clothes won't satisfy us for the rest of our life. The temporary needs of one day can't cover our entire life. It's impossible. We have to keep working continuously because worldly happiness keeps finishing. We're always running on a treadmill, where nothing is new, going round and round and round.

Like eating and defecating, something we must do in an endless round, over and over and over again, the search for samsaric happiness never finishes. Until we cut off the karma created by ignorance, as long as we still have the cause to take rebirth again, we'll keep dying and being reborn, keep cycling around, forever.

Not only does samsaric pleasure neither increase nor last, when it degenerates it becomes the suffering of suffering because, as we have seen, we're labeling "pleasure" on a feeling that is actually suffering in nature. As we continue the action, putting effort into it again and again, as we must, it leads to dissatisfaction. Even though, in the view of our hallucinated mind of attachment, what we're experiencing is real happiness, pure happiness, through meditation we can discover for ourselves that it's actually suffering, and our clinging to it is the cause of samsara, is what's making us die and be reborn continuously.

Worldly happiness must *always* turn into suffering. We get pleasure from swimming on a hot day but if we stay in the water too long we get cold and crave warmth. We're happy eating food, but if we eat more and more, we lose the taste, our stomach fills up and we vomit. Sherpa people who enjoy drinking *chang* drink one cup, then another because they liked the first, then more and more until they completely lose all control and discipline. They often end up fighting and shouting nonsensical words and breaking things that were usually obtained with much difficulty. Their minds are not happy because of the wrong belief that does not see the true nature of suffering. The same can be said about people who use drugs.

Conversely, true Dharma happiness—the happiness that comes from renouncing the thought of the eight worldly dharmas—never ends but there's an end to the work we need to do to obtain it. The more we experience Dharma happiness, the more enjoyment we get and it can never be used up, which is the complete opposite of worldly pleasure.

Enjoying worldly pleasure depends on maintaining something that is not a continuum, so it always finishes, but the pleasure of enjoying the holy Dharma is a continuum, so it's unceasing. And whereas none of the worldly possessions we worked very hard to obtain and are so attached to can be taken with us to our future life, all of our Dharma possessions—the merit we create by practicing Dharma—can be.

As we gradually progress in our Dharma practice, slowly working toward the path of the higher capable being,[26] our happiness increases more and more. When we finally achieve enlightenment, our work has finished but the enjoyment we receive from Dharma practice lasts forever; it never finishes. Achieving the ultimate goal, enlightenment, does not mean, as some people think, that everything becomes nothingness, like space. It's not at all like that; if it were, there'd be no way for us to help other beings after getting enlightened.

To stop ourselves from being attached to things and creating the cause of more suffering when we're experiencing worldly pleasure, we can think, "It's only my wrong conception that believes this to be true pleasure. In fact, it's not true pleasure but only suffering. It never gives satisfaction; it never lasts. It never gives unending satisfaction. Therefore, being attached to this samsaric pleasure will only keep me continuously in the bondage of samsaric suffering and cause me to be reborn in the three lower realms and suffer there forever. This pleasure is trivial and I should not be attached to it."

When we finally achieve enlightenment, our work has finished; we've achieved the highest pleasure and it's unchangeable and can never revert to anything less. Because there's not one atom of delusion in the enlightened mind, there's no way it can slip back. There's no creator to change it and bring it down; there's no higher state we still need to work toward. Therefore, just as the enlightened state never changes, so the happiness received from Dharma practice never finishes.

Therefore, after we start to practice Dharma and face and eventually

[26] According to the lam-rim teachings there are three levels of practice: the path of the lower capable being seeking the happiness of future lives; the path of the medium capable being seeking individual liberation, or nirvana; and the path of the higher capable being seeking full enlightenment for the sake of all sentient beings.

destroy the enemy, the thought of the worldly dharmas, there's a big difference in the happiness we receive. The very rough and dangerous water of samsaric pleasures becomes a vast ocean—blue, calm and very clear.

To use another analogy, if we pull a thorn out of our foot there's no more pain—with the thorn removed, it's natural that the problem ceases. It's logical. In the same way, we need to see samsaric pleasure as suffering or we won't try to remove it. The actual thing is to see this through our own experience, then we'll understand that what the Dharma explains is really true.

The real happiness of life, real peace of mind, is renunciation. Whenever we start to practice renouncing the desire for this life, real peace of mind starts. So holy Dharma and worldly dharma are complete opposites: holy Dharma is renouncing the thought of the eight worldly dharmas; the thought of the eight worldly dharmas is renouncing the holy Dharma.

RELYING ON THE UNRELIABLE

Wanting peace on the rollercoaster

With the thought of the eight worldly dharmas there's no way we can have peace of mind. We wake up in the morning happy, smiling, feeling kind of high, almost flying. Then, within an hour, our mind has totally crashed. It goes on like this day after day, some days happy all day, other days miserable, sometimes happy in the morning but by evening completely berserk, ridiculous.

Our life becomes a wild goose chase, running after what we think will make us happy and running away from what we don't like, constantly fluctuating between wishes fulfilled and wishes frustrated, constantly up and down. Even though all we want is peace and happiness, we're on a constant rollercoaster of emotions. Praise brings happiness, criticism brings misery; a good reputation makes us feel really good, a bad one makes us feel terrible. We're happy when things go our way and we have the four desirable objects and we plunge into depression and misery when things don't go our way and we have to face the four undesirable objects. Happy, unhappy, excited, depressed—up, down, up, down, even in the space of one day. In this way our life is never balanced, peaceful or happy. As long as we crave things, it will always be like this. We're living in a house built out of the evil thought of the eight worldly dharmas and all our confusion stems from that. We want peace but our worldly concern robs us of it, making our mind extremely unstable.

Actually, if we really understand this subject, we can see our life as a movie—funny, interesting, awful, disgusting. If we analyze it we can easily see that the thought of the eight worldly dharmas is what makes life so difficult, so suffocating. This evil thought is the reason we have no freedom, no peace of mind.

We're completely reliant on external conditions, objects of desire, for our happiness but they're not dependable; the conditions are always changing. Dependent on ever-changing conditions, our mind is uncontrollable, a weak animal that can't carry its load and is always staggering, falling first this way, then that, as the conditions change. As a result, one minute we're up, the next minute we're down. This is the nature of samsara.

Our main entertainment—television, movies, books and so forth—is based on the drama that this crazy fluctuation creates. Almost every book in airport bookshops is about the ups and downs of people's lives and how all their problems are based on attachment clinging to this life. Stories on television are based on people's lives going out of control—one day happy, the next day unhappy; in the morning happy, in the afternoon unhappy. Listening to other people's problems, we can see how they all come from discrimination or anger that in turn arise out of clinging to this life, the attachment and aversion associated with one of these eight objects.

One of the things I've noticed traveling around the world is that the lives of people in materially developed countries are quite complicated and unstable whereas the lives of those in primitive countries where there are few modern appliances—sometimes not even matches—seem much more stable. Of course, they have problems—after all, they're also living in samsara, where just having a body is a problem. But they don't have problems like people in the West, where it seems that their mood changes minute by minute: up one minute, down the next.

Many of the great yogis of the past chose to lead a simple life at the beginning of their practice. It wasn't because they were fools or didn't know how to live a worldly life or how to be political, cunning or smart. The purpose of choosing that life was to fight the evil thought of the eight worldly dharmas. If at the beginning of our practice we live among temporal needs and have everything we like, we find it extremely difficult to practice Dharma purely; invariably, the thought of eight worldly dharmas interferes with our attempts to do so.

If you read the autobiography of the great yogi Milarepa, who achieved enlightenment in one lifetime, he explains how the great peace in his life came from practicing Dharma. His songs are full of this. There are many other great yogis who also explain their own experiences and they all say how only by practicing pure Dharma unstained by the thought of the eight worldly dharmas can one find real happiness in this and future lives.

Expecting happiness from the unreliable

Unlike Dharma happiness, which can never be stolen, worldly pleasures can be taken away by an enemy. Whatever we have—friends, wealth, possessions and so forth—will inevitably get lost for one reason or another. If our house is full of wonderful things, other people get jealous and steal them; if we're rich, there are always robbers around waiting to take our wealth. Everywhere we look there are people wanting what we have, looking for ways to rob us of our pleasure.

Sometimes desirable objects themselves become undesirable. Many actions done with worldly concern eventually lead to the four undesirable results. For example, in business, we may have success after success and because of that act more and more with the thought of the eight worldly dharmas. Then after some time our karma to be successful finishes and our karma for failure ripens. In a day we become a pauper—one day we're a millionaire, the next we don't even know how we'll pay our rent or take care of our family. Our whole life collapses. Thogme Zangpo said,

> Even if everybody could obtain the perfections of this life, there's
> no guarantee that they could freely enjoy them. The only thing
> that's certain is death.

We might be able to get whatever it is we think will bring us pleasure in our life but there's no certainty that we'll be able to freely enjoy it. Even if others don't try to steal our treasured possession, the object itself—a fast car, perhaps—can become a danger to our life.

We make many arrangements and work very hard for years and years to obtain the perfections of this life but what is more certain, the realization of our plan or death? Death is *definitely* more certain than our plan. And at the time of death, none of this life's perfections can benefit us and, because we're clinging to this life, there's much suffering. Thogme Zangpo encourages us to understand this and to strongly renounce this life.[27]

---

[27] See the meditation at the end of this chapter.

The great pandit Asanga said that there's no way to compare worldly pleasure with the pleasure of enjoying the holy Dharma. For example, no worldly pleasure covers the whole body. The pleasure we experience from an object of attachment is extremely limited—to a very short duration and a very small area. The most delicious food in the world is delicious only between the tongue and the throat, lasts only for the time it takes to swallow and there's no way the rest of the body can enjoy it: our feet can't, our arms can't, and our stomach might even end up in pain if the food is too rich.

Ordinary samsaric happiness derives from external objects and doesn't arise if the object isn't nearby. This is what "not covering the whole body" means. Dharma happiness, on the other hand, can be permanently increased without depending on external objects and does cover the whole body. As such, it is pure happiness and causes us to receive the transcendent realizations of the noble beings in this very life. Enjoying worldly pleasures doesn't help develop realizations either in this life or in future lives.

It is also useful to remember what Guru Shakyamuni Buddha said:

> If you wish all happiness, renounce all attachment. If you renounce all attachment, you will achieve the supreme happiness.

The pleasure of enjoying the holy Dharma gives satisfaction because it pacifies the disturbed, unsubdued mind of attachment, thus eliminating the problems of this and all future lives.

In his *Precious Garland*, Nagarjuna advises the king to do his work according to Dharma and that by freeing himself from the dissatisfied mind of desire he will receive respect, a good reputation and everything he needs and, furthermore, will benefit all other sentient beings greatly. If done with desire, even the work of a king has no meaning.

MEDITATION

Meditating on the eight worldly dharmas and impermanence and death

Without question, the quickest, most powerful technique to destroy the thought of the eight worldly dharmas is meditation on impermanence and death.[28] People are naturally afraid of death. In that, they are the same as

---

[28] See the forthcoming LYWA book by Rinpoche on impermanence and death, various FPMT

animals. When a dog is attacked by another dog, it's afraid of death; when it's beaten by a person, it's afraid of death; when it gets too close to a cliff, it's afraid of death. Ordinary people who don't practice Dharma have the same fear of death, but that fear is useless, simply because it brings no solution, no method to stop the cause. The fear generated when we meditate on the impermanence of life and the certainty of death is different. It's a vital tool to completely stop the greater fear and to free ourselves from the endless circle of death and rebirth.[29]

Death will definitely happen; we're definitely going to die. Death is something we all have to experience, something we can experience at any time. There's no use ignoring it and unless we prepare for death in this life we cannot possibly die with a happy mind.

Without meditating on the impermanence of life and death, even though we might want to practice Dharma, we become lazy and always put it off. We think Dharma is not so important, that there's no rush, and constantly keep ourselves busy with all the many worldly things that seem more urgent. And even when we do try to practice Dharma, our actions become worldly because our motivation never goes beyond the happiness of this life. His Holiness the Dalai Lama says,

> If we don't renounce the temporal life through the practice of meditation on impermanence, the Dharma actions we perform become a service to the eight worldly dharmas.

We might know logically that we're going to die, but unless we've really studied this subject, our death seems so remote and far away—twenty, thirty, forty years—that it's not real to us. Intuitively, we feel as if we're going to live forever. We follow this wrong concept of permanence and thus make many mistakes, trusting in the untrustworthy.

If we strongly remember that we're definitely going to die and that the time of death is indefinite and may in fact happen at any moment, then everything meaningless falls away and we naturally abandon all the pointless concerns of this life—the need for a good reputation, admiration, possessions and so forth. We immediately see that everything we do *must* prepare

---

materials on this topic and related teachings in Tsongkhapa's *Great Treatise,* Pabongka's *Liberation in the Palm of Your Hand* and other lam-rim books.

[29] This is the subject of the book *Wholesome Fear.*

us for death and our next life, and even though the things we do might have the aspect of worldly actions, they automatically become holy Dharma. Living like this leads us to have a happy mind at the time of death and to happiness in our future lives and also lays the foundation for enlightenment.

Meditations to abandon attachment

Contemplate how rarely you even think about death. Normally you act as if you're going to live forever but this is completely deluded. Everybody dies and you're no exception. Furthermore, you have no idea when you will die. It might be in a few years but it might also be tomorrow or even today. Contemplate that you really have no idea when you will die.

Think of a present or some praise that you've recently received and how it made you happy. That happiness feels permanent, but which is more definite, that you'll be separated from the object of your attachment or that you'll never be separated from it? In the same way, ask yourself which is more definite, to be born in the lower realms or the upper? Because you've created far more negative karma than positive, it's much more likely that you'll be born in the lower realms.

Then visualize as clearly and strongly as possible the suffering of the hells.[30] Don't just think the words but really try to get a clear picture and feel the experience. Think, "This terrible place of unbelievable suffering is where I'm about to be reborn." This is a very quick way of controlling attachment. If you can generate a strong picture of the suffering of the hells and see it as somewhere you *will* end up very soon because of your attachment, your attachment will automatically disappear.

Then draw the conclusion that you gain absolutely no benefit from being attached, especially since your attachment will lead you to such a place of suffering. Therefore, the object of attachment, such as the gift or praise you have received, is worse than useless.

This meditation can also be used whenever you're angry—for example, when somebody criticizes you. Watch your mind as anger arises. Observe how your mind can change. If that person had praised you, you would have

---

[30] There are many descriptions of the lower realms by Rinpoche and many other great masters. See the forthcoming LYWA book by Rinpoche on the three lower realms and lam-rim books such as Tsongkhapa's *Great Treatise* and Pabongka's *Liberation in the Palm of Your Hand*.

been happy, but as soon as she criticized you, you got really angry. See how changeable your mind is depending on the object and see how this, not the object, is the cause of suffering. From that, go on to do the death meditation as above.

When you have a clear visualization of the hell realms that your anger is leading you to, your anger will automatically go away. Conclude by thinking that there's no reason at all to ever get angry.

Meditate, too, on the impermanent nature of phenomena. It is in the nature of samsara that we lose things we want and encounter things we don't. Padmasambhava said,

> The vision of this life is like last night's dream.
> All meaningless actions are like ripples on a lake.[31]

Whenever there's a problem, instead of worrying about it, building it up and giving yourself a nervous breakdown, just see that problem as a dream; you are simply *dreaming* you are having a problem. You should think about it in the way that Padmasambhava said. You may have a dream that lasts only a few moments, but within the dream itself it seems to last a very long time, maybe a hundred thousand years. You live somewhere and grow from a child to an adult, become middle-aged, then your hair turns white. You see your whole life over many years and during that time there are many pleasures and many problems. Yet the actual duration of the dream is perhaps five minutes. When you wake up you realize it has just been a short time and it's empty; whatever problem or excitement you had in the dream is empty.

Similarly, this life appears to last a long time, but at the time of death you suddenly experience that your life has gone and you feel as if you're waking from a dream. You see that, in fact, your life was very short. You're definitely going to experience this when you die, therefore you should remember it now in order to control your delusions and prepare yourself for death. If you do, you can die happy and you'll be happy in your future lives, all the way to liberation and enlightenment.

Reflecting on impermanence and death is the most powerful thing. Not just that you might die sometime in the vague future but that death can happen *now*, at this very moment, while you're eating, while you're on the toilet,

---

[31] Quoted in Rinpoche's *Wish-fulfilling Golden Sun* in the section on the nine-point death meditation.

while you're drinking tea, while you're walking, while you're going home—death can happen at any time. From here to there, just a few steps, you might die. You might even die before your meditation session has finished.

You need to relate this to karma, otherwise it's just the consciousness separating from the body and what then? When you think about the vast amount of negative karma you've created in this life alone, the moment after the moment of death will almost certainly be in the lower realms amid all those unimaginable sufferings. It's extremely terrifying. Nobody even wants to have a terrifying dream; we all want our dreams to be pleasant and nice. We can't even stand the sufferings of the human realm. So how will we bear the unimaginable sufferings of the lower realms?

For instance, maybe a woman is thinking of killing herself because she's so attached to her husband that she can't stand the thought of his dying one day and being left on her own. Being with her husband is the only thing that's important to her, so her fear of losing him completely overwhelms her to the point where she really contemplates suicide. By remembering impermanence and death in the Dharma way, she will see that, in fact, he *is* going leave her. Everybody dies, and he must separate from her, so what is the point of being attached? If she can remember impermanence and death, right at that moment, all that big hassle will dissipate like a cloud in the sky.

Thinking that death might happen this hour, this minute, this moment cuts the thought of the eight worldly dharmas, which means peace arises in your heart immediately; your mind *immediately* lets go of the attachment clinging to the pleasures of this life. All your fear and worry, all those hundreds of thousands of expectations and superstitions caused by the thought of the eight worldly dharmas, are cut. Then, when you think back how worried you were, you just have to laugh because it was so childish. Your mind is free from confusion; whatever you do becomes pure Dharma, like pure gold.

If your Dharma practice isn't developing, then no matter what you study or meditate on, whether it's bodhicitta or emptiness or whatever, the reason will be because you've not started with this most basic meditation on impermanence and death. If you omit the first part then there's no chance that the more advanced practices will succeed. You need to cut the thought of the eight worldly dharmas and to do that you need a technique like meditating on the impermanence of life and the certainty of death. If you avoid these meditations because you think that they're boring or you're afraid to do them, that's a big mistake.

5. The Problems Desire Brings

Seeking happiness, we create negative karma

Looking for happiness by following the thought of the eight worldly dharmas not only fails to bring us the happiness we want, it usually also leads to our creating more negative karma.

We might be sleeping comfortably when suddenly our sleep is disturbed by a mosquito. All we want is peace and comfort and this little bug is doing its best to destroy all that, so of course we're annoyed. And yet, all we're getting is one tiny nip from one little mosquito. Generally speaking, it's nothing dangerous, nothing that can cause any serious disease. The mosquito takes one tiny drop of blood from our body. But seeing that mosquito's body filled with our own blood, we're enraged. When we move, it bites us in another place. We try to catch it but we can't. Then, finally, after hours of this mosquito buzzing around and biting us and evading our attempts to catch it, we find it. We really want to kill that bug. For sure! We find it, crush it and are very happy, incredibly happy. *Now* we have peace. And so we've done a nonvirtuous action with great joy. It becomes a very powerful karma. But of course we don't see it that way.

Our job should be the source of our worldly happiness but for most of us it not only fails to bring us that happiness, it also brings suffering to many other beings as well. We probably don't think we're a negative person but neither does a butcher, whose job is to slaughter sentient beings. While honestly thinking that he's just taking care of his and his family's immediate needs, he's creating powerful negative karma that will cause him incredible suffering in future. This is a double negative action that brings suffering to himself and others.

Like the butcher, we do negative things to get what we want and not only fail to achieve the happiness we seek but also create the cause for future suffering. The things we do to avoid poverty and hunger, the results of previous negative karma, create more negative karma. In other words, we create negative karma to stop negative karma—an impossible thing. This is nobody's fault, but by trying to end our suffering in this unskillful way, suffering perpetuates suffering, endlessly.

Expecting from the depths of their heart to achieve happiness, people all over the world cheat, lie, steal and even kill. Because of his dissatisfied mind, somebody who actually has enough to live on still feels that he doesn't have enough and that the only way to be happy is to rob a bank. Then, by stealing what belongs to others, he creates negative karma, causing difficulties for himself and many others. He risks getting caught, shot, killed, thrown into prison and tortured. He might have murdered somebody to get that person's property, the police might have captured him and the judge might have sentenced him, but it's actually the evil thought of the eight worldly dharmas that has landed him in prison. The notoriety and hatred that his acts bring him all started because he wanted to be happy. His ignorance led him to crime. Our ignorance might not lead us that far but it still demands that we create lots of negative karma.

Acts of terrorism, kidnapping and hijacking are terrible and bring not one single atom of benefit to anybody, either the criminal or the victim, but it's completely the thought of the worldly dharmas that forces people to act like this.

Following the thought of the eight worldly dharmas, a person who kills others has no peace. He himself is always in danger of being killed by his victim's relatives or friends. He receives a bad reputation and has to go into exile, to flee his country to avoid getting thrown into prison. That's his life. And the suffering he'll experience in future lives is truly terrible. It's as if he has purposely made himself a path straight to the lower realms. All this is caused by the evil thought attached to the comfort of this life.

This is happening nowadays even in India. People see kidnappings in the West on television and learn from them; they learn how to be skilful and clever at harming other sentient beings. How terrible it is to kidnap another person, then make a phone call to the poor parents: "If you don't give me a million dollars, I'm going to kill your daughter." The family have to accept that their daughter is in the hands of other people and in danger of being killed, so of course they say they will pay. But when the kidnappers get the money, they still kill the daughter. Even if she's not killed, what happens? The parents can't repay the money and then have to work hard for the rest of their lives but can never repay the debt.

It's often the case that the rich have gained their great wealth through negative actions such as lying, cheating and stealing, but even though they might have every possible comfort, what kind of life is it really and what happens when they die? There's no real peace at all.

We can easily see this if we look at very rich people in the West. They're unable to relax. A poor family has much more time than the rich do. They're always busy, they have many worries and there's always the possibility that their business will fail and they'll lose everything they've worked for. They're never sure that the economy won't collapse or that their competitors won't develop something better.

Clinging to worldly pleasures, we discriminate against others based on whether they help or harm us and this is the cause of all disharmony and fighting between individuals and even countries. This person gives me what I want, so he is good; this person stops me from getting what I want, so she is bad. This is the main way we judge people. It has nothing to do with their qualities and everything to do with the fulfillment of our selfish desires.

If we check, we'll find that we discriminate like this all the time. These people are good, those people are bad; this country is good, that country is bad. Our discrimination is not based on concern for the other person's happiness but on concern for only our own, so it's very selfish. Discriminating like this, we wish our enemies harm. We don't want to be criticized or abused ourselves, but for our enemies it's the opposite. We want them to meet *all* four undesirable objects as much as possible.

Our potential is wasted

It took us an enormous amount of energy to create the causes for this perfect human existence yet the thought of the eight worldly dharmas makes all that effort meaningless. Furthermore, by wasting this present life we waste all our future lives and destroy the possibility of receiving better rebirths and the many things that we can achieve with them, especially the ultimate happiness of liberation and enlightenment.

One way we squander our incredible potential is by using all our energy in confused, unskillful ways simply to get rid of mundane hardships. For instance, it's natural to wash when we get up in the morning. Nobody wants to smell, but what kind of mind do we wash with? With the thought of the eight worldly dharmas. We don't have any higher, special reason to wash or way of washing.

Then, when we have tea—all of a sudden a desire for tea arises—that, too, has no special reason, no pure motivation. We just drink, unconsciously, with attachment, with the thought of the eight worldly dharmas. It's the same with breakfast or going for a walk—again there's no pure motivation there at all. Then, our whole day is spent working: during that time we're incredibly busy but without any real understanding of whether our actions are positive or negative.

Probably our motivation is to earn money to get what we want for the comfort of this life and to not be fired. There's no pure motivation, nothing to do with Dharma practice, nothing to do with benefiting other sentient beings. Our mind is concerned with only one thing—me. All the time, the great big me. If we truthfully check up from the depths of our heart, this is why we work.

And while we're working all kinds of negative thoughts arise: hatred, jealousy, attachment and the rest. We gossip with a jealous mind or anger, with the thought of the eight worldly dharmas. Then, at lunch time, we eat with attachment to worldly pleasure, with the thought of the eight worldly dharmas. We go shopping with the eight worldly dharmas, buying things with attachment for the great big me, seeking only the comfort of this life.

In the evening we throw a party, but again there's no virtuous reason for doing so; we're partying with the thought of the eight worldly dharmas. Maybe we hope to get presents from the people we invite, but the presents are for our enjoyment, not for our enlightenment. Maybe we're looking for praise or a good reputation. But whether we do that or go to a movie, watch television or phone our friends, everything we do is the same trip, working for the thought of the eight worldly dharmas.

And when we finally go to bed we're still out of control, too tired to think of anything virtuous. Again there's no pure motivation, just unconsciously, "I'm tired," just seeking comfort of this life, and so with attachment, we go to bed. And then become like a dead person.

Here we're just looking at a normal day's activities when nothing terrible has happened. It doesn't include anything done that hurts another being, like killing, hunting or fighting. Even these very normal everyday actions are done with the thought of the eight worldly dharmas. Slaves to attachment, we do nothing that brings beneficial results or happiness and many of our actions destroy the very happiness they're designed to get.

We think that there's no time to practice Dharma. "I have to do this, I have to do that, and after that, I have to do this and that, this and that," all very clearly controlled by the thought of the eight worldly dharmas. Not counting our job, we have time for all these other things, for watching television and so forth, but somehow there's no time for meditation. We can see very clearly that this is a creation of our own mind, the thought of the eight worldly dharmas not wanting to bear the difficulties of meditation.

There are so many things that seem harmless but are in fact doing us great harm because they waste our life. When one of the previous Ganden Tripas came to the United States he discovered television. He was amazed at what a waste of time it was and advised Western students never to watch TV.

I do watch television—and it *is* a great waste of time—but we can watch television from a lam-rim perspective. Looking at the programs, we can see how the nature of samsara traps us. The actors in the programs show us; they have parties, get killed, are tortured, cheat each other, make wars—whatever they do, it's all suffering.

Dawa Dragpa

Once in Tibet there was a servant for a rich family. During the years he worked for them he received a monthly wage of one plate of barley. Each month he saved some of the barley and then, finally, one year, he had saved a big sack of barley. He took this sack back to his home and hung it from the ceiling by a rope. As he was lying on his bed feeling very happy at having all this barley he thought, "Now I'm rich, *incredibly* rich, with this big sack of barley. What should I do?" He made plans. He thought he should get married and have a child and wondered what he should call that child.

As he was thinking, the moon came out, sending moonbeams through the window onto the floor. Suddenly, looking at the moonlight, the name for the child came to him. "Fantastic! I shall name my child after the moon! Famous Moon (Dawa Dragpa)." After so much thinking, the name seemed perfect and he couldn't contain his joy. He jumped up, grabbed a stick and started dancing around the room, swinging the stick over his head. The stick struck the bag of barley and it dropped down on his head, killing him instantly.

So, after working for so many years, he didn't have the chance to enjoy his barley—not even one plate—or to get married and have a child. And this was all the fault of his uncontrolled mind. He was attached to the barley and the sense that he was rich, attached to his future plans and attached to his future child and its beautiful name. Unable to control the thought of the eight worldly dharmas, he killed himself unnecessarily. He was killed by the thought of the eight worldly dharmas. If we don't control our mind, this can easily happen to us as well.

HARMING OTHERS WITH OUR OWN NEEDS

The misery of a relationship based on selfishness

Thogme Zangpo said,

> Always quarreling and fighting with leaders, teachers, friends, relatives, unable to bear suffering, bad reputation and being without enjoyments. The evil thought alone causes a person to do this uncontrollably.

Even though we might have studied psychology extensively and feel we're an expert, as long as we don't recognize the thought of the eight worldly dharmas, there's no way to recognize the main source of our relationship problems and therefore no way to work to solve them. In fact, attacking them unskillfully will only make them worse.

We see in newspapers and on television how all the time people in relationships have so many incredible problems: fighting, quarrelling, being unfaithful, breaking up, killing each other. If we look for the source of these problems we will see that they all stem from the thought of the eight worldly dharmas.

I once read in a newspaper about an old man in Greece who married twenty times, always changing from one young girl to another. The article said he wanted to take another wife, this time a young girl in prison. In the East, there are fewer problems like this because many marriages are arranged. Right from the start the parents check the whole of their child's life with lamas or astrologers in order for there to be harmony.

We create many problems for ourselves in our quest for friends. For instance, we move to a new country and feel very lonely. We don't know anyone; we don't have any friends. After a while we get to know some people and feel happy for a while, but before long we begin to dislike them. They no longer live up to our expectations and we don't get on with them any more. We complain that they're no good, that they have such bad personalities and so forth. Expecting supportive relationships, when they don't work out we get angry and friends become enemies. In addition to the lack of peace from the very beginning, the suffering has now doubled.

Relationship problems go on and on as long as we keep the thought of the worldly dharmas in our heart. Basing relationships on *my* needs alone, seeing them through our own selfishness, of course our partners can never give us what we want. We're so obsessed by our own problems that we can't eat, can't work, can't sleep. We even develop physical problems such as back and chest pains. When we lose our object of desire—our friend doesn't love us any more and leaves us or something else happens—if we can't do anything to control the situation, such as kill the person who has interfered with our desire, we go crazy or have a nervous breakdown. Desire doesn't give our mind space for anything but the thought of suicide. We take refuge in an overdose of sleeping pills, a rope with which hang ourselves, the roof of a tall building or a high bridge from which we can throw ourselves, such as the famous Golden Gate or Sydney Harbour bridges.

There was a Swiss student who spoke and taught Tibetan and was translating texts and receiving teachings from Geshe Rabten Rinpoche, my first teacher and one of Lama Yeshe's teachers as well. One day his wife left him and, unable to bear the pain and anger, he hung himself in his house. That's how he ended his life. He couldn't stand the desire for his object of his attachment being frustrated. If he hadn't been so attached to his wife, her leaving him wouldn't have seemed such a tragedy. Nobody else came there to hang him; he hung himself. Actually, the thought of the eight worldly dharmas hung him. The real problem in his life was not his wife but his own mind. He didn't practice the antidote to attachment. He didn't let go of attachment. He didn't give it up. His attachment was so strong that it tortured him, bringing him so much pain that he committed suicide.

I once met a man in Singapore who told me he had a huge problem and wasn't sure whether he'd be alive the next day. His wife had left him and taken up with somebody else. She told him that she was going to be coming back to their house to pick up some things and he was planning to kill her there. He told me that he was going to the temple to tell the Buddha he was going to take her with him, meaning he was going to kill her first and then himself. Anyway, he kept on telling me that he wasn't sure whether or not he'd be alive the next day.

I tried to explain to him that this was the complete opposite of what the Buddha had taught, but I haven't met him since so I don't know what happened. Maybe he's in another realm by now; maybe they both are. I'm not sure. It's incredible how somebody we're totally attached to, somebody we can't bear to be separated from, can become an object to kill. Attachment brings one problem after another, on and on.

Jealousy between married couples is common. This is the most familiar theme of novels, and many films on television and in the cinema are about jealousy and infidelity. This is really funny, because the people who watch these movies are involved in such real-life situations themselves. They themselves are living in a movie but when they watch the on-screen version they have no idea how much like their own life that movie is and they watch it as if they're not involved in the kind of life it portrays, as if they've transcended that life. The world is full of such people but they never check up the root of the problem.

Perhaps a man is married but he's not satisfied with his wife so he starts seeing somebody else. He thinks that his new relationship is better, that this woman is more beautiful, the pleasure more intense. Whatever the thought of the eight worldly dharmas tells him to do, he does, uncontrollably. But maybe after a while the new person no longer satisfies him, so he starts another relationship, then another, like this all the time, because of the dissatisfaction caused by attachment. He creates much confusion in his life—with himself, his wife and the other women.

He's like a bee buzzing around in a field of flowers, flying from flower to flower, taking a little pollen from one, then moving on to the next and then the next and the next, never able to settle anywhere, always causing confusion for himself and others. And if he's like this then he's also worried that his wife might be the same; that she might be unfaithful too and run off with somebody else. So his life is full of worry that he will lose what he has. This also comes from the thought of the worldly eight dharmas.

His strong attachment causes him to be very fearful whenever his wife goes out, even for a short time, perhaps just for one or two hours. He stays home worrying that she will be seduced by another man. If she goes away for a few days' holiday without him, he's out of his mind with worry. He can't stand it; he can't wait for her return. He can't relax. If she doesn't come back as scheduled he starts calling all their friends, "Where is she? Where is she?" He keeps everybody busy. His mind is so nervous; his whole body is so nervous.

Maybe she does have an affair that she has to keep a secret, like the Vajrayana teachings. But one day he hears from a friend, "Oh yes, I saw your wife with another man, blah, blah, blah. Your wife was drinking at this party, blah, blah, blah," all these things. He gets furious waiting for her to return, his face extremely red. He's unable to do any work; he just paces about wringing his hands. And when she comes back, there's a huge argument. All the families in the other flats, downstairs, upstairs, can hear. What's happening? What movie is being shown in that house? The other families finally get so fed up with this couple who are always screaming and fighting that they move to another place where there's more peace.

The couple keep fighting and it gets worse and worse. He says something, she says something, they pull each other's hair, they beat each other up. Maybe they end up killing each other or maybe she escapes. She goes to the wardrobe, grabs her clothes, throws them into a suitcase and leaves, slamming the door loudly behind her.

Then he hears she's flown to Chicago or Hawaii with another man. He can't stand it; his body shakes violently. In his view this other guy is now the most evil being in the world. He wants to kill him, blow him up, make him completely non-existent. If he had the power, he'd do this. He's so upset he can't eat. Even though there's plenty of food in the kitchen—even if somebody cooks a meal and brings it to him—he has no appetite. His mind is full of worry, completely concentrated on that enemy and his wife.

He can't sleep at all; he tosses and turns in bed the whole night. He spends the entire night meditating single-pointedly on those two objects, his wife and her boyfriend. He's so upset he can't relax at all. Then he decides he has to fly to where they are. No matter how much it costs, he's going to get a ticket and go there right away. So now he's completely concentrated on that problem.

After arriving, he goes around and around, around and around, checking everywhere, searching anxiously, completely spaced out. Everybody can see from his face the problem he has. When he finds his wife and her boyfriend, he creates a huge scene and finishes up shooting the boyfriend. Or perhaps before he can kill his rival he himself gets killed. Then it's finished. All that worry, all that effort was completely unsuccessful.

Like this, relationships involve a huge amount of suffering. A man goes to a psychiatrist because his wife has left him and all the psychiatrist can tell him to do is to go find another woman, another object of desire. But even if he manages to acquire another wife or girlfriend, he might stay with her for some time, but because of his fickle mind, it doesn't last. Things change again, he gets another divorce, and many more problems arise—his children are taken away from him and so forth.

From his wife's side, his jealousy makes her so crazy that her need for kindness drives her to look for somebody else who might provide it. All her fear and worry, too, is caused by attachment. Maybe she gets pregnant— even if she's on the pill, it can still happen without choice or control. Then there's incredibly more worry in her mind. Abortions are very expensive and she has no money, so what to do? She can't tell her husband or her parents because they'll be furious and kick her out, and the guy who made her pregnant won't help either. So she has to steal the money for an abortion.

For people like this, all these problems—with children, wives, husbands, boyfriends, girlfriends—arise over and over again. Even if a person is over sixty, he still hasn't finished working and has to start his life over again. The second round. All these problems are caused by the thought of the eight worldly dharmas, attachment to the pleasure of this life.

Even couples who stay together can be tortured by fears that their spouse will be unfaithful. Their relationship is full of suspicion, jealousy and rivalry. The husband feels his wife is forever hurting his pride; the wife feels that he doesn't have a good enough job or that their status in society isn't high enough.

Perhaps they want to build a house, but they have different ideas about what they want. Each wants to do things according to his or her own idea, so even if the house gets built it doesn't suit either one. Because the need to have their own way is rooted in both their minds, neither listens to the other's ideas and they both get really angry. And pride arises because they feel their own ideas are better than the other's, and then many other negative minds arise. We can easily see how confused life becomes when it's ruled by the thought of the eight worldly dharmas.

Maybe it's nothing so big. The husband and wife just fight and argue, day after day, over anything, even breakfast. She wants muesli, he wants bread; he says muesli makes him sick, she says bread makes her sick. In fact, they're both sick. Whatever they end up having, neither is happy and they spend breakfast arguing with each other. Maybe they even end up fighting physically. That can happen. Many times insignificant incidents build up into major arguments and big fights. To us it might seem insignificant but to the couple it's a really big thing. But it's like children fighting. Children know very little and are only concerned with getting what they want, so they often fight over small things.

Even when the wife gets him his bread, he's not happy; he's still confused and sick with attachment. Getting the bread might solve the problem of not having bread but it doesn't solve the problem of attachment. In the same way, because the wife wants muesli, she thinks he's being selfish wanting bread. She's following her own desire, her own attachment. During their whole life that problem is never solved, and so life passes. They continue to experience the problems of attachment and then they die. And whatever rebirths they take, the problems caused by attachment continue.

Imagining what would happen if, for instance, instead of insisting on bread the husband just accepted the muesli, thinking, "I think my desire is important but really, her desire is just as important as mine." Simply by renouncing the thought that his desire is more important that his wife's, by not following his attachment, the problem is solved. He feels happy and doesn't upset his wife. It's just a matter of changing the way of thinking, a matter of conception.

By the husband's accepting what his wife offers, neither of them creates negative karma by getting angry. Both are at peace and relaxed; both are happy. This is scientific experience, not some religious superstition that we're asked to believe. This is the way the mind works; it's simple psychology.

When we're attached to somebody, even if that person is suffering we don't have the space to feel real compassion for them. When we're overwhelmed by our own needs we can never generate compassion and bodhicitta, the heart-felt wish to achieve enlightenment for the sake of other sentient beings. But if we can lessen our attachment to temporal pleasures, there will be less confusion in our relationships. With more peace and more satisfaction, we can bring more peace and satisfaction to our partner and our friends.

Society's problems come from the eight worldly dharmas

Disharmony in relationships doesn't just happen between two individuals; whole groups of people fight—families, gangs, communities, even countries—all because of the evil thought of the eight worldly dharmas. The main stories in newspapers are always about disputes, whether they're between political parties, companies or countries. Most of the images television news brings us are of fighting, murders and wars. All the hostility of this world comes from the need to get what we want and the willingness to harm others to get it.

For instance, a university, which should be a place of wisdom, can be a hotbed of rivalry and pettiness, caused by pride, anger and all the other negative minds. A student might be consumed with jealousy and hatred for those with more knowledge. She thinks that all the other students have more knowledge, a greater reputation and more friends than she does. She can't stand how they seem to enjoy wonderful reputations and warm friendships while she's left out, so she plans how to harm them, maybe even kill them. She doesn't want them to exist. Even though they might have done nothing wrong, she picks fights with them. She tries to undermine them and destroy their reputation so she can gain favor with the teachers and get the position that is rightfully theirs. But nothing brings her satisfaction.

Even lecturers have many problems. They dislike each other and are consumed with rivalry. One who has more ambition gets promoted and the others become jealous of him; another has great knowledge and is renowned in the community but is hated by the others, who feel insecure because they could lose their jobs. All these negative minds—jealousy, pride, fear, suffering—come from the thought of the eight worldly dharmas seeking only the happiness of this life.

Every country on earth is full of problems. There are disputes between workers and bosses, demonstrators and police, and riots so big that the government needs to call in the army to put them down.

As soon as somebody gets into power he's the target of abuse. Whether he does his job well or badly, others blame him for all the problems of the country and do everything possible to give him a bad reputation and bring him down. In the West this often goes on in parliament or in the media, but in other counties it can be far nastier. A person is voted into office to lead a country and gets the name "president" and the power, but it also brings enemies who plot to overthrow him, even if it means harming his family or worse. But even killing him doesn't bring them peace. It doesn't destroy their jealousy or their wish to have the power and possessions of others. It just becomes the cause of more problems, such as the relatives of the dead leader plotting revenge on them. Or if they do get power for themselves, then they in turn are killed by somebody else wanting their power. This is common; we hear about this sort of thing all the time.

When two countries fight, their leaders invariably say it is to bring happiness to their own people, but war can never become a pure action and bring happiness to other living beings. Despite what they say, in the depths of their heart the leaders are doing it for their own reputation and power. They want to have a big name; they want to have power over people; they want to be rich. They are not really concerned with the welfare of the people of their own country and definitely not concerned with that of the people of the country they're fighting.

One person, like Hitler or Mao, can create incredibly heavy negative karma by destroying whole countries and killing millions and millions of people. And not just human beings but numberless other sentient beings as well.

Where does all this greed and desire for power come from? For us, it's quite difficult to see the whole situation. We're really only aware of the physical manifestations—the results—of the greed and hatred; we don't recognize the root problem. We are *all* capable of being jealous of what others have and equally capable of reasoning that we have more right to it than they do and entitled to harm them to get it.

There are so many people in the world whose life is engaged in harming others, without caring, without thinking of this as a negative action. Thieves take others' possessions without even a thought of how it harms the owners. Mercenaries kill other people thoughtlessly. No matter how much danger there is, they just don't care. They think only of reputation and money. This is ridiculous and tragic, because such people are using their incredible human potential in such meaningless and senseless ways. They think that possessions are more important than life.

There are also many other people who don't actively try to harm others but nonetheless cause much pain and suffering by doing meaningless and dangerous actions, such as climbing mountains or going on expeditions. Just to get a thrill or for their own reputation, they risk their own lives and those of the people who guide them. I'm not criticizing them. I'm just talking about how many of us lead our lives, because usually we're not conscious. All these problems are due to the thought of the eight worldly dharmas.

Whether capitalist or socialist, all societies have many problems. The aim of a capitalist society is to make this life comfortable and free of material troubles, such as poverty and starvation, by increasing wealth and developing technologies. This is the ethos of such a society, from the poorest worker to the richest industrialist. Material comfort and leisure, freedom from sickness and poverty—the capitalist seeks nothing higher than this.

Socialists, on the other hand, say that they're concerned for the wellbeing of others. They say that everybody needs material things equally for there to be peace. But no matter how much they use the term "equality" and ideologically seem to be concerned with other beings, they are still controlled by attachment to comfort. If we look at both systems, capitalism and socialism, at a deeper level, we can see that both sides are just trying to make life more materially comfortable, for the individual or for society. Both aim solely for comfort for this life alone. I find it quite strange that they fight each other when their goal is exactly the same.

Even if they were to resolve their differences there would still be no real peace because the source of the problem is within the mind, not in the distribution of wealth. As long as the evil thought of the eight worldly dharmas exists in people's minds there can be no peace, no matter what the system of government.

The thought of the eight worldly dharmas obliges us to waste our life, to create negative karma; it makes our life empty. The biggest countries in the world, with the biggest buildings, the greatest wealth, the most people, still fight each other; there is still much disharmony. This is true of any group—couples, companies, governments—ruled by self-interest.

DYING WITH A NEEDY MIND

The great guru Padmasambhava said,

> The meditator who does not realize that his mind is a liar takes
> the wrong path at the time of death.

He saw that unless we clearly understand the role that the thought of the eight worldly dharmas plays in creating all suffering, we will suffer terribly when we die. Although at the time of death meditators are supposed to be free to take whatever path they choose, unless they've destroyed the thought of the eight worldly dharmas they actually go on the wrong path. Despite the profundity of the subject they might be practicing—Highest Yoga Tantra, controlling the *nadis* or achieving magical powers, such as the ability to fly—they are really only on the road to more suffering.

Death from its own side is not difficult or scary. Our own mind, the desire clinging to this life, is what makes it so fearful. This is the cause of our continuous reincarnation, of our always being chained to samsara—again and again, again and again. It's as if we have a huge block of fiercely burning wood chained to our back, where the fire is the suffering of samsara and the chain tying it to us is our craving for continued existence.

Because of clinging to this life, our mind doesn't want to separate from any aspect of it—our body, possessions, properties, friends, relatives, parents or anything else. So although dying is a natural process, we make it almost impossible to experience death peacefully. Prevented from practicing Dharma and purifying past negative karma by constantly being distracted by the things of this life, we continually create countless causes for rebirth in the lower realms and make our death extremely difficult. We have great fear at the time of death.

MEDITATION

Meditating on the eight worldly dharmas past and present

A very useful meditation to do before going to bed and falling asleep is to check up on each action you did during the day to see how many were done with pure motivation and how many with the thought of the eight worldly dharmas. Check every action done from morning to night: talking to others, drinking, eating, working, playing, watching television. Ask yourself, "Did I do anything at all with a pure motivation, the mind *not* expecting the comfort of this life?" Check up, check up. If you find a positive action done with this pure motivation, with the mind renouncing this life, it is very worthwhile to rejoice.

Investigate the problems you experienced today. If you had an issue with somebody, look to see if it was caused by thought of eight worldly dharmas, if the mind attached to worldly happiness was at the root of it.

Then try to remember what happened yesterday. If you experienced some confusion, some problem or unhappiness, check to see if it was caused by the thought of the eight worldly dharmas. Then go back to the beginning of this year and look at all the problems you've had, then those of the year before and so forth, like this. Go back as far as you can, remembering all the past problems you can, checking back to their source to see if they came from the thought of the eight worldly dharmas.

Check how the thought of the eight worldly dharmas blocks the practice of Dharma. Check how it disturbs your practice of morality, the cause of the body of the happy transmigratory being. Whatever positive action you try to do—meditating, making offerings to holy objects, making charity, helping others—this evil thought arises and disturbs you, preventing that action from becoming the cause of happiness. Thoroughly investigate to see whether or not this is so.

If you're aware, if you keep your mind focused on your inner thought processes, you can recognize clearly how unhappiness, loneliness, lack of peace, depression, aggression and all the other negative minds are caused by this attachment. Study your mind as if it were a book: read and study it.

Then you'll understand. That you don't understand this now is not because nobody has explained it to you; it's simply because you've never meditated in this way before.

This is not just dry doctrine, some kind of abstract philosophy that doesn't relate to real life. It's not something you're asked to believe that has no basis in fact. These teachings are real; what they explain is really true.

After you've checked like this you'll recognize the real enemy, the thought of the eight worldly dharmas, and it will be a lot easier for you not to follow that enemy. Then, when that enemy tells you something pleasing, shows you something tempting, you'll be able to recognize it and think, "This is the evil thought of the eight worldly dharmas telling me to do this." Understanding its shortcomings, you'll naturally not want to follow it any more and will naturally gain much more control over your life. Your life will become more stable and you'll finally start to experience real satisfaction.

6. Mixing Worldly and Holy Dharma

DHARMA PRACTICE IS IMPOSSIBLE WITH THE EIGHT WORLDLY DHARMAS

THE GREAT BODHISATTVA Thogme Zangpo said,

> There is no greater hindrance to taking the holy Dharma on the path to liberation than the evil thought that completely concentrates on obtaining the perfections of this life. Therefore, it is necessary to always avoid this.

The thought of the eight worldly dharmas is the greatest hindrance to Dharma practice. Mix the work for enlightenment with the work of this life and enlightenment is lost, just as food becomes inedible if it's mixed with poison.

We honestly try to do virtuous things—listening to the teachings, studying, reflecting or meditating—but somehow things never work out well because the thought of the eight worldly dharmas always disturbs us. Here is the most delicious food, but it's tainted with poison. It looks enticing but it's inedible. We have to throw it out.

With poison in our system, we're sick with pain and headaches and nothing tastes good. As long as our mind is under the control of the eight worldly dharmas, everything we do is poisoned and no matter how much we try to manipulate our external conditions and acquire material comfort, it doesn't stop the problem. In the same way that we can't be healthy until we've flushed the poison from our body, we can't really be happy until we've flushed the poison of the eight worldly dharmas from our mind.

Until then, we might act renounced but it's all just show. Even if we fast, keep silent or live in an isolated place, all these activities become worldly dharma because the motivation is worldly.

If we wash a white shirt with a black one, the color runs. The black stays black but the white goes grey. When we Tibetans spill butter tea on the white page of a Dharma book, it's impossible for the paper to be white after that. In the same way, a mind mixed with both holy Dharma and the eight worldly dharmas can never be pure; the mind is stained throughout by the evil thought of the eight worldly dharmas.

Thogme Zangpo also said,

> Even though we hold the lamp of the teachings in our hand, we still obscure our mind. The clouded, evil thought blinds our eye and leads us over the precipice of sin, creating problems for ourselves and those around us.

Dharma teachings are likened to a lamp because they dispel the darkness that prevents us from seeing things as they are. However, even though we know many words of the teachings and can explain them to others, still, somehow, we do not practice and our mind does not become one with the Dharma. So even though we hold the lamp in our hand, we still can't see though the darkness. It's as if we have eyes but they're damaged in some way, say by cataracts that make us see falling hairs or by something that makes us see two images where there's only one. Obscured from seeing reality by the eight worldly dharmas, we create all sorts of problems for ourselves and others.

Every negative action we create brings us one step closer to the precipice; every negative action we do makes our appointment with the suffering lower realms more certain. As long as we fail to recognize and avoid this, our mind cannot become one with the Dharma—like milk and water mixing—and we will always have problems.

The Dharma becomes our enemy. Not understanding that this is the only method to subdue our mind, we interpret what is explained by our teachers as something harmful. If we could become more friendly with Dharma wisdom, then when we heard the teachings that explain wrong conduct we'd see them as an antidote to the three poisonous minds. However, if we remain friendlier with the thought of the eight worldly dharmas, then to our disturbed, unsubdued mind the holy Dharma seems just the opposite. Our attachment doesn't want to be pacified. Controlled by the eight worldly dharmas, our mind sees the Dharma as a threat.

In this way, by not letting one single action that we ever do become Dharma, the thought of the eight worldly dharmas destroys the incredible potential of this precious human life. Even if it's been a long time since we met the Buddhadharma, so far we've been unable to gain any realizations. We work and work but somehow there's still no change in our mind; it's still the same old mind. If it hadn't been following the thought of the eight worldly dharmas then there would definitely have been a profound change by now.

We try to practice but somehow our mind is too weak. We haven't done enough meditation on impermanence and death, the suffering of the lower realms or the general shortcomings of samsara. Somehow, in the depths of our heart, we don't want to face it, afraid that if we renounce samsaric pleasure we'll lose all our fun, all our happiness. This gap between logical understanding and heart yearning can make us feel quite strange. And so we ignore the meditations on the various kinds of samsaric suffering and concentrate only on visualizing beautiful objects. This can really make us crazy.

When there's a battle between the worldly mind and the holy mind there are great hindrances to our Dharma practice. Somehow, we never seem to have time to do our practice; we can't even manage to recite one mala of a mantra. We sincerely want to meditate but always find a reason to postpone it. This is completely the fault of the thought of the eight worldly dharmas. There's always something else we have to do.

It's quite funny when you look at it. We always manage to find time to sleep, eat, talk, go to the movies, do unnecessary things, but, because we're following the thought of the eight worldly dharmas, we always find a thousand important reasons for not meditating.

Weeks, months and years go by without our practicing Dharma; we always plan to do it later. Later, later, later; after some time, after some time, after some time. Then suddenly death arrives. The Lord of Death doesn't say, "Oh, you haven't finished your Dharma practice. I'll give you special dispensation. I'll wait until you've finished." Death doesn't wait.

Living in the West amidst much material development, it's very easy to blame the external conditions, as if we're completely pure and it's the outside world that's making us suffer. However, we should not blame society or our material wealth. Nobody makes it difficult for us to practice Dharma but ourselves.

When we first come back home from a stay in India or Nepal, we might have a lot of energy to practice Dharma but, working in the city surrounded by people with a completely different attitude from ours, we get lonely. Even though we're trying to not be concerned with the affairs of this life, everybody else we work and socialize with is totally obsessed with worldly pleasure, the happiness of this life alone. This makes it very difficult for us to maintain our pure motivation.

When our life is too comfortable, too luxurious, our mind gets out of control because there are too many distractions to our Dharma practice. And when we have personal problems, illness, family and relationship difficulties, again it is very hard to keep our mind quiet and practice Dharma. To live a life that has neither too much comfort nor too little is extremely rare. Our Dharma practice depends upon our having good, continued meditation and for that we need a stable life. We need control over the distractions of this life and this is exactly what the thought of the eight worldly dharmas robs us of.

The main reason for getting ordained is renunciation of this life, but for those who become monks and nuns without renunciation, ordination is just another attraction to this life: wearing warm robes, saying lots of prayers, making a big noise like a tiger roaring. It's possible that we enjoy the beautiful robes and the interesting customs and feel good just because other people respect us. Things that lay people find hard to obtain—food, clothes, a good reputation—come to us easily.

We might wear robes, hold a mala, shave our head, show the form of a perfect Dharma practitioner on the surface—externally everybody can see that we're a seeker of liberation—but with a mind clinging to this life we're unable to engage in the actions of a Dharma practitioner, we never do anything of great meaning. No matter how much Dharma education we receive, instead of our mind becoming more subtle, more pliant, it becomes more rigid, like iron. We become more tough skinned.

The thought of the eight worldly dharmas is *the* thing that stops us practicing Dharma, so the first step on our spiritual journey has to be renunciation of the attachment that clings to this life. If we want to fly to California we have to start by getting out of bed. We can't step into the airplane from our bedroom—we need to get up, get dressed, get into a taxi and go to the airport. In the same way, if we really want to practice holy Dharma, the very first step is to renounce this life, to renounce the attachment seeking the happiness of this life.

Pure meditation is impossible with the eight worldly dharmas

When we try to meditate, the thought of the eight worldly dharmas makes it impossible to concentrate. It continuously distracts us, taking us away from our object of meditation and directing us to an object of attachment.

We even find it hard to start meditating. We have the thought that it's time to meditate but it somehow takes us too long to get around to it. We're about to start but there's a distraction, so we put it off. We try again but then there's another distraction—ten minutes, half an hour—just one more little thing and then we can meditate…and then one more little thing. Our attachment tells us we'll be able to meditate much better once we've cleared our mind of that concern. "Do the practice later," it tells us; "First you need to do this for me." And so it gives us such wonderful advice.

We think that we need to sleep well to remain healthy and have a clear mind. It's so hard to meditate when our mind is foggy with exhaustion. This is true, but is that the real reason we stay in bed longer or is it because our bed is so warm and comfortable? We feel resentful that everybody else in the whole world is sleeping but we have to get up in the cold and sit on a hard floor. Nobody is forcing us to do this, so why are we being so masochistic? Thinking like this, the minutes tick by and we're still under the covers. Then it's time to have breakfast and suddenly we have to rush to get to work. Being late and having no time to meditate was not caused by lack of time but by seeing comfort as more important than practicing Dharma.

Maybe we force ourselves onto the meditation cushion and try to meditate but our mind gets bored. We can't stick with it. We tell ourselves it's not working. "I've been meditating for over a week and I still don't have any realizations." And so we find excuses to quit—we'll meditate tomorrow or some other time when we have more energy; today we're a bit tired so it might be better to go to the beach.

I hear from many students, especially when I'm in America, that they have no time to meditate. However, they do have time to sleep—a lot of time. They do have time to eat—a lot of time. And to drink, and to talk. The mind preoccupied with worldly concern blocks the sense that meditation is more important than the worldly activities that fill their day. Being too busy is not the main reason for lack of space for Dharma; following the thought of the eight worldly dharmas is. The more we follow our attachment to this life, the less time we have to practice Dharma and the more difficult we find it. And conversely, the less we follow attachment to this life, the more space we have for Dharma.

Even if we know all this intellectually, somehow we still can't do it. We have no energy to overcome our reluctance. There's no fuel to get the plane to fly—nothing to persuade us to have the courage to practice. Delusions take over our mind and become more and more powerful. We become a slave to the thought of the eight worldly dharmas and everything, even studying Dharma, even doing retreat, becomes a means to serve and feed it.

Even when we manage to start a meditation session with a pure motivation, the thought of the eight worldly dharmas sneaks in slowly, like a cat coming into a room. Just like a cat, there's no noise, it's utterly silent. Only after some time do we notice that the cat has taken things. Just like this, the thought of the worldly dharmas arises very quietly and spoils our motivation.

We try to calm our mind but the thought of the eight worldly dharmas won't let it happen. Our mind remains agitated, like boiling water or dust caught in a strong wind, whipped around, unable to relax. We can't concentrate for even a minute without its wandering off to an object of attachment. Our mind is full of expectations, full of clinging to this and that, full of so many things that our thoughts scatter everywhere.

Maybe we've decided to meditate for an hour, but for the first thirty minutes, forty minutes, even fifty minutes, we still can't bring the object of our meditation up in our mind. And if we manage to do so, it's only there for a second and then it's gone, like a fly landing on a table and then flying off. We bring it back and the next second it's gone again, over and over like this. We have so much distraction. Even if we sit for two hours, the time that we're actually concentrating on the object of meditation is no more than a few seconds or a few minutes at most.

And what's worse, not only does our mind not dwell on its intended object but it focuses on some object of attachment, so it's a negative mind. While we're sitting there trying to do a breathing meditation, the thought of the eight worldly dharmas is busy creating nonvirtue. We sit up straight and wonder whether people are watching and thinking what a great meditator we are. They *must* be envious of how good we are; surely they'll ask us to teach some meditation classes.

Most of the images that come into our mind are images of either attraction or aversion, and with them come the associated emotions of pleasure or anger. Without our consciously thinking about it, these images arise all the time, and because we still have strong attachment to the happiness of this life, we find it very hard to forget them.

We might be trying to meditate but a friend is talking to somebody else in the next room. Their conversation is so interesting that our mind can no longer remain in meditation. We want to listen. Talking and listening are much more appealing. If we know something that our friend doesn't, then because of our pride we can't wait to leave the meditation to tell her. She hasn't ruined our meditation; the thought of the eight worldly dharmas has. Even if there's no conversation to distract us, there's still that little insect biting us.

The stronger our attachment seeking the happiness of this life, the more uncontrolled our mind and the greater the distractions that arise. It's much more difficult to keep our mind calm. If we remain aware of the distractions and images that appear in our mind when we try to meditate, we'll easily recognize all this from our own experience.

Even if we can concentrate for five minutes at the beginning of our meditation, soon after that we find ourselves on a big trip. Sometimes we're in the East, sometimes in the West, sometimes traveling in India, sometimes traveling in Nepal, sometimes traveling in Indonesia. We might be trying to visualize Shakyamuni Buddha but within a few minutes we're in America, visiting family, talking to friends, doing the things we enjoy. Completely unconscious of our body, which is here, we're away on holiday. Then, however long we spend meditating—five minutes, five hours—it all becomes worldly meditation, a meditation to create more causes of suffering. We're meditating to remain longer in samsara. And of course, during this time we have no awareness of the object we're supposed to be meditating on.

The thought of the eight worldly dharmas can become a hindrance even after our meditation has finished. Say we've managed to meditate with pure motivation and the action has become a pure Dharma action but later we get angry because we remember something worldly we could have done instead. In that way the thought of the eight worldly dharmas destroys whatever merit we might have created in the session. The result of anger is only suffering; it destroys any chance we have of achieving liberation. So it's very important to be mindful even after we've finished meditating.

The eight worldly dharmas make enlightenment impossible

This thought of the eight worldly dharmas also prevents us from realizing the absolute nature, emptiness, which means we have no way to attain enlightenment. One of the great Indian pandits, Dharmakirti, explains that by its very nature, attachment distorts reality because under its influence our mind exaggerates the qualities of the object to which it's attached by seeing intrinsically real positive qualities that are simply not there. Because of our delusions we're unable to see the false projection we place on an object of attachment as false—to us it's real and intrinsic—and so we're unable to overcome this false view.

In particular, the thought of the eight worldly dharmas obscures our realization of the false nature of the self-existent I. Therefore, this is a fundamental wrong view. Even if we meditate on the absolute nature of reality in order to realize the emptiness of the self, the thought of the eight worldly dharma always arises to block our realization. It doesn't want to be destroyed, it doesn't want to be smashed, it doesn't want to be extinguished. The stronger our attachment to this life, the more difficult it is to even *understand* the ultimate nature of the I, let alone realize it. That's how attachment makes it difficult to be free from samsara.

If we were ever to actually realize the emptiness of the self, we would immediately see how the thought of the eight worldly dharmas has been deceiving us. It's like a really skilful liar, one who everybody trusts completely because his lies are so believable. He lives in our house and we think he's a good friend, but actually he's constantly stealing our stuff. Because we trust him so much we never suspect him and always blame others for the theft. Only when we really investigate do we discover that all the time it's our "friend" who's been the liar and the thief, the cause of all our problems. We get a big shock because we never suspected him. So right then and there we decide to kick him out, destroy him, because there's no place for such a person in our home.

In the same way, it's only by realizing the emptiness of the self that we can come to understand just how completely false the thought of the eight worldly dharmas is. When we see how it's the most damaging wrong view and the root of all the other problems we face, we'll have the courage to destroy it so completely that even the name "attachment" does not exist in our mind. This is why the worldly mind that sees external things as true happiness is so afraid of the meditation on emptiness, why whenever we think about doing it, attachment begs us, "Please don't." It's afraid for its very existence.

Like the thought of the eight worldly dharmas, self-cherishing is also a very harmful wrong conception, but we can harbor a subtle form of self-cherishing and still become free from samsara and achieve nirvana. Even with self-cherishing, even holding the wrong view of the self-existent I, we can still create virtuous actions and be reborn as a happy transmigrator, but we can't achieve this with the thought of the eight worldly dharmas, which blocks us from not only transient happiness but also the happiness of future lives, including, of course, liberation and the ultimate happiness of enlightenment.

Achieving enlightenment depends on realizing bodhicitta, which in turn depends on realizing the mind renouncing samsara. And as long as the thought of the eight worldly dharmas is present in our mind, there's no way to realize the mind renouncing samsara.

Just as where there's water there can't be fire, so where there is *seeking* the temporal happiness of this life, there can't be *renunciation* of the temporal happiness of this life. Thus by clinging to the happiness of this life we destroy our chances of creating happiness both now and in the future.

That's why Manjushri explained that if we cling to this life we cannot be considered a Dharma practitioner.[32] Besides a few exceptional actions done without pure motivation due to the power of the object, anything we do with the thought of the eight worldly dharmas becomes the cause only for samsara, not enlightenment. We should therefore reflect deeply on the teachings of the Buddha that show the path to attain enlightenment and firmly resolve to cut off any wrong understanding.

At present we're like babies. A mother can't give her baby meat until his teeth have developed. If he can't chew or digest strong food, it can really harm him, so his mother needs to feed him milk or soft food. We want to bite into enlightenment but we haven't developed the strong teeth of renunciation. Only when our daily practice is pure and free from clinging to this life can we become excited about trying to achieve enlightenment. The problem is that many of us fail to check our motivation and therefore fail to really understand what actions are harmful or beneficial.

We want enlightenment and we want it quickly, but we must make sure that all the conditions are there. If we want to go to India we have to fly— any other way takes too long—so we really need to make sure we have enough money for the ticket. The flight is the tantric path and realizing

---

[32] In the famous Sakya teaching, *Parting from the Four Attachments* (*zhen-pa-zhi-drel*): "If you desire this life, you are not a religious person; if you desire the round of existence, you have not turned about with conviction; if you desire for the sake of self, you do not have the enlightenment thought; if grasping ensues, you do not have the view." See also *Mind Training*, pp. 517–66.

bodhicitta and emptiness are like the ticket. Buying the ticket depends on having enough money, the mind that has fully renounced the evil thought of the eight worldly dharmas.

Thus the practice of tantra is impossible while we follow the mind of the eight worldly dharmas. The fundamental tantric practice is living in the practice of avoiding the impure thought that projects the impure view. Just as we need a strong foundation before we can build a house, this practice is the ground upon which all of tantra is based. And it's far more difficult to avoid this impure thought than it is to avoid self-cherishing.

There's no doubt that tantra is the quickest path, but we need to develop all the other practices before we can even consider it. We might be able to go from one country to another by sneaking past customs but that doesn't work with Dharma practice. All the fundamental elements need to be in place if we want to achieve enlightenment.

Retreating with the eight worldly dharmas

Perhaps we've made it as far as a retreat hut and feel we're beyond the influence of the thought of the eight worldly dharmas. Far from it. Here, desire can be stronger, pride can be stronger, all our delusions can come to torture us. Retreat is a wonderful way to turn our mind toward the Dharma but there are traps.

We set ourselves a big goal for our retreat—lots of prostrations, a very strict timetable, precepts every day, the determination to do the long sessions very strongly—and feel very happy about that. In fact, we start thinking we're very special and feeling proud. When pride and ego creep into our retreat we lose much of benefit we might have gained from all our hard work and the only difference between us—alone, isolated, spending hours and hours each day prostrating and meditating—and somebody working in the city and spending every evening drinking and having fun is the location.

Maybe, jealous of our friends who've done a retreat in Nepal, we're desperate to collect some beautiful stories for our retreat diary so that we can impress them. We put a big sign outside our retreat hut for everybody to see: "RETREAT" or "STRICT RETREAT" or "VERY STRICT RETREAT." But I'm not so sure just how strict our mind is. This is a sign to our friends: "Look at me! I'm doing a retreat!" We think it's us doing the retreat but in fact it's the thought of the eight worldly dharmas that's doing it.

If we're not constantly aware of what our mind is doing, pride and the need for reputation can creep in, making all our hard work meaningless. Even if all our doors and windows have been sealed with mud and we're living without air vents like insects in a hole,[33] if our mind is attached to such a tiny transient thing as reputation, the need for people to respect us, it's all for nothing.

Where there's a need for comfort, there will always be distractions; somebody will always be making a noise outside to disturb our profound meditations. If it's not an adult or a child, it's a bird, a dog or a goat. We try not to listen but inside we get angrier and angrier. We're doing retreat for the sake of all sentient beings, but while we're saying those words we're secretly wanting to kill the noisy sentient being outside disturbing our meditation.

Then there's the danger that during the break between sessions we might actively seek out that sentient being and we'd better pray that there are no stones or other weapons around or we could become very dangerous. When we're angry, that person or animal is the ultimate enemy, but when our anger subsides we realize it's not like that at all. It's the same object, but one moment that sentient being is an enemy and the next it's not.

Even in retreat, hatred, anger and even the thought of killing can arise. Our mouth can be reciting a mantra but our mind can be back with the harm somebody has done us in the past, thinking how if we ever meet that person again we'll definitely kill him. We're holding a mala in our hand but in our mind it's a knife. I haven't actually heard a story where somebody on retreat has killed somebody else—not actually killed.

While the constraints of the retreat mean that our body is tied to moral discipline, our mind can easily be tied to attachment. Unless we're retreating away from the thought of the eight worldly dharmas, all we're doing is simply locking our body in a room, unable to talk to anyone, like in a prison. If that was all that was required to be in retreat, then everybody in prison would be in retreat. And every time we slept we'd be in retreat. Trapped in our retreat hut, we're both unable to get what attachment wants but also unable to enjoy the benefits of the moral life that the retreat conditions impose upon us. We can't find inner happiness, we can't follow the advice of our spiritual friend and we're unable to do service to other sentient beings.

It can even make us crazy. A retreat is supposed to make us calmer and more relaxed each day, but instead, denied the objects of our attachment, our mind becomes worse. We sit in our tiny room meditating on the whole

---

[33] A practice done in the Tibetan tradition when somebody goes into very strict retreat.

world, remembering all the objects we've had contact with in past—friends, countries, jobs and things like that—and our unsubdued mind uses these objects to develop more and more attachment. The more we think about those objects, the stronger our attachment grows. Isolated, with nothing else to distract us, the electricity of attachment is generated by these objects and gets stronger and stronger.

Our retreat hut becomes like a pressure cooker, with the pressure inside our mind building until we're about to explode. We can't meditate at all but we've committed to doing the retreat in our small room, so we can't go outside. Maybe we ineffectually recite some mantras, but since we're not practicing the remedies, our mind gets tighter and tighter and our mood darker and darker. Soon we're starting to look very strange and say very funny things. We're like a prisoner in a cell. Our eyes roll around and we make pipi and kaka in the room. Finally, we're sedated by injection and taken to hospital and that's the end of our retreat.

Retreating away from the eight worldly dharmas

Attachment comes up in any retreat, but we must deal with it by practicing the inner remedies. Unless we're skilled at countering the thought of the eight worldly dharmas when it arises we really can go mad. Meditating on the lam-rim, contemplating impermanence and death and remedies like this will move our mind away from the eight worldly dharmas and help us renounce this life. Otherwise when we meditate it's like we're shooting an arrow at a target but hitting ourselves instead.

The word "retreat" means retreating away from the thought of the eight worldly dharmas. When we retreat this is exactly what we should be doing. Retreating away from the thought of the eight worldly dharmas means living in renunciation, letting go of attachment to this life. During this precious time we give freedom to ourselves, not to the thought of the eight worldly dharmas.

Usually the time that we have for retreat is very short. Therefore it's unbelievably important to put all our effort into making sure that our retreat, our attitude and everything we do within the retreat become pure Dharma. Otherwise, even if we believe we're a Dharma practitioner doing a retreat, actually we're just fooling ourselves. If we don't watch our mind and turn every action of our body, speech and mind into Dharma during that precious, short time, then it will be almost impossible to do so at other times, with all the distractions, superstitions and delusions that life throws at us in a normal day.

For our retreat to be really effective we need to see the very nature of suffering and determine to be free of it. We need to see how the whole of samsara is in the nature of suffering and how samsaric pleasures trick us. Then we can really retreat away from the self-cherishing thought and attachment to the pleasures of this life and keep our mind in bodhicitta.

I find the following quotation very effective for the mind. It's advice given by Heruka to the great yogi Luipa, one of the lineage lamas of the Heruka Chakrasamvara teachings. It's a short verse but it contains the essence of the lam-rim and of the tantric path.

> Give up stretching the legs
> And give up being a servant to samsara.
> Vajrasattva, the great king, exhorts us to do this again and again.[34]

This is not saying that we can't sleep during retreat, that we can't lie down and stretch out our legs at night. This is not what Heruka's advising. "Give up stretching the legs" means giving up allowing the mind to be controlled by the thought of the eight worldly dharmas, which seeks only the comfort of this life.

For example, when we're studying or meditating with other people we can't stretch out our legs, but if we're alone and start to feel a little tired, the thought of the worldly dharmas, the thought of seeking comfort, arises, and because our mind follows that thought, we naturally physically "stretch the legs." In this way we can easily skip sessions or not do our commitments or even spend our whole time sleeping, which is *completely* stretching the legs. This is an incredible waste of time, because instead of making our life highly meaningful during that period we've lost the great benefit we might otherwise have gained. The fundamental mistake is allowing our mind to be under the control of the thought of the eight worldly dharmas.

Like this, we waste one day, one week, one month, one year, until we've wasted our whole life. If we add it up, like making a bill, the total amount of time that we've actually spent making our life meaningful is very small. Even

---

[34] Rinpoche has translated this verse in various ways over the years. See the extensive treatment of it in *Bodhisattva Attitude*.

when we try to practice Dharma, apart from some exceptional actions that, as mentioned above, do become Dharma due to the power of the object, our actions are rarely pure Dharma. Our greatest enemy, the one that makes us waste our life, however, is the thought of the eight worldly dharmas, the mind that wants to "stretch its legs."

Everything we do in retreat should be an antidote to the thought of the eight worldly dharmas. An effective way of doing this is to practice the meditations on the graduated path of the being of lower capability, such as those we've seen above. In particular, these are thinking about the perfect human rebirth (the eight freedoms and ten richnesses, its great usefulness and the difficulty of receiving it again) and contemplating impermanence—always thinking that since we're going to die soon, even today, even this hour, there's no point in following the delusions; from that perspective it all seems quite childish and silly.

A more advanced retreat is our mind retreating away from attachment to future lives' samsaric perfections and happiness by living in renunciation of the whole of samsara. Then, on the basis of this foundation, we retreat away from the ego and self-cherishing thought by living in bodhicitta, the thought of cherishing and benefiting other sentient beings—working for others rather than self, seeking the happiness of others rather than our own.

Then, more advanced still is retreating away from ignorance, the root of samsara, which is the ignorance apprehending the I to exist from its own side. While the I is totally empty of existing from its own side, it appears to exist that way and ignorance apprehends that appearance as true. It's the same with the aggregates and whatever appears to the senses—forms, sounds, smells, tastes or tangible objects. Even though they are totally empty, devoid of existing from their own side, to the hallucinated mind they appear to exist from their own side and then ignorance holds onto that as true.

We can do a retreat, retreat away from this ignorance, by practicing mindfulness in daily life, looking at all these things as empty or as hallucinations. We examine the hallucination we put on the merely imputed I, the merely imputed aggregates, merely imputed forms, merely imputed sounds, merely imputed smells, tastes, tangible objects, merely imputed hell, merely imputed enlightenment, merely imputed liberation from samsara and so forth. We examine the hallucination we place on all these merely imputed phenomena and see them as such—as nothing more than hallucinations—because the way our mind perceives them *is* a hallucination.

Even though these phenomena appear truly existent, by practicing mindfulness in this way we don't allow our mind to apprehend the false view as reality and don't allow ourselves to believe appearances are true in the way that they appear. We can also practice mindfulness by looking at all these phenomena—I, action, object—as dependent arisings, phenomena that arise in dependence on cause and conditions or on base and label.

Meditating on subtle dependent arising or in any of these ways stops our mind from holding onto phenomena, including the I, which appear to be inherently existent, as true, which is a false view. Working with all these ideas is another form of retreat.

This is retreating by keeping our mind in renunciation, bodhicitta and emptiness. In Lama Tsongkhapa's tradition these are the three principal aspects of the path, the three things that encompass the whole Buddhist path. When these three are there, there's nothing missing. Retreat is living with our mind in these three principal aspects, retreating away from attachment to this life, from the whole of samsara and from the self-cherishing thought and ignorance.

What I want to emphasize, however, is that if we retreat with a good heart there will be good results, even if we can't rid ourselves of the mind clinging to this life. Even though our motivation is still muddied by attachment to this life, at least we're trying honestly. And because we're *trying* to practice morality with a good heart, which protects our mind, we can still have great peace and no major obstacles to our Dharma practice. Then, whether our retreat is long or short, it's still a good life and will bring a good result.

THE THREE TYPES OF EIGHT WORLDLY DHARMAS

Talking about the great guru Lama Tsongkhapa, Pabongka Dechen Nyingpo said,

> Leave aside the eight black worldly dharmas and eight mixed
>   dharmas,
> He is even unstained by the eight white dharmas.
> He made the complete teaching of the Buddha pure, like refined
>   gold, with hundreds of quotations and reasonings.
> In your life story, Lama Tsongkhapa, I rejoice!

In praising Lama Tsongkhapa, he mentions the three types of worldly dharma, black, mixed and white. The eight *black* worldly dharmas are what we have been talking about: liking comfort and disliking discomfort; wishing for a good reputation, disliking a bad one or none at all; wanting praise, disliking criticism; wanting to receive material things, disliking not receiving material things. An action done out of these worldly concerns is one of the black eight worldly dharmas.

The eight *mixed* worldly dharmas are actions done without worldly concern but with the self-cherishing thought. The eight *white* worldly dharmas are actions done without the self-cherishing thought but with the wrong conception of clinging to things as truly existent. In Lama Tsongkhapa's biography, all his actions, twenty-four hours a day, were not only unstained by the black and mixed eight worldly dharmas, they were unstained by the eight white worldly dharmas as well.

A story that illustrates how Lama Tsongkhapa abandoned the black, mixed and white worldly dharmas comes from when he was at Tölung, near Lhasa, which is the birthplace of my virtuous friend, Lama Yeshe, who was kinder than all the buddhas of the three times. When Lama Tsongkhapa was there giving teachings to one hundred and eight learned monks, great practitioners who were holders of the three baskets of teachings, Manjushri sent a message to Pawo Dorje to tell Lama Tsongkhapa to stop the teaching and go to a solitary place to practice. Because they were in the middle of the teachings, Pawo Dorje said to Manjushri, "How can I request this of Lama Tsongkhapa? He is now doing great things for the teachings of the Buddha. How can I interfere with his teachings? I'll be criticized if I do. Please don't ask me to do this."

Manjushri then replied, "How do you know whether it benefits the teachings of the Buddha or not? If this is continued, after Lama Tsongkhapa has passed away, there won't be much benefit to the teachings of the Buddha. This is not sufficient. One must attempt to benefit sentient beings equal to the extent of space." What he meant was that simply saying the words alone cannot benefit others.

As soon as Pawo Dorje gave him Manjushri's message, Lama Tsongkhapa stopped abruptly in the middle of the teaching he was giving and immediately left for an isolated place to live an ascetic life, taking with him only eight disciples and the essential robes of a monk.[35]

---

[35] This refers to Lama Tsongkhapa's famous retreat at Olka Chölung, where he and his eight

MEDITATIONS

Meditation on how the mind moves toward objects of attraction

There are two main hindrances to meditation: sluggishness, which is a lack of clarity and a kind of dark fogginess, and scattering, or mental wandering, where the mind can't stay on the object of meditation. The thought of the eight worldly dharmas is generally responsible for the latter, so when meditating, it's very worthwhile to observe how the mind habitually moves toward objects of attachment.

For example, when doing breathing meditation, it's normal to check frequently that the mind is still on the object of meditation, the breath. You can extend this a little by watching what actually happens. Use your introspection—the part of the mind that observes the rest of the mind's activities—to spy on what's happening while you're supposed to be watching your breath. Check what pictures come into your mind and I'm sure you'll find that they're objects to which your senses are attached.

The object comes up, your mind jumps on it and you make up a story about it: "Oh, that was very nice, I enjoyed it, I'd love to do it again," and so on and so forth—a long, long story. Then you think about the present and maybe the future, and your object of attachment is part of all that story too.

So don't get involved in the story but rather observe how your mind gets attracted to things. Watch how, as soon as you return to your breath, another object of attraction pops up and again your mind wants to jump onto that one, like a child in a playground.

Just this objective observation of the process creates some space between your mind and its object. It helps you to disassociate from distracting images and thoughts and strengthens your meditation practice.

Meditation on how the mind reacts to the eight worldly dharmas

This meditation is a little different from the previous one, where you simply observed whatever naturally arose in your mind. Here you actively bring up an object of either attraction or aversion and observe both how and why your mind reacts to it.

In meditation, imagine meeting a sense object to which you're attached and that you'd like to have. Visualize that you have it in your possession and

---

disciples remained for four years doing hundreds of thousands of prostrations, mandala offerings and other practices.

watch how your mind reacts. When you feel pleasure, check whether your mind is attached to that pleasure or not. Then analyze the pleasure. What is its nature? Is it peaceful or unpeaceful, calm or uptight? You can meditate on the suffering of encountering an undesirable object in the same way. When you experience suffering, watch how your mind reacts.

Try to be aware; that's the main thing. For instance, visualize somebody praising you and investigate how your mind reacts, whether your mind is attached to those words or not. Observe how good the feeling is and how it comes from the thought of the eight worldly dharmas. It feels pleasurable, so check the nature of that pleasure. Is it peaceful and relaxed or is it uptight? Then, again, imagine an undesirable situation, such as somebody criticizing you. How does your mind react? If you had no expectation of or attachment to praise, would you get upset when criticized?

In the same way, meditate on the other pairs of opposites: receiving and not receiving material things, reputation and notoriety, and so forth. Check how your mind feels when the imagined situation arises and, most importantly, check the nature of the pleasure or aversion you feel. If it's pleasure, is it real happiness, peaceful and calm, or a lifting of your mind that's actually an uptight, agitated sensation?

Then try to understand that what you call pleasure when you meet a desirable object of the senses is suffering in just the same way that not meeting an object of desire is suffering. Try to see how the suffering that we call suffering, which we easily recognize, and the suffering that we call pleasure by being attached are related, how both feelings are in the nature of suffering. Try to understand this fact as it is and see how, in our normal relationships with sense objects, we exaggerate their qualities and discriminate. See how it's a completely wrong belief that the desirable object of the senses is in the nature of everlasting happiness and not in the nature of suffering. Try to see things as they are. Try to be aware instead of ignorant.

Then check whether your mind would change if you could lose your attachment to the object. Would you still suffer if you didn't have the object? Would your mind be unhappy if the object changed in some way or you lost it?

It's vital to understand your own mind in this way. Such analytical meditation is the real way to study your mind, the true research into the nature of your mind. Your own research is the way to prove the validity of the teachings, to see that they're not just some fabricated theory that has nothing to do with reality.

Become aware of your mind in order to recognize how all the undesirable things that you experience are caused by attachment to the pleasures of this life. Loneliness, depression, unhappiness, aggression—all negative states come from attachment. It's not that difficult to check up in this way. The concept is not difficult, nor does it require a profound meditation like that on emptiness; it's just a matter of being aware, of just watching your mind. Our eyes are constantly watching things anyway—books, television, scenery and so forth—so now turn your attention to the mind. Become an observer: watch your mental processes; watch how your mind flips from happiness to unhappiness depending on circumstances and the objects it encounters.

7. How Worldly Dharma and Holy Dharma Differ

THE IMPORTANCE OF KNOWING WHAT DHARMA IS

EVEN IF WE UNDERSTAND nothing else, if, by recognizing the eight worldly dharmas, we can clearly differentiate between what is Dharma and what is not Dharma, we're very fortunate. This is the essential point. This knowledge alone gives us a great chance to really put Dharma practice into our daily life and create an incredible amount of merit.

Buddhism is a house full of treasures—practices for gaining the happiness of future lives, the bliss of liberation and the supreme happiness of enlightenment—but knowing the difference between Dharma and non-Dharma is the key that opens the door to all those treasures. No matter how much we know about emptiness, the chakras or controlling our vital energy through *kundalini* yoga, it's all pointless without this crucial understanding of how to practice Dharma, how to correct our actions. There are vast numbers of people who delude themselves and waste their entire life studying the most esoteric aspects of Buddhism but never understand the most fundamental point, the distinction between Dharma and non-Dharma.

It is very easy to do Dharma activities such as reciting mantras, saying prayers, making offerings and things like that with the thought of the eight worldly dharmas. That happens. But in reality, the holy Dharma, which includes all these activities, actually means renouncing this life. Therefore holy Dharma and worldly dharma can *never* be done together. Nobody can do these two things—renounce this life *and* seek the happiness of this life with the eight worldly dharmas—at once. We can do one and then the other but never both together in the one mind at the same time.

It's better to practice Dharma

Whenever different benefactors wrote to Pabongka Dechen Nyingpo asking for advice, it seems that he always advised them to persuade other sentient beings to practice Dharma, especially lam-rim, as much as possible, by giving the very heart instructions on how to make their life most meaningful.

Because the eight worldly dharmas are the source of every problem we ever encounter, if Dharma practice means renouncing suffering it means renouncing the eight worldly dharmas. "I'm practicing Dharma" really means "I'm renouncing all the suffering of this and all future lives; I'm renouncing the thought of the eight worldly dharmas."

In previous times, Dromtönpa, Atisha's close disciple and translator, saw an old man walking around the temple at Reting (Radreng) Monastery. The old man thought that he was practicing Dharma. So Dromtönpa said, "Circumambulating the temple is good, but wouldn't it be better to practice Dharma?" After hearing this the old man gave up going around the temple and started reading scriptures, thinking that that was what practicing Dharma meant. Again Dromtönpa saw him and said, "Reading the scriptures is good, but wouldn't it be better to practice Dharma?" At that the old man gave up reading Dharma texts and, thinking that maybe meditation was practicing Dharma, sat cross-legged with his eyes closed. Again Dromtönpa saw him and said, "Meditation is good, but wouldn't it be better to practice Dharma?"

This made the old man really confused. He couldn't think of any other way of practicing Dharma if it wasn't circumambulating, reading scriptures or meditating. So, a little exasperated, he exclaimed to Dromtönpa, "Practice Dharma! Practice Dharma! What do you mean, practice Dharma?" Dromtönpa replied, "Renounce this life. Renounce it now, for if you do not renounce attachment to this life, whatever you do will not be the practice of Dharma because you will not have passed beyond the eight worldly dharmas. Once you have renounced this life's habitual thoughts and are no longer distracted by the eight worldly dharmas, whatever you do will advance you on the path of liberation."

Dromtönpa advised the old man to renounce this life because without renouncing this life nobody can practice pure Dharma. With renunciation, however, pure Dharma practice, which brings happiness in this and all future lives, is possible. Renouncing this life doesn't mean running away from home or throwing away all our material possessions; it means running away from the cause of the suffering. That alone can cut our suffering. As long as we follow the eight worldly dharmas, whether we separate from this physical body or not, without question we will still suffer.

In a similar vein, when Lama Atisha was about to pass away, one of his followers, a yogi called Naljor Chaktri Chok, said to him, "After you have passed away I will dedicate myself to meditation." Lama Atisha answered, "Give up anything that is a bad action." Atisha did not say whether it was good or bad to meditate, just to give up all bad actions. Naljor Chaktri Chok then said to Atisha, "In that case, sometimes I will explain Dharma and sometimes I will meditate." Again Atisha gave the same answer. The yogi thought some more, then made another suggestion. But no matter what he said, Atisha just kept on giving him the same answer. Finally he asked, "Well, what should I do?" Lama Atisha answered, "Give up this life in your mind!"

Keeping this advice in his heart, Naljor Chaktri Chok lived in a juniper forest rear Reting Monastery, physically no different from the way the forest animals lived. Living alone, not seeing even one other human face, he passed his life there.[36]

But giving up this life doesn't necessarily mean leaving everything behind and escaping from this world, this entire planet, and going somewhere else. Giving away all our possessions—even all the possessions that exist in the world—is not giving up this life. Taking our body away from our home or country is not giving up this life. Even living in a cave with no possessions at all, with only the body, is not giving up this life. Even separating from our body—as we do every time we die—is not giving up the worldly life. Giving up this life does not depend on physical things; it is a mental change.

THE DIFFERENCE BETWEEN THE EIGHT WORLDLY DHARMAS AND DHARMA

Without renouncing the thought of the eight worldly dharmas, any action—circumambulating a stupa, meditating, reading a Dharma book—is a negative action, a worldly action. It is not spiritual, it is not Dharma; it is the opposite of Dharma. In other words, the action itself does not determine whether something is Dharma. Dromtönpa shows us clearly that practic-

[36] See *The Door to Satisfaction*, p. 34.

ing Dharma is nothing more than renouncing the evil thought of the eight worldly dharmas.

We need to be very clear about the distinction between Dharma and non-Dharma. We know that anger is negative, of course, but we aren't angry all the time. What really wastes our precious life isn't anger but attachment, being attached to the eight worldly dharmas.

Without clearly understanding what Dharma is, even though we try to practice it our whole life, nothing becomes Dharma because we still have the wrong motivation. The definition of non-Dharma is simply anything that is done for the happiness of this life alone; it is whatever we do motivated by attachment to the eight worldly dharmas. The definition of Dharma is exactly the opposite: it is anything that is done for happiness beyond this life, whatever is unstained by attachment to the eight worldly dharmas. I repeat: whatever action we do with the thought of the eight worldly dharmas is not Dharma; whatever we do unstained by the thought of the eight worldly dharmas is Dharma. Every action we do from morning to night is either Dharma or non-Dharma depending on this.

If we clearly see the borderline between Dharma and non-Dharma, between a Dharma action and a worldly action, we're very fortunate. Until we reach that point, despite all the suffering we've endured and all our attempts to stop it, we have no route out of our unhappiness. Once we do reach that point we can start to do something about it. In the past we've probably wanted to do many good things, like meditation, but because we've lacked this fundamental understanding we've made many mistakes. Even if we never understand one other Dharma subject, learning just this one thing is like opening our eyes for the first time.

Pure Dharma is any action that is a remedy for or an antidote to the delusions. Basically, practicing Dharma benefits future lives, unlike the meaningless activities of this life, which might possibly bring some temporary happiness in this life but nothing more. Achieving the happiness of this life is nothing special. Even animals and insects as tiny as ants can do that, so if we never do more than that we're no more special than an insect. No matter how expert in our field we are, without practicing Dharma we can't fulfill our human potential, especially that of this perfect human rebirth. The special purposes of having a perfect human rebirth are achievement of the happiness of future lives, liberation from samsara and full enlightenment, something we can do because we can create the causes of those results every second of our lives.

Virtue and nonvirtue are defined on this basis. Every action done renouncing attachment to this life is virtue; every action done with attachment to this life is nonvirtue. If we renounce the attachment that clings to the pleasures of this life, our attitude becomes pure and everything we do becomes Dharma. Nothing we do is done for just this life.

As soon as we renounce the evil thought of the eight worldly dharmas we find peace. There's no need to wait until tomorrow or the day after. It's not as if we renounce the eight worldly dharmas today but need to wait for a few years or the next life to receive happiness.

When our mind is not mixed with the thought of the worldly dharmas, every action we do becomes Dharma. The deeper we see the cause of our suffering, the more our wisdom grows and the more we can put Dharma into our everyday life. Then we have much more energy to make every action we do Dharma. Even if we live in a big family with twenty children and many possessions, everything we do becomes a remedy to the delusions and we can be said to be living in renunciation of this life.

Nobody can tell from external appearances who has renounced this life and who hasn't. Renunciation is a state of mind and having lots of possessions is no indication at all. Even though somebody is a king with countless servants, stores of jewels and possessions and many rich apartments, we can't conclude that his mind is not living in renunciation. Renouncing this life is a mental action, not a physical one.

If it were only a question of not owning anything, all the animals and insects who have no possessions and live in holes without food to eat should be regarded as highly renounced beings. At Lawudo Retreat Center near Everest there are many caves that used to be the homes of great yogis. When I went to see them I found that they were full of kaka because yaks had used them to sleep in, probably because they're warm. If the definition of a yogi is somebody who lives in a cave, perhaps we should consider yaks to be great yogis.

Another way of defining Dharma is anything that does not accord with the actions of worldly people. If we do something that normal people do, it's not Dharma; if we do something that normal people don't do, it's Dharma. This is how the great teacher Dromtönpa explained it to Potowa:

> It is Dharma if it becomes an antidote to delusion; it is not Dharma if it does not. If all worldly people disagree with it, it is Dharma; if they agree with it, it is not Dharma.[37]

---

[37] Quoted in *Liberation in the Palm of Your Hand*, p. 298.

Most worldly people have an interpretation of what constitutes a good life based on attachment and filtered through the ego. And so more wealth, more success, more friends, more children, more cars—such things are seen as part of a good life. They measure their happiness by how many possessions they have, by their external development. Children, and then grandchildren, and then great-grandchildren—the more of everything they have, the happier they are.

This is the exact opposite of what Dharma wisdom, based on the fundamental understanding of karma and the lam-rim, considers to be a good life. What attachment doesn't consider important in its view of a good life is having peace in the heart, having real satisfaction. Actually, this is what we're all looking for, but very few people know this and even fewer actually know how to achieve it.

The importance of motivation

I once asked an abbot about the meaning of "worldly dharma." He replied that it meant gambling, working in the fields and so forth—these are worldly activities. It is very common to think of worldly actions in this way, relating to just the action and not the motivation, the attitude. If done with pure motivation, however, such actions can become pure Dharma.

Dromtönpa's example above is extremely important to keep in mind because it so clearly shows the border between Dharma and non-Dharma. It is easy to think of worldly actions as playing football, smoking, drinking, having sex and so forth but that is not what defines a worldly action. We therefore need to become very aware of the motivation for all the actions we do in daily life to see what is and what is not Dharma.

If our motivation is worldly concern, then the action becomes a worldly activity. It can't be Dharma, even if the action is reciting prayers, meditating and so forth. It can be *like* Dharma but it's not Dharma. And a person who "practices" Dharma with a motivation of worldly concern is *like* a Dharma practitioner but is not a real Dharma practitioner. There's a big difference.

Somebody once gave me plastic ice cream. It looked exactly like ice cream and even ran down the spoon like melting ice cream does. When Ueli, the former director of FPMT's Mongolian projects, came to lunch I offered it to him and he was completely fooled. It was so well made. But of course, it was completely inedible. It's the same thing with the person who practices Dharma but pollutes it with the mind clinging to this life. His activities might look exactly like Dharma—listening to teachings, reflecting, meditating, going on retreat, even teaching Dharma—but in fact they are not Dharma. He might look like a Dharma practitioner but in fact he is not a Dharma practitioner.

Since we're seeking liberation, this is the most important point to know. It's like a radio dial that can be tuned to all the different stations. Without understanding the distinction between Dharma and non-Dharma, no matter how many different spiritual actions we do, no matter how long we do things such as building monasteries, making prostrations and so forth—even if we do them until we die—there's the real danger that our whole life will become filled with negative actions, causing us to be trapped in samsara, bound to suffering. Without this knowledge we're in great danger of cheating ourselves.

In itself, no action can be defined as a worldly action. It can be either holy Dharma or worldly dharma, virtuous or nonvirtuous. It all depends on the motivation. Enjoying sense pleasures can be positive or negative; having wealth can be positive or negative. Two people can do exactly the same thing and for one person it can be a positive action, for the other, negative. It all depends on attitude.

A politician with a good motivation can do a lot of good but if his motivation is the thought of the eight worldly dharmas—the wish for power, reputation, wealth and so forth—then his politics become negative, harming both himself and the people around him. Without the worldly mind, his politics become Dharma. And if his motivation is unstained by self-cherishing and is one of bodhicitta, then those politics become pure Mahayana Dharma, pure service for other sentient beings and a cause for him to achieve enlightenment.

No matter how it looks on the surface, any action done without involvement in the eight worldly dharmas is a Dharma action. Whatever method we use to renounce the thought of the eight worldly dharmas becomes a method to stop the continuity of bad karma, which leads to escape from suffering and enlightenment. This is the perfect, true method.

And so before we start any Dharma practice, the most important thing is to cultivate a pure motivation. Just understanding this crucial point is very important. It opens our wisdom eye; it is the first thing we need to do to follow the path. Even if we don't have a pure motivation from the very beginning, just understanding what Dharma means and how it makes life meaningful is very beneficial. As we practice more, we can develop a better and purer motivation based on this understanding. Then we have the chance to act correctly without mistake.

We can't become like those exalted yogis of the past in just a few days or even a few months, but it's very beneficial simply knowing how they gained their great freedom and peace by practicing Dharma. This gives us some insight into how we can start to lead our life. We can watch and ensure all our actions are as pure as possible, not controlled by the thought of the eight worldly dharmas.

What is a nonvirtuous action?

What is a nonvirtuous action? The shortest definition is: any action that results only in suffering. To make the definition clearer, we can say it is any action motivated by a nonvirtuous thought, a nonvirtuous thought being a thought based on one of the three poisonous minds of ignorance—particularly ignorance of karma—anger or attachment. And as we have seen, it is not anger but attachment that dominates our life—day in and day out, we live with the thought of the eight worldly dharmas, attached to the happiness of this life.

It's not just that we have the thought of seeking a good reputation, material rewards, praise and comfort—we can seek these out of a good heart, out of a wish to benefit others. Here it's the thought of seeking these things simply for the happiness of this life, out of the attachment that clings to this life.

Every action we do—walking, sitting, sleeping, working and so forth, even prayers and meditation—is transformed into nonvirtue by being stained with attachment to the happiness of this life and will only result in suffering, not happiness. The thought of the eight worldly dharmas not only blocks us from ultimate happiness, it blocks us from temporary happiness as well. Delusions pour down on us with the incredible force of a large waterfall. Even if we don't want to get angry, strong anger still arises, showing us how we're under the control of delusions most of the time.

We might know the meditation techniques that are the antidotes to the delusions, but if we don't apply them in our daily life when situations arise, we won't be able to protect our mind and will have missed a precious opportunity. We might try to practice Dharma, but if our mind is still overwhelmed by delusions, most of our actions will become nonvirtuous. It's even more difficult to generate a virtuous thought when we go to sleep, so even our sleep becomes nonvirtuous. However many hours we sleep, we create that many hours of nonvirtue.

As we're talking about motivation, I'd like to ask a question. Somebody is dying of starvation and we give her food, not with a virtuous thought but with a nonvirtuous thought of worldly concern, with attachment to our reputation and with the hope that other people will praise us. Is that action virtuous or nonvirtuous?

You might think that the action is virtuous because we're helping somebody, but the motivation is nonvirtuous because it's done for praise. If it were the case that such an action was virtuous, then if somebody wanted to be killed and you killed him, that would also be a virtuous action because it brought happiness to another being. It's similar to the previous example, where filling a starving person's stomach made her happy. Perhaps you agree that the motivation is nonvirtuous but my question is whether the action itself is virtuous or nonvirtuous.

Here's another example. Let's say that you have cancer and take medicine to prolong your life. Your motivation for taking the medicine is simply attachment clinging to the pleasure of this life. You want to have a long life but the long life is just for yourself; you're not thinking of having a long life to benefit other sentient beings. Is that virtuous?

If it were, then everything you did to help yourself survive would be virtuous—eating, sleeping, going to the toilet, doing your job—because you do all these things to give yourself a long and comfortable life. None of them involves killing or any other violent action toward other sentient beings. Eating and drinking stop your hunger and thirst, having a house protects you and gives you comfort, clothes give you warmth, and doing a job gives you money, which helps you get the pleasures you desire. Since everything you do twenty-four hours a day helps you survive without harming others in any way, all these actions should become virtue. But they don't.

In a text of questions and answers by the first Panchen Lama, Panchen Losang Chökyi Gyaltsen,[38] there's the question "What is the beginning of meditation?" He replies, "The beginning of meditation is motivation."

If an action were virtuous simply because it didn't involve harming others through killing and so forth, then whenever we meditated there'd be no need to generate a virtuous motivation because just doing the meditation itself would be virtuous. This mistake would arise. That's why there's so much emphasis on watching the mind and transforming it into not just a

---

[38] The first Panchen Lama (1570–1662) composed *Guru Puja (Lama Chöpa)* and *Path to Bliss Leading to Omniscience*, a famous lam-rim text. He was a tutor of the Fifth Dalai Lama.

virtuous thought but into renunciation of the whole of samsara. And not just into that, but also into bodhicitta.

If you believe that an action can be virtuous even with a nonvirtuous motivation because it doesn't hurt others, what about the opposite, an action involving harm done with a virtuous motivation, such as when a bodhisattva kills somebody? Since there's violence and the other person is hurt, that would have to be nonvirtuous even though the bodhisattva had bodhicitta.

For example, in one of his past lives Shakyamuni Buddha was the bodhisattva captain of a ship and killed a man he saw was planning to kill the other five hundred traders on the ship. By killing him, that bodhisattva collected great merit and shortened the duration of his time in samsara by one hundred thousand eons; he came one hundred thousand eons closer to liberation and enlightenment. This happened not because of his action but because of his motivation of great compassion. His great compassion transformed that action. What determines whether an action is a virtue or a nonvirtue is its motivation.

Therefore, with respect to the charitable act of feeding a starving person, even though the food enables her to survive and have a long life, the act itself becomes nonvirtuous because of the power of the nonvirtuous motivation. It's the same in our everyday life when we eat food or take medicine that help us to be healthy and live long—if the motivation is nonvirtuous, the action is nonvirtuous.

For example, there's the story of two people who were doing a very long Yamantaka retreat in Penpo when one of them died. Every evening after that, the other meditator did the *sur* practice, which involves burning *tsampa* and making charity of the smell to the hungry ghosts.[39] One evening he didn't do the practice and a terrifying hungry ghost with many arms that looked just like Yamantaka appeared. When the meditator asked who he was, the hungry ghost replied, "I am your friend, the one who was doing retreat with you." Even though the one who died had done retreat on the deity for many years, he didn't know how to practice properly. He'd done it with attachment, omitting the lam-rim and bodhicitta motivation. There wasn't even the virtuous thought seeking the happiness of future lives, which would at least make the motivation Dharma and save him from being reborn as a hungry ghost.

---

[39] See *Aroma Charity for Spirits.*

This is why motivation is so important. Motivation controls the action. As *The Treasury of Precious Qualities* says,

> If the root is medicinal, so are its shoots,
> If poisonous, no need to say its shoots will be the same.
> What makes an act positive or negative is not how it looks
> Or its size, but the good or bad intention behind it.[40]

If the root of a plant is medicinal, the flowers, fruit and the rest of the plant will be medicinal, but if the root is poisonous, the rest of the plant will be poisonous too. The result of an action depends on the motivation with which it's done. A great bodhisattva is permitted to do the seven actions of killing, stealing, sexual misconduct, telling lies, slandering, gossiping and speaking harshly because he or she has such great compassion for others that all actions are transformed into virtue.

If we have no idea what a virtuous action is, then whatever we do will be based on ignorance. Even if we try to meditate using some simple physical yoga or watching the breath, since we lack Dharma wisdom we're really just imitating Dharma practitioners, like monkeys imitate people, and it's extremely difficult to make our actions pure.

We really need to be mindful of every action, to check why we're about to do something to see if there's the taint of the thought of the eight worldly dharmas. If there is and we see that doing the action will become the cause of suffering, we can change our motivation to a virtuous one and the resulting action will then become the cause of perfect peace, enlightenment. A Kadampa geshe, Lama Gyamaba, said,

> Renouncing this life is the very start of Dharma. When you take pride in being a Dharma practitioner without actually doing a single Dharma practice, how foolish you are. Therefore, from the beginning, always check whether your mental continuum contains this very first step of renouncing this life.[41]

This very effective instruction comes from the deep experience of this yogi and shows that he lived in his practice, renunciation of this life. Whenever

---

[40] Quoted in *The Words of My Perfect Teacher*, p. 125.
[41] See also *The Door to Satisfaction*, p. 64, and *Liberation in the Palm of Your Hand*, p. 296.

we do any action, we should check the motivation and see whether we're about to do the action with the mind renouncing this life or not. Check, because then this is really practicing Dharma. Without exploring our motivation like this, just knowing the words doesn't help our mind.

Let me take my own life as an example. I think I'm a Dharma practitioner, but as soon as I get up, rather than immediately focusing on renouncing this life, all I think about is my first cup of tea. And so I drink that first cup of tea with the thought of the eight worldly dharmas and then it's time for breakfast. And from then on, slowly, my whole day—eating lunch, drinking tea, going outside, coming inside, washing, putting clothes on, talking, going to bed—is spent completely in service of the eight worldly dharmas. I might think I'm leading a spiritual life but really I'm not. Perhaps I've not created even one Dharma action the whole day; my entire day is completely empty, blank. The only firm arrangement I've managed to make is to be reborn quickly and continuously in the suffering lower realms. If we live each day like this, we can expect nothing good from our future lives, and when we die—and we can die suddenly and at any time—we will die with great upset.

The same action with four motivations

There's a quote that says that all existence depends on motivation.[42] This means that everything we experience comes from the motivation we create with our mind: hell comes from motivation, liberation and enlightenment come from motivation; what is called happiness and what is called suffering come from motivation. Everything comes from our mind; everything depends on our intention, our attitude, our motivation.

Let's take the example of four people—it doesn't matter whether they're rich or poor—who give money to a beggar. The first person gives with the motivation of achieving full enlightenment, the omniscient mind with fully developed wisdom, compassion and perfect power, so that she can completely free all sentient beings from suffering and obscuration and lead them to the peerless happiness of full enlightenment. Her action of giving becomes the cause of achieving full enlightenment.

The second person gives money not with the motivation of achieving full enlightenment for the sake of all sentient beings but to achieve ultimate liberation, which means liberation from just his own suffering and its causes,

---

[42] Sometimes expressed as "everything exists on the tip of a wish."

from just his own samsara. His action of giving doesn't become the cause of enlightenment but simply liberation for himself.

The third person gives money with the motivation not for liberation or enlightenment but only to obtain happiness in future lives. There's no question that the previous two people's actions of giving money become the cause of happiness, but even this person's action still becomes the cause of happiness, the happiness of future lives.

Finally, the fourth person gives money with the motivation of getting a good reputation, expecting that later, when he's in trouble and needs help, the other person will help him. It's done in order to get the four desirable objects and avoid the four undesirable ones. His motivation is the desire clinging only to the temporary happiness of this life.

In a similar example in *Liberation in the Palm of Your Hand*, Pabongka Dechen Nyingpo talks about four people reciting praises to Tara with those four motivations.[43] The first person recites the prayer with the motivation to achieve enlightenment for the sake of other sentient beings, the second to achieve individual liberation, the third to achieve happiness in future lives and the fourth seeking only the happiness of this life.

The actions of the first three people are all actions of holy Dharma. The fourth person's action, however, is not holy Dharma; it is worldly dharma because it is done with worldly concern, clinging to this life. The motivation is nonvirtuous and the result will be rebirth in the hell, hungry ghost or animal realms. So, even though the prayer itself is Dharma, the person's action does not become holy Dharma.

Here we can clearly see the borderline between Dharma and non-Dharma, between what is virtue and nonvirtue, between the cause of happiness and the cause of suffering. The fourth person's action of giving money (or reciting Tara prayers) does not become the cause of enlightenment for the sake of all sentient beings, does not become the cause of ultimate liberation and does not even become the cause of happiness in future lives. It is done only with the thought of the worldly dharmas, clinging to the temporary happiness of this life, and is therefore nonvirtuous and not the cause of happiness, now or in the future.

People who steal generally think that stealing is a way to obtain happiness. The enjoyment they get from the stolen money, however, is not the result of stealing but of a virtuous action done in the past. Stealing is just the

---

[43] *Liberation*, pp. 154–55.

condition, not the main cause of the enjoyment. Because it is done with the motivation of self-cherishing, seeking happiness only for the self and wishing harm to others, with one of the poisonous minds—ignorance, anger or attachment—the action of stealing is negative and leaves on the mind an imprint that results in future suffering. Therefore, even though the person believes that stealing is a way of obtaining happiness, what he believes and the reality of it are two completely opposite things.

And here it is the same with the fourth person in our example, who gives money to others but with the thought of the eight worldly dharmas. He is seeking happiness, but only for himself, and only for this life, and only temporary happiness. That motivation is nonvirtuous—it is not Dharma—and its result is only suffering.

As the great bodhisattva Shantideva said in *A Guide to the Bodhisattva's Way of Life*,

> Even those who wish to find happiness and overcome misery
> Will wander with no aim or meaning
> If they do not comprehend the secret of the mind—
> The paramount significance of Dharma.[44]

Here "secret of the mind" does not mean some high realization such as the unification of clear light and illusory body;[45] it's not talking about anything very complicated. We can interpret it as meaning the different levels of motivation I have just described. This verse emphasizes the importance of watching and protecting our mind, keeping it in virtue, because happiness and suffering are dependent upon our own mind, our own positive and negative thoughts. One way of thinking creates happiness; the other way produces suffering and problems. Everything depends on our mind, from day-to-day problems and the sufferings of the six realms up to liberation and enlightenment.

Don't mix Dharma with the eight worldly dharmas

Marpa granted the complete teachings on receiving enlightenment in one lifetime to his disciple Milarepa. Once when Milarepa was going away, Marpa instructed him,

---

[44] Ch. 5, v. 17.
[45] The most profound practice in tantra, done just before achieving enlightenment.

Son, don't mix the Dharma and this life's work. If they are mixed you will lose the Dharma. Think on that: you, the son, are suffering in samsara. Even if I were to try to explain the nature of suffering an infinite number of times, I could not. It is inexpressible; it is infinite. Even if I were to manifest hundreds of mouths and tongues to explain it for hundreds of thousands of eons, I could never finish. So, my instruction to you is don't waste the Dharma, don't mix this life and Dharma.

This has great taste, but if we don't know the actual meaning of Dharma, if our Dharma is only mouth Dharma, then what Marpa said won't mean much to us. No matter how much we work for enlightenment, if our practice is mixed with the work for this life, it is meaningless. That action cannot bring the result we expect; it's like milking a goat's horn—even if we milk it for eons, we'll never get any milk. There's no living being who can obtain both the work of this life and the holy Dharma. No matter how much we try to do both without losing either, we're only deluding ourselves.

There's the story of one of the ancient yogis, a Kadampa geshe called Ben Gungyal,[46] who always watched his motivation. In his early life he was completely crooked, a robber by day and a thief by night, but when he eventually met holy gurus living in the practice, he totally changed his life. He became a monk and spent his life in a cave practicing the graduated path. His robes were all he owned, nothing else. One day he received an invitation to a nearby monastery where a benefactor was offering curd. All the monks were sitting in a line and because of his junior status he was seated somewhere down near the end. As the people offering the curd moved down the line he heard how much curd was plopping into the cups of the people before him and became more and more worried that it would run out before they got to him. Then he checked his motivation and, realizing what was happening in his mind, turned his bowl upside down. So when they got to him and told him to turn his bowl the right way up, he said, "It's OK, I've had mine." Here, his attachment to the curd was telling him that the others were getting too much and he was going to miss out, so he turned his bowl over to punish his negative mind, to tell it that he wouldn't let it destroy his peace. Instead of following the negative mind, he fought it.

Another time, as a monk, he'd been invited to a family's house to do

---

[46] See also Ben Gungyal's story in the section "We always have what we need," p. 147–48.

puja and was left alone in the living room while they were outside working. Suddenly he found his hand in a sack of wheat, an unconscious reaction from the days when he was a thief. When he realized what was happening he shouted loudly, "Thief! Thief!" When the people came running back in looking around for the thief, saying, "Where? Where?" he pointed to his hand in the sack and said, "Here he is!" It sounds silly, but actually he was practicing purely, trying to fight the negative mind, the thought of the eight worldly dharmas, the mind that's attached to the happiness of just this temporal life.

There's also the story of the day his benefactor was coming to his hermitage.[47] He cleaned his room ahead of time, set up his altar nicely and made sure everything was very neat and clean. Then, as soon as he sat down and examined his motivation, he saw that he'd cleaned the room in order to impress his benefactor so that he'd continue supporting him and that his motivation was the thought of the eight worldly dharmas. Realizing this, he suddenly stood up, took a handful of ashes from the fireplace and threw them all over his altar, making a real mess. He had recognized that what he had done had the form of a Dharma action but in reality wasn't. So, to immediately practice the antidote and let go of the attachment, he scattered ash over his altar.

At that moment, Padampa Sangye, one of Geshe Ben Gungyal's teachers and a great yogi like Milarepa, was teaching at a far distant place. Suddenly, in the middle of his teachings, he smiled, and when his students asked why he was smiling, he said, "This morning, my student Ben Gungyal made the best offering in Tibet. He threw dirt in the mouth of the eight worldly dharmas."

Any action is either holy Dharma or worldly dharma. Nothing can be both. We can do both, but not at the same time. One action cannot become both holy Dharma *and* worldly dharma. Those two are complete opposites and if we try to do them together, we lose the holy Dharma. If we don't renounce the thought that clings to this life, it's difficult even to stop rebirth in the lower realms let alone make our Dharma practice the path to nirvana.

The Kadampa geshe Potowa said that "a two-pointed needle cannot be used to sew cloth." Holy Dharma and worldly dharma are completely opposite, so no matter how we try to mix the two, we can't do it. We might think that we're practicing holy Dharma and also doing the work of this life at the

---

[47] See also *Liberation in the Palm of Your Hand*, p.117.

same time, but the two can never come together, just as a two-pointed needle—a needle without an eye—can't sew. We want both. We want enlightenment and we also want the comfort of this life. We try to have both, but when we do, we lose. As Marpa advised Milarepa, when holy Dharma and worldly dharma are mixed, the holy Dharma is lost.

As long as our mind is involved in the thought of the eight worldly dharmas, we're a worldly person and whatever action we do—meditating, studying, teaching—is negative. Therefore the great Indian pandits and Tibetan yogis of old always instructed their followers that the very first step in Dharma practice is avoidance of the thought of the eight worldly dharmas.

There are many wonderful life stories of the ancient yogis showing how they practiced by renouncing the eight worldly dharmas. In *The Jewel Ornament of Liberation,* the great Gampopa said,

> Nobody has attained both the holy Dharma and the work of this life. There's no doubt that the person who wishes to obtain both together cheats himself. Even if I were to meet you face to face I'd have nothing to say other than this. Keep your body and mind in virtue at your own place.

Gampopa shows us that it's impossible to practice holy Dharma and worldly dharma at the same time. If, for example, we read a Dharma text with attachment, expecting a good reputation, we're only cheating ourselves. We might think that our action is Dharma but the holy Dharma is lost. He then says that the only worthwhile topic of conversation is the true meaning of Dharma, so even if we were to meet somewhere, he'd have nothing else to talk about, and when we separated we should go to our respective places and keep our body, speech and mind pure and in virtue.

Living in renunciation of the thought of the eight worldly dharmas, we produce only pure actions that continually make our life meaningful, no matter what the external appearances might be. Following worldly concerns, however, we only use up the result of previous lives' good karma and don't make any arrangements for our future lives. Once the result of our previous good karma has finished, the future results will be only suffering. Like trying to drink the water of a mirage can never quench the suffering of thirst, trying to do good actions polluted by the thought of the eight worldly dharmas can never bring happiness. Such actions can never become Dharma.

The thought of the eight worldly dharmas is something that we have within our own mind right now, so it's important to be conscious of our emotions and feelings as they arise and deal with this problem. We need all our skill to stop attachment arising. In this way, we become our own guide. In fact, by being conscious of attachment when it arises and dealing with it immediately, we become our own savior.

Evil people can be subdued by Dharma, tough-skinned ones cannot

The *Request to the Supreme Compassionate One* from the *nyung-nä* practice says,

> Behold with compassion tough-skinned beings like me
> Who maintain a religious manner but do not achieve the great
>   meaning,
> Being overwhelmed by attachment, hatred, and the eight worldly
>   concerns,
> Without having subdued our minds by observing cause and result.[48]

We assume the form of a Dharma practitioner but our actions can never obtain the three great meanings that Dharma practice should bring: happiness in future lives, liberation and enlightenment. In truth, the thought of the eight worldly dharmas is our practice.

Butter is very important in Tibet. When Tibetans use leather to make shoes or clothing they treat it with butter to make it flexible. The rancid butter they use has a very bad taste and a kind of blue-green color. They stretch a skin out on the ground and make it flexible by rubbing the butter into it with their feet and leaving it in the hot sun. But they also use leather as a container for the butter itself and that kind of leather is different. Because it's permeated by butter it becomes very hard and inflexible.

And so it is said that greatly evil beings can be subdued by the Dharma but a "tough-skinned" person cannot. Even though evil beings accumulate much negative karma, when they hear Dharma for the first time there's a chance that they'll feel regret. They can understand that what they've done is very negative and can change their mind, purify their negativities, practice confession and determine never to do evil actions again. In that way, no matter how evil they are, their mind can be subdued by the Dharma.

---

[48] From *Nyung Nä: The Means of Achievement of the Great Eleven-Faced Compassionate One,* p. 41.

But that doesn't happen with tough-skinned people.[49] Even though they might be living in a monastery or some other Dharma environment where everybody is practicing continuously and listening to teachings all the time, somehow, nothing penetrates their tough skin. Just as our daily life can become dull and routine—breakfast, coffee and so forth—in the same way, listening to Dharma becomes nothing special for them. Whatever they hear, it's always, "Oh yeah, sure, sure, I know that, oh yeah." Instead of becoming medicine to subdue their unsubdued minds of attachment and anger, Dharma becomes medicine to nourish their self-cherishing.

We listen to so much Dharma, read so many Dharma books, but our mind never changes, there's never any progress. That's not the fault of the lama who reveals the teachings. It's not the fault of the teachings. It's our own fault. If we make no progress it's because we're making the mistake of following the thought of the eight worldly dharmas. A teaching says,

> You have hundreds of qualities, but you're still under the control of the one mistake. You have a hundred thoughts, but the mistake is not having thought the one thought.

We might have many great qualities and an incredible education but still be under the control of the one mistake of letting ourselves be ruled by the thought of the eight worldly dharmas. No matter how high our degree, no matter how knowledgeable we are in Dharma, we have never learned how to create happiness, how to accumulate virtue. Instead of using our incredible education for that, it's all directed toward accumulating nonvirtue as we seek just the happiness of this life.

Rather than subduing our mind, our education makes us more tough-skinned, full of pride and arrogance. Under the control of that one mistake, we waste our education and our Dharma knowledge, and because of that we waste our life. We have so many thoughts all the time, so many ideas, so many, so many—the "hundred thoughts" of the quote—so why do we still have so many problems? Because we miss this one crucial thought of renouncing the thought of the eight worldly dharmas. It's like we have a heavy stone fastened to our legs—we have no freedom to go where we wish. Because of that one mistake we have no liberty to develop our mind.

---

[49] Rinpoche sometimes calls such people "Dharma thick skulls."

The long road ahead

Practicing Dharma is the best way—the only way—of really taking care of ourselves. His Holiness the Dalai Lama often says that if we want to be self-ish we should be *wisely* selfish. That means if we want happiness then we should not only never harm others but always benefit them, finding the best ways to serve them. In other words, the best way to take care of ourselves is to fully dedicate ourselves to the welfare of others.

Practicing Dharma in this way has an element of selfishness in it. Along with our wish for the happiness of future lives, liberation from samsara and full enlightenment we have the wish for the happiness of this life. It's there in our heart even as we do service for others. Because of the delusions we still have in our mind, our motivation is not completely cleansed of attach-ment. But, even if we can't find full satisfaction in our life because of this, we're still performing positive actions and still being useful to others.

Therefore, there's no reason to stop helping others, even if our motiva-tion is impure and we're still full of delusions. If we were to wait until we had a completely pure motivation before we tried to do positive things, we'd probably never do anything beneficial. Even with a mixed motivation, it's still a good life because we're helping others. Stopping benefiting others because we don't yet have a pure motivation is crazy. It would mean that instead of doing positive actions we'd be completely wasting every action we did; all the time, energy and expense we put into obtaining shelter, food, medicine, clothes and so forth would be completely wasted. We wouldn't have benefited ourselves and we wouldn't have benefited others.

If you're new to Dharma you might feel like giving up because you think it doesn't work. You feel lonely, depressed and alienated from your friends. This actually comes from not having enough understanding of Dharma. You're applying the remedy to your delusions but not strongly enough. You're surrounded by people always trying to develop their three poison-ous minds and working only for worldly concerns and you're trying to do the complete opposite, trying to diminish your poisonous minds and be free from worldly concern. You might think that it's impossible to practice Dharma and live a normal life, that the only thing you can do is to physically separate yourself from this life.

However, when your mind gets a little closer to Dharma, you start to find that you have less interest in the happiness of this life. You don't need to get so involved with worldly concerns. The attitudes of the people around you affect you less. Things that go on around you—all the pride, jealousy, attachment, anger, ill will and so forth that you see others display—mean less to you. You find that you no longer act or think like the people around you. With less contact with such people, of course you have more time to practice Dharma, but it can seem strange at first. You can feel lonely when your old friends no longer come around.

The point is, however, that it's not necessary to give up your job and your life, but it *is* necessary to change your attitude. You can practice morality and charity just as well where you are. But as long as you follow the thought of the eight worldly dharmas you cannot achieve liberation. The door of the path to liberation is the mind renouncing samsara, and renunciation of the happiness of this life is the first renunciation you need to generate in our mind.

I heard that once in Switzerland, where there are a lot of Tibetan people, including some incarnate lamas who have disrobed, the factories where they worked were shut down for a week. During that week nobody earned any money and most people were really worried about this—the Swiss workers as well as the Tibetans. But there were some who were Dharma practitioners and very happy to have the break, especially one man who found a lot of time to do Dharma activities. He told me that when he met the other factory workers they were very unhappy but he had an incredibly good time.

When we stayed with His Holiness Song Rinpoche's family in Canada once, I saw how hard they worked, day and night, not only to earn money for the family but also to sponsor monks in the tantric college and the big monasteries in India, to make offerings and to sponsor big statues. Each year they also found time to go to the East to visit the monasteries and see their lamas and sponsor teachings. With such strong faith in the Triple Gem, they used as much of their money as possible to accumulate merit. This is such a worthwhile thing to do. Their lives are not empty, not wasted, and the merit they create is something they can carry with them to their future lives.

Perhaps we are a monk or a nun living for years in a monastery or nunnery but, because our mind is not completely renounced, we're still not really happy. I still say that this is a good life because all the practices we do will bring a good result in future lives. We're still living in moral discipline and following the advice of our spiritual friend. If, on the other hand, we get so disillusioned that we want to give it all up, we can create big suffering for ourselves. Maybe we think, "Oh, I've been living in ordination for years and it doesn't give me any satisfaction. Studying Tibetan Buddhism doesn't work. Maybe I'll try being a Muslim." Maybe we think like this or that living our life as a "free" person—no rules, just doing whatever we want whenever we want—is the way to happiness. Before, we were trying to be free from attachment, but now we've given in and allowed ourselves to become a slave to attachment again. We interpret happiness from the point of view of the eight worldly dharmas, not from the point of view of Dharma wisdom.

And perhaps, in the short term, if we leave our monastic environment and give up our vows, we might have more fun and seem to be enjoying ourselves more, but really, this is just a total hallucination. We close our eyes to our motivation and to our long-term happiness and don't see how much this current, temporary enjoyment is costing us. It only appears to be pleasure but the karmic result will be strong suffering. Therefore we should define happiness only by its motivation and whether it brings a good result.

When we read Milarepa's biography we can understand how many hardships he had to bear, how hard he practiced under his great guru Marpa, how he completely put his whole life in Marpa's hands. He had to build and rebuild a nine-storey tower many times. When he completed it the first time his guru told him to tear it down and put the stones back in their original places. Then when he had done that he had to build it again. He was made to do this several times, but by practicing in this way all his negativity was completely purified in one lifetime.

Just like Milarepa, Naropa and many other great yogis also went through incredible hardships in the practice of Dharma. Understanding why we have to go through such hardships helps us understand how to practice.

When we live within the various vows, such as ordination in a monastery or nunnery, we have to bear a lot of hardship because we can't make our mind pure in one day. It takes time. However, if everything we do is aimed at benefiting our mind, we will definitely progress. Then when we meditate continuously on the graduated path of the lower capable being and live in morality, we'll be protecting our mind. This is discipline, but completely different from the discipline an army imposes. The discipline in monasteries such as Sera, Ganden or Drepung, or in Gyume or Gyuto, the Lower and Upper Tantric Colleges, has been made by those incredible, learned holy beings, and everything is aimed at benefiting the mind, to not give harm to others but to benefit them. Even if we find such discipline hard and don't think we're happy, the result of our practice of abstaining from killing, stealing and so forth will definitely have a good result in the future.

Of course, it takes time for this to happen and we need to develop a continual and strong meditation practice, especially on subjects like the perfect human rebirth, impermanence and death, karma, the lower realms' sufferings and the general suffering of samsara. As we strengthen our understanding of these subjects within our mind, our clinging to this life will lessen and meeting the objects of the eight worldly dharmas will not disturb our mind as much.

Changing a deep-seated habit doesn't happen all of a sudden. Meditating on renunciation of attachment once or twice doesn't work, and even after one year, two years, ten, thirty, forty years, it might not completely turn our life around.

From beginningless lifetimes we've been working for attachment, our mind always under its control, and even in this life attachment has been arising continuously, making our mind more and more habituated to it, so how can we expect the problem to be solved instantaneously? Even physical habits such as smoking cigarettes are difficult to stop. So we shouldn't have a fickle mind when we try to practice Dharma. We shouldn't become discouraged because we don't see much progress after meditating for a month or two. When we do a month's retreat and a thousand prostrations and *still* our mind hasn't completely changed, we shouldn't decide that the methods don't work, give up and go back to our old life and just put more kaka in our mind.

And in the same way that feeling regret for a negative action is a positive thing to do, it's negative to feel regret for having done the very positive actions we did in trying to transform our mind. That sort of negative regret destroys the merit we created from doing the practice.

It's very helpful to understand that we will naturally encounter many difficulties when trying to overcome attachment because of our habituation to negative actions. Really understanding this will give us continued energy to practice, even though we don't feel good and seem to be making very little progress—even if we still haven't received any *siddhis!*

Milarepa received enlightenment in one lifetime but he had meditated extensively on emptiness, the fully renounced mind and so forth in previous lifetimes; his mind was already well trained in those things. Shakyamuni Buddha, too, created merits for many eons before he achieved enlightenment for the sake of sentient beings. We build up our practice drop by drop, like putting drops of water in the ocean, creating one or two merits, doing a retreat or a daily Dharma practice and so forth. Therefore it is totally unrealistic to think that we can receive realizations instantaneously. This is the expectation of a small mind. When we're feeling discouraged, it's useful to think of holy beings such as Guru Shakyamuni Buddha and how they practiced for such a long, long time.

MEDITATION

Meditation on the objects of the eight worldly dharmas as repulsive

Our attachment to an object depends on the aspect of the object we relate to, so a useful technique to eliminate attachment is to change the aspect of the object the mind focuses on. The most effective way of doing this, of course, is to meditate on the emptiness of the object, to see that the object, the beauty we ascribe to it and the pleasure we gain from it are all completely empty of existing in the way we think they exist, that what we think of as real is in fact an utter hallucination. Normally we see objects of attachment and their beauty as independent and self-existent, which is simply not true. That is how attachment is just a wrong conception.

An easier way of changing the aspect of the object of our attachment is simply to imagine it as something else. For instance, if you have an object to which you're attached, imagine it as made of stone or wood, as just an ordinary object that doesn't cause attachment to arise. Or you can focus on the ugly aspect of the object rather than its beauty, effectively countering your attachment to the object. Then you won't have to get rid of it. The problem isn't in the object but in the creator, the mind that superimposes "beautiful" onto that object.

If somebody brings you a gift and your mind just freaks out, flying with attachment to the gift, you can change the aspect of the gift from "wonderful" to something dangerous. Imagine that the thing in your hands is made of red-hot iron. If you do, the incredible attachment that made your mind so uptight and stressed suddenly decreases and you can control it. You make yourself happy and relaxed and don't create negative karma. This practice itself is a pure Dharma practice. Also think, "This red-hot iron may burn my hands but it can't cause me to be reborn in the suffering realms; it can't cause me to continuously suffer in samsara. But this object I'm attached to has been causing me to suffer in countless previous lifetimes until now and will continuously cause me to remain trapped in samsara and suffer." If you meditate like this, it's quite easy to lose your attachment.

A similar technique can be used when there are problems such as attachment arising by hearing sounds to which you're attached, like music. When you hear the sound, visualize it as a red-hot burning needle and think, "This red-hot burning needle can't cause me to be reborn in the suffering realms of samsara but this sound has been causing delusions and attachment to arise in me from numberless previous lifetimes until now and will continuously cause delusions to arise and make me experience continual suffering, even in future lives."

This simple technique to stop attachment from rising can really help. If you could see the actual nature of the sound there'd be no way for attachment to arise, but that's difficult; you need understanding, you need wisdom, and sometimes your wisdom is not strong enough to work. At such times, simple techniques like this can be very helpful and are quicker at stopping attachment. The main problem is not the sound; it's your mind, your attachment—but by using techniques such as these you can lose that attachment.

Whenever you hear personal praise that makes your heart burst with pride, try to be conscious of what's happening in your mind. If you have a painful open wound on your hand and you're in a bustling crowd of people, you protect your wounded hand very carefully in case somebody bumps into it and makes it worse. Your mind is like that vulnerable wound. If you don't take care of it, there's the danger of all kinds of things happening with your mind, then with your speech and then with your body.

So when you hear praise, as before, try to visualize it as a thunderbolt or a red-hot needle that destroys things. You don't have to say anything, you can still listen to the person praising you, but at the same time work with your mind, because the problem is in your mind. Understand that these pleasing words cause your pride to get bigger and greed and many other negative minds to arise and at the same time visualize the words in the terrifying form of a thunderbolt or a red-hot needle. Then what's happening in your mind becomes quite different. Before, your mind was lifted up, like a piece of paper caught by the wind. Just as the paper is powerless and has to go wherever the wind takes it, so your mind is made powerless by the praise. But just by changing the object, visualizing it in a different way, all of a sudden it changes your mind; it comes down and becomes peaceful and relaxed.

Then think, "Compared to being attached to praise, this red-hot needle is nothing, because even if it pierces my body it can harm only this present life's body, not my future lives' bodies. But praise has caused me to experience the infinite sufferings of samsara countless times, preventing happiness, realizations and enlightenment, is still doing so now and will continue do so in future." If you think this strongly and don't just say the words, it will be very useful. No matter how much praise you receive, there'll be no problem in your mind, no confusion—it will be peaceful, relaxed.

Many of us have too much attachment to food. Again, the problem isn't with the food but with the mind. A human being shouldn't eat food like a dog does. A dog sees food and just gobbles it up, expecting happiness. Our motivation for eating food should be higher than this. In everything we do, including eating, our fundamental motivation should be to achieve happiness and peace, so we should find a method of eating that brings peace, not more suffering through attachment. In this way, eating becomes worthwhile; it becomes wise eating.

Again, visualize the food as something disgusting, like kaka. This will definitely bring down the strong attachment you have for the food immediately. Then, as before, think, "This object, the kaka, may cause some harm to this present life but it cannot harm me as much as the food, which has been causing me to experience suffering since beginningless previous lives, preventing me from experiencing happiness and enlightenment, is still doing so now and will continue to do so in future." Practicing like this, you keep yourself from mental danger, from the attachment that causes you to be reborn in the three lower realms. In particular, attachment to food causes rebirth as a hungry ghost, so you're protecting yourself from that danger and making a huge profit.

You can use any of the four undesirable objects, such as displeasing words, abuse and criticism, to destroy the negative mind. Let them harm your attachment rather than you. Feel that they're your allies in the fight against your negative mind.

Even if you don't meditate or say mantras, even you don't have an altar, even if all your daily life is spent eating, sleeping and making kaka and pipi—it can still be Dharma practice fighting the negative mind, depending on your skill and mental power. This is better than sitting in a cave meditating without any possessions but still holding onto the evil thought of the eight worldly dharmas.

8. Turning Away from Worldly Concern

HAPPINESS COMES WHEN WE RENOUNCE THE EIGHT WORLDLY DHARMAS

In the West, the main emphasis is on external appearances and whether something makes us happy right now. The main goal seems to be happiness *now*. It has to be *now*. *Now!* At this moment! That's what the main thing in life is. That's old style psychology, cherishing ourselves. However, the best way to love ourselves, the best way to take care of ourselves, is to practice Dharma. That doesn't mean denying ourselves but practicing renunciation so that we can become liberated from samsara. That's what we all need, otherwise we'll experience suffering again and again, continuously, without end.

Attachment to the eight worldly dharmas makes us anxious that we'll be unable to fulfill our desire. Renunciation means the cessation of such worry. If we want to worry, there are more important things to worry about, such as creating bad karma or the suffering of the three lower realms. As long as the thought of the eight worldly dharmas is not renounced, life is full of problems. The moment we start to renounce this evil thought is the moment real happiness begins.

The peace of renunciation is inexpensive and doesn't depend on factories, rockets, weapons, armies or presidents. Such peace continues until enlightenment, growing stronger and stronger. Renouncing the eight worldly dharmas is like opening a door—a simple step that requires an understanding mind. We need to know the evolution of such an action, understanding its causes and expected results. Unlike most actions done ignorant of their results, such as taking drugs, which make us progressively crazier, renunciation makes us progressively saner. It's like a saw, cutting through problems and confusion.

Many people who have no experience of Dharma are shocked by those who follow a spiritual path and give up temporal things. This is especially true of the parents of Western Dharma students. They see renunciation as a great suffering and something only a limited mind would engage in. They think that those who renounce worldly concerns are foolish, that they're leading a nonsensical life that will lead to more problems. However, all this is judged with ignorance, without understanding the true benefits of renunciation. Since they have not been through the experience they cannot know. Rather than being just the causes of misery, as they seem to think, in reality such actions bring both future benefits and immediate help by releasing us from our confusion.

Any problems we might have with our Dharma practice come from our attitude to the practice, not from the practice itself. If we feel we were happier before we started practicing Dharma, we need to look at where this thought comes from and sort it out. Such thoughts are dangerous because they can destroy the merit of positive actions.

If we live in pure Dharma practice we simply won't have the common problems of people who lead a mundane life. A recent lam-rim lineage lama said,

> One who has renounced this life does not return anger when somebody is angry with him. When somebody insults him, he doesn't return the insult. When somebody beats him, he doesn't retaliate with a beating in return. The person who is able to practice like this is renounced.

As we practice Dharma and see the truth that all problems come from attachment to this life, we discover great calmness and peace, as opposed to the clinging, dissatisfied mind that never has enough. Freed from our desires, there's no painful mind, no stuck mind; it's like being released from prison. We feel incredibly happy when we're finally released from the painful emotional mind of desire.

In the absence of desire, we no longer have all the other problems that we normally experience: the suffering that lack of comfort brings, the pain of being criticized and so forth. There's only peace. This is the renunciation that is defined in the graduated path of the middle capable being, as clearly explained by Lama Tsongkhapa in *The Three Principal Aspects of the Path*.

With the great stability that renouncing this life brings, there is very little difference between meeting the four desirable objects and the four undesirable objects. If there's praise, we're happy; if there's criticism, we're happy. If we receive material things, we're happy; if we don't, we're happy. Neither good reputation nor bad reputation can disturb our mind; we have equalized them. However the conditions of life change, our mind remains undisturbed, so we experience great peace, great relaxation and freedom from anxiety.

Actually, this is the best way to stay healthy. With the relaxation and lack of worry that come with freedom from attachment, we're unlikely to have a sudden heart attack in the street and lie there, surrounded by people, our family upset and crying, waiting to get rushed off to the hospital in an ambulance with sirens blaring, this noise we hear all the time. Dharma saves us from all this. It not only protects us, it protects others and saves them from problems too.

With renunciation, any action, mundane or spiritual, becomes a pure Dharma action. While devoting all our energy to achieving enlightenment, we still need food, clothing and shelter to survive, but obtaining them is no longer the prime motivation for our actions. Moreover, living in the pure, essential practice of Dharma, the necessities of life come to us by the way, without too much effort on our part. They are like the many things we see on the way as we are traveling to a distant country that are enjoyable but not the purpose of our journey.

Understanding how only Dharma has the power to diminish and finally eliminate all delusions, we can see that there's no method other than Dharma if we want to be truly happy. We can practice Dharma anywhere, not just in Tibetan monasteries but in the West, in the East, in space, under the earth, wherever. It doesn't require sitting cross-legged with our eyes closed, saying prayers; it doesn't necessarily mean giving our possessions away. There's no specific form of action. Whatever we do, the power of our mind, a correct motivation, can make the actions of our daily life the remedy to our delusions.

There's great benefit if we can renounce our attachment to this life for even a second, so if we can do it for longer—a minute, an hour, twenty-four hours—then our life can really have great meaning. The benefit we can be to other sentient beings is unbelievable. There's so much we can do, especially by meditating on the lam-rim. Even if we don't achieve the actual realizations in this life, at least we'll be that much closer and well prepared to achieve realizations in our next life, which will happen without much hardship.

The higher the realizations we can actualize, the greater the benefit we can be to other sentient beings, who equal the limitless sky; those most precious sentient beings, from whom we have received all our past, present and future happiness and every single comfort.

Developing determination

This life is not long. In fact, it is very short. We might have only a few days left, a few months, at the most a few years. So what's the big deal with all these objects of attachment? Why should we care so much? Why should we be so concerned? With so much attachment and aversion we make ourselves crazy, so crazy, all the time thinking *bad, bad, bad;* these things are *bad, bad, bad.* Every day labeling *bad, bad, bad,* believing they are *bad, bad, bad.* We label them *bad, bad, bad* and they appear to our consciousness as *bad, bad, bad.* Like this, we make ourselves completely neurotic and paranoid.

And life is constantly changing around us. Every day, every hour, every minute, every second there are new good things and bad things to experience. We open our eyes and we see so many things around us: beautiful objects, ugly objects, indifferent objects. We are not deaf and so our ears are always hearing sounds: good sounds, bad sounds, indifferent sounds. As long as our nose consciousness is functioning, then again we smell good smells, bad smells, indifferent smells; and as long as our tactile consciousness is functioning, we are surrounded by objects that feel good to touch, or bad, or indifferent.

Whatever happens, whatever we experience, whichever of the four desirable objects or the four undesirable objects we encounter, we should be very aware of how short life is. The appearance of life is like a dream, like a finger-snap. So there's absolutely no point in caring about any of these things. There's no point in clinging to these ephemeral experiences. Otherwise it's like we're staying in a house for only a couple of days but spending all our time and effort making extensive improvements—renovating, decorating, furnishing—and not making any preparations for the onward journey. Knowing that we're leaving today, there's no point in trying to fix it up as if we were going to live there for many years. We don't paint the hotel or dormitory rooms we stay in.

The whole thing is a question of determination. Without determination there's no development. My first alphabet teacher, whose holy name was Aku Ngawang Lekshe,[50] used to tell me that the whole problem is being unable to make the determination to practice Dharma. He explained this to me the very first time he taught me the alphabet and he was still saying it the last time I saw him, not long before he passed away.

The inability to make this determination is the source of all our problems and obstacles. Our own mind creates the difficulty. Our own mind makes it difficult to practice and generate the realizations of the path. If we make the determination to practice, we won't have any difficulties; if we don't, we will. There are no difficulties from the side of the Dharma. There are no external difficulties. The difficulties in practicing Dharma come from our own mind, from our own inability to make the necessary determination. And what makes us unable to make that determination is the thought of the eight worldly dharmas.

The very moment we make the determination to not follow desire and to practice Dharma, we find peace. On this very seat, at this very second, there's peace. Really, there's no other choice; there's no other solution.

Renouncing the eight worldly dharmas is not only a Buddhist practice

Everybody wants satisfaction, so everybody needs to renounce the eight worldly dharmas, whether they're a religious practitioner or not. It's the one route out of suffering to happiness, so there's no other choice. This is psychology, not religion.

When somebody has a headache, a painkiller will stop it. It doesn't depend on that person's race or religion. There isn't an analgesic just for Buddhists. Similarly, the practice of renouncing the eight worldly dharmas is the psychological remedy to the suffering of attachment. Therefore this teaching is universal education. Everybody, Buddhist or not, needs this practice.

When we first come across Buddhism we might think that Dharma is easy; it's just a matter of sitting cross-legged with eyes closed and imitating that person over there. But the real Dharma is to create actions that are undefiled by the eight worldly dharmas and free of greed, hatred and ignorance. Those actions don't need the label "Buddhist," "Hindu," "Christian" or "Muslim." People might even call us "evil," but if our actions arise from a pure motivation and have the power to destroy the negative mind and

---

[50] Aku is a honorific, meaning "uncle." See *The Lawudo Lama*, pp. 140–42.

create positive karma, such actions are called Dharma because they allow us to escape from ignorance and reach enlightenment.

Dharma is not a prescribed set of actions only for Buddhists but something that everybody can do if their mind is open enough. It has nothing to do with class, caste, occupation, title, religion or skin color. But we sentient beings block the ability to help ourselves. Our ignorance alone stops us from creating positive karma. If we feel that the Dharma teachings we read are too deep and profound to be relevant to us, it's only our mind that has labeled them such. The Buddha didn't deliberately make them hard to follow. The level of Dharma that we can practice depends on our level of wisdom.

You might be worried about becoming a Buddhist because of what you think you have to do. If you are scared of the word, you don't have to be called "Buddhist." It's just a name. Scientists experiment on external phenomena, trying to improve the world, but experimenting with your mind is much more worthwhile. Instead of going around with a confused mind spending a lot of money rearranging material things, it's much more beneficial to experiment on your mind—hundreds, thousands, billions of times more beneficial—and much more interesting, too.

Check to see whether the scientists who work with external phenomena have discovered any methods that will completely cut off greed, hatred and ignorance. Have they ever discovered a method that will definitely destroy the cause of all mental and physical problems, such as old age and death? Of course, these people themselves, as wise as they are in science or whatever their field is, are afraid of aging and death. That's because there's something missing in the way they do their experiments; they can't recognize the root cause of these problems. If they had already discovered the cause of old age, which nobody wants, they would have developed a cure for it and there wouldn't be any old people any more; everybody would be young and eternally youthful looking. But there's no choice—everybody, no matter what religion or belief, has to go through old age, death and all these other sufferings.

Give up the clinging, not the object

Many people think that the Buddhist teachings on renunciation mean that we have to deny ourselves what we like, that Buddhism says we're not allowed to enjoy ourselves any more and therefore think that Dharma practitioners must be miserable people, always denying themselves pleasure.

From the practitioner's side, however, the limited-minded person who says such things is only an object of derision, because the experience of renunciation is not at all like that. Such a concept is completely wrong, completely opposite to the logical experience gained from this practice. Rather than bringing misery, renouncing attachment to worldly comfort brings great happiness in this and future lives.

Renunciation doesn't mean giving up all physical things and running away from life. We shouldn't eat, we shouldn't drink, we shouldn't wear clothes, we shouldn't live in our house, we need to give up our body...of course it doesn't mean that. If it did, how could we exist? How could we practice Dharma? Impossible! How is it possible to practice without relying on immediate needs? Perhaps it's possible if we're practicing Dharma in a dream; perhaps it would be easier to renounce the eight worldly dharmas while asleep.

Having money is not the problem, but clinging to money is. Having friends is not the problem, but attachment to them is. Whenever we cling to something, that mind of desire becomes very dangerous. The object isn't dangerous, but, like a contagious disease, the mind of desire is.

Without worldly concern, having the four desirable objects is not a problem. Not receiving gifts becomes a problem when there's the desire to receive them. Discomfort becomes a problem when there's desire for comfort. The problem isn't having a friend but having the need for friendship.

Perhaps we've had a friend for years and always thought that she loves us but suddenly find out that she's never really loved us at all. While we thought that our friend loved us we were happy, but now, suddenly, it has all changed and we're miserable. The object hasn't changed—our friend's love was never there in the first place—but the mind perceiving it has. Our friend's love (or lack of it) is not the problem. When our mind interprets a situation as "bad," *then* the problem starts, *then* there's unhappiness in our life. It's not just finding out that the person doesn't love us; it's our interpretation of that fact and our labeling it "bad" and "negative." Then we feel as if an arrow has been shot into our heart.

This shows clearly that the suffering has been brought on not by the external object, the friend, but our own mind. Not practicing Dharma but following the self-cherishing thought instead, we interpret the situation as negative and our own mind makes this external object the condition upon which we base our suffering. It could equally be a condition for happiness, but our mind makes it the opposite.

I once saw on TV a story about a man who lived quite close to Man-jushri Institute,[51] in England. He was very rich, with a huge property and bodyguards and dogs that bit people who tried to sneak onto his land. His house had hundreds of rooms but nobody else lived there. He slept in each of the many bedrooms one at a time, a different bedroom each night. He ate very little food but drank quite a lot of alcohol, four or five bottles a day. Not eating but getting very drunk, he then cried and felt very aggressive, very depressed. As the tears poured down his cheeks he moaned about how meaningless his life was. He had all these possessions, he was so rich, yet he was so depressed and felt that life was meaningless. He'd become rich through the car business but he was very bored with it and blamed the business for all his problems.

One Sunday he took his huge collection of toy cars outside. As his bodyguard held each car individually, he poured kerosene on it and set it alight, thinking that as he burned each car he was destroying the root of his problem. He was angry with the car business for making him miserable and thought that destroying his toy cars would make him happy.

Beggars wear ragged clothes and street dogs eat poor food, but this doesn't mean they have renounced this life. Only by watching our mind can we be sure we're living a renounced life. Otherwise, with our ragged clothes and poor food we may look renounced, but we could be putting it all on just to gain a reputation as an ascetic meditator. As we have seen, we can't judge renunciation from external appearances. It has nothing to do with being naked in a cave or throwing all our material possessions out the window—sleeping bag, jacket, cameras, shoes, bags, everything—until we're sitting in a completely empty room. If it did, we'd have to throw our body out the window as well.

Renunciation means renouncing the cause of suffering—throwing the dissatisfied mind out the window. Whatever our external appearance, richly clothed or utterly without clothes or possessions, if we have renounced attachment we have the great happiness that comes from practicing Dharma.

Renouncing attachment to a person means that we no longer have desire for that person. It doesn't mean that we give up on that person as an object of compassion. These are two completely different things. It's a common experience in our lives that we can have compassion and loving kindness for somebody without desiring him.

[51] One of the first FPMT centers. It was in Cumbria, north England, and operated between 1976 and 1983.

One of my teachers was Gen Jampa Wangdu, who also had many Western students and taught them "taking the essence," the *chu-len* pill retreat. In particular, this practice helps with the realization of calm abiding and the quick development of mind by using substances such as flower pills instead of food.[52] He had the lineage of the chu-len retreat and had himself accomplished the practice in Penpo, Tibet.

Even though he kept very quiet about his practice, Gen Jampa Wangdu had great success in achieving realizations. He generated bodhicitta, attained perfect calm abiding and realized emptiness—not just the common realization but tantric *mahamudra*, the completion stage realization that is generated on the basis of the generation stage. He also had experience of the Six Yogas of Naropa.

For many years he lived underneath a rocky outcrop just below His Holiness Ling Rinpoche's house. There was no cave below the rock; the earth was just dug out so that it became a cave. For some years he also lived in a hut way back on the mountain.

He was Lama Yeshe's and my best friend in Dharamsala. Whenever Gen Jampa Wangdu came to see us we had the best time. He was a very old meditator—not "old" in terms of age but in terms of meditation experience.

Even when he was at Buxa he was totally different from the other monks. I saw him from time to time walking around outside or going to the toilet. Just behind where I lived there was a long line of toilets. It was very difficult to keep them clean and they gave out such an intense smell that at lunchtime we'd have to hold our noses to eat. Even at that time Gen Jampa Wangdu's conduct and appearance were very different from those of the other monks. The way he wore his robes was very proper, in accordance with the *Vinaya*, and he walked the way an *arhat* walks, as described in the lam-rim teachings. You could see that his mind was totally concentrated. He did not have a monkey mind or a bird mind. A bird looks here for one second, there for one second, here for one second; it's impossible for it to concentrate. You could see just from Gen Jampa Wangdu's proper manner when went to the toilet that he practiced Dharma continuously, with full awareness of his body, speech and mind.

One day, even though he lived such a simple life, he gave up his tattered, faded robes and started wearing more expensive ones. He told me, "The reason I wear good robes now is that people complain when I wear them.

[52] See more on the chu-len practice in the section on Geshe Lama Konchog, p. 148 ff. See also LamaYeshe.com for Lama Yeshe's *Taking the Essence* teaching.

They say that I'm supposed to be an ascetic but because I'm wearing such rich clothes I can't be. They think I have plenty of money so they don't come making offerings as much as they used to. This is very good for me."

Going completely against the self-cherishing thought and worldly concern, which wants a good reputation, is a real sign of renunciation. By wearing fancy robes Gen Jampa Wangdu faced criticism instead of the praise he received before by looking like an ascetic monk. In that way he completely opposed worldly concern and self-cherishing. Renunciation depends on the mind, not on the external appearance.

In the 1970s and '80s many young people came to Asia from the West after being inspired by Milarepa's autobiography, but they didn't understand what renouncing this life meant. They saw that renunciation had certain benefits and that not having possessions could help their life but didn't understand the process, the way of doing it. They thought that Milarepa's amazing powers came from simply giving away all his possessions, so they threw theirs away too. Then, because of their lack of wisdom, not understanding what it means to "give up this life," they got into problems. They had no possessions but still had the thought of the eight worldly dharmas. They took good care of that. So they missed the things they'd thrown away and their minds got into a lot of trouble thinking and worrying about how they could get them back. Giving up this life doesn't work like that.

Their problems got bigger and bigger because their minds were not renounced. They tried to give things up physically but mentally couldn't stand being without possessions. Not understanding Dharma, they almost always gave up and returned home, thinking that renunciation doesn't work, that it isn't a solution to life's problems.

There was one Italian student who, before reading the biography of Milarepa, was a communist who took many drugs. He was so inspired by the book that he wanted to experience the great peace that Milarepa did, but because he had nobody to show him how to practice he thought that renunciation meant getting rid of all his material possessions. So he gave everything away and went to India with the book. He didn't have much money to start with and by the time he got to Bombay or Madras had only forty rupees left. He put it under his pillow and went to sleep but somebody stole it. His mind was extremely confused. Never having had any lam-rim teachings he had no method to stop the confusion, so his life was miserable. He only discovered that what he'd done was completely wrong after receiving lam-rim teachings from Lama Yeshe.

We should not understand renunciation in that way. This is a big mistake and only causes confusion in our mind. In ancient times in Tibet there were many bodhisattva kings who lived in avoidance of the thought of the eight worldly dharmas while surrounded by incredible possessions. Amidst all this opulence they worked for and guided the people of the country with kindness while still maintaining a pure Dharma practice.

A fabulously wealthy king can still live in renunciation; a beggar with nothing can live full of attachment for this life. What we look like on the outside has nothing to do with whether we have renounced this life or not. We can look like a monk or nun, we can be freaky or straight looking, it doesn't matter. If our mind is living in avoidance of the eight worldly dharmas, we're a pure Dharma practitioner, we have a pure Dharma mind.

It's definitely possible to live a busy life in the city with a renounced mind. His Holiness the Dalai Lama is the perfect example of this. While he is so busy looking after the problems of his people, guiding countless others, teaching almost continuously, his mind is still fully renounced, where not one single action he ever does is meaningless.

Renouncing attachment to the temporal pleasures of this life doesn't mean not experiencing the happiness of this life. As long as our mind has no thought of clinging to this life, there's nothing wrong with pleasure.

In *A Guide to the Bodhisattva's Way of Life*, Shantideva said,

> Having found by some coincidence
> This beneficial state that is so hard to find,
> If now while able to discriminate
> I once again am led into the hells,
>
> Then as though I were hypnotized by a spell
> I shall reduce this mind to nothing.
> Even I do not know what is causing me confusion,
> What is dwelling there inside me.[53]

So it is our choice whether we want to renounce the cause of suffering or not. Just knowing the words is not enough; it's necessary to recognize the evil thought of the eight worldly dharmas within us.

It's not a problem to find the thought of the eight worldly dharmas. Our

---

[53] Ch 4, vv. 26, 27.

mind is living in it the whole time; we're always working with it. So first we have to make a scientific experiment and learn how to recognize the evil thought when it arises. If we can't recognize it, how can we change it into Dharma?

To gradually move toward renunciation we need to be very careful when we encounter the eight objects and try to use whatever Dharma understanding we have to solve the confusion, to not let confusion with the object arise. This is very important. While we're together with the object, we should try to be conscious of what's happening. Better still, we should try to see what is about to happen just before the confusion arises. We should be like soldiers setting an ambush. Before encountering an enemy army, they know it's coming, so they hide and prepare themselves to destroy it before it has a chance to harm them.

This is where introspection is so important. If we can constantly watch our mind and see when the thought of the eight worldly dharmas arises, we can break the habit of clinging to this life. We can take an objective view of what's happening around us.

For instance, if a football player falls and injures himself, the spectators don't feel his pain. The player, who was so excited by the match that he thought he was happy, suddenly becomes very unhappy when he's injured and causes his side to lose. But the spectators don't share his excitement or unhappiness. They're just observers outside the actual experience of the match.

It's the same here. You "the observer" watch you "the doer" doing the actions, getting inflated or deflated by your experiences with external objects. You "the observer" are not involved in all that; you just watch the process. Thinking like this helps you control your mind and not get upset when conditions change. Your mind just watches impassively, not thinking "I want" when an object of attachment is experienced or "I am" when a feeling of happiness arises.

It's difficult to control the thought of the eight worldly dharmas without maintaining this impassive observer-mind. Without introspection, attachment and aversion can easily arise, flipping the mind out of control again. The teachings are like a mirror for the mind. Just as we use a mirror to check if our face is dirty or clean, the teaching shows us the truth of our life: what our mind is, how it works and whether it's perfect or imperfect.

No matter how much time we spend studying at university, researching the mind, studying psychology and things like that, it's extremely difficult to really understand how the mind works until we understand the teachings. Somebody who studies psychology academically doesn't actually study her own mind; she doesn't check from her own experience, which is the correct way of doing it. It's not very helpful just believing a book written about the mind by an author who doesn't even recognize his or her own problems.

Students who have studied psychology at university for three or four years and then done just a one-month meditation course have told me that they now realize that what they studied at university taught them nothing significant about the mind. Their university years were empty. Psychiatrists, people who are considered guides of the mind, are paid a lot of money for even a few words of advice, yet when they're asked about the root of the problems such as anxiety, schizophrenia and so forth, they get extremely vague. They can never point out the actual cause of unhappiness. They point to other things. Of course, this is not true of all psychiatrists, but many have little real understanding of the mind, of the cause of happiness and suffering, so it's extremely difficult for them to really help people and offer lasting solutions to their problems.

If we delay our Dharma practice until we've completely cleared all confusion from our mind, we may never reach that point. The only way to treat problems is to work on our mind right now. We need to start countering the thought of the eight worldly dharmas immediately. In that way we can become our own psychologist. We can be the best psychologist. I'm not denigrating Western methods or saying that there's never any need for external treatment, but most of us can control our own suffering by the power of the mind.

If your problems are too severe and cannot be controlled by the power of the mind alone, then take external treatment, but even then that treatment should be done with the pure thought of avoiding the eight worldly dharmas. Your motivation should be to receive enlightenment, and in order to accomplish that it's necessary to have a long life. If you undergo treatment with the motivation that has enlightenment as its final goal, then it becomes a very beneficial action.

This is how the great yogis and high Tibetan lamas studied Dharma: listening, checking and trying to understand the subject and actualize it in their mind. First they listened to the subject from somebody experienced, somebody living in the practice who had received teachings from a perfect teacher. Then they tried to understand the meaning, checking up whether it's like that or not, checking against their own life's experience. Then, after they had understood the teaching clearly, they meditated on it to actualize it in their mind, to try to make their mind become the path. This is what we should do.

HAPPINESS STARTS WHEN WE RENOUNCE THIS LIFE

The terms "renouncing this life" or "renouncing suffering" both mean renouncing the mind that is the cause of the problems, the thought of the eight worldly dharmas. Therefore "Dharma" includes even pragmatic, transient techniques to stop attachment from arising. This is the actual Dharma, the method that immediately solves our confusion and mental illness. Bringing clarity and lack of confusion to our mind is the best way of bringing happiness to our life. Renouncing suffering doesn't mean we'll never have stomach or knee pain, a headache or a cold. It doesn't mean wishing to be free of all pain but wishing to be free from the very cause of all suffering.

It has been the experience of these great yogis that we don't have to wait until our future lives to experience this happiness. As soon as we stop the dissatisfied mind, immediately—*immediately*—there's the result, happiness.

At first we might be nervous about letting go of desire because we normally equate desire with happiness. In fact, it's exactly the opposite. As soon as we let go of desire we achieve inner peace, satisfaction and happiness; we become independent. Before, we were dictated to and controlled by desire but now we have achieved real freedom.

We can see in the biographies of the great yogis Tilopa, Marpa, Milarepa, Lama Tsongkhapa and many of those other highly realized beings whose holy minds passed into enlightenment how, even without material possessions, they generated great tranquility and peace and through that were able to realize the great achievements of the path. They didn't have even the scent of the eight worldly dharmas about them but by completely renouncing desire for this life, they received everything—the best reputation, perfect surroundings and sufficient material comfort.

In Milarepa's *Hundred Thousand Songs* he often says how renouncing this life's worldly activities automatically stops all the thousands of problems associated with the worldly life and brings great bliss.

Without any possessions at all, he led an ascetic life in solitary places. Although he lived like an animal, he spent his life in great happiness, his mind always peaceful, without confusion or problems. He didn't have even one sack of tsampa but lived on nettles alone. Living without food, clothing or reputation didn't cause him any problems because of his Dharma practice. He achieved all the high realizations and then enlightenment in that one lifetime, all due to the power of his pure Dharma practice of renouncing suffering, renouncing this life. His mind was incomparably happier than that of the king who has great power and many bodyguards, soldiers and weapons.

Therefore, it's completely wrong to think that Dharma only brings happiness in future lifetimes but not in this one. We experience peace and happiness the very moment we begin to practice and live in the Dharma. We feel its effects immediately.

If we want to enjoy a beautiful apartment, we first have to work to collect lots of money and then put a great deal of time and effort into renovating and decorating it. Worldly actions require a huge amount of energy, yet we can't be sure whether or not they will bring us any pleasure. Whenever we do Dharma actions, however, we immediately feel the real peace and happiness they bring to our life.

It's so silly to allow ourselves to feel upset when we don't get what we want, angry when somebody criticizes us or happy when somebody praises us. It's so silly to worry about what others think, to discriminate, deciding one thing's good and another's bad. If we really examine this we can understand how it's just our mind projecting and believing its own projections.

Perhaps we feel dissatisfied with our partner and think we can't be happy until we get another one. When such dissatisfied, unrealistic expectations arise we should see the uncomfortable, uptight mind for what it is and think, "What's the point in accumulating more negative karma in addition to that which I've already collected from the beginningless past? Why make another deposit into my negative karma savings account and create more suffering for myself?"

With the inner peace that Dharma brings, the subtle wind, which is the vehicle of the mind, no longer gets disturbed and so the four elements of the body—earth, water, fire and air—are in balance. When our elements are in balance we don't suffer from illness and enjoy good health. First we develop a healthy mind, then our body becomes healthy as a side effect.

There once was a lay yogi, Kharak Gomchung, who contracted leprosy. He was sick for a long time and his family got scared and kicked him out, so his mind was terribly upset. With no family and nobody else to look after him, he thought that he should make his being thrown out beneficial, so he made the strong determination to live by the roadside, recite Chenrezig mantras and beg for food, no matter what happened. He came upon a cave in a rock near a village called Gemo Trong, where he slept that first night. There, he had a dream of a man dressed completely in white putting him on the rock while heavy rain fell, making everything wet. When he awoke he found that all the pus had come out of his sores and made the whole area around him wet. Without the need of medicine, he was completely cured of leprosy by the power of his mind alone—living in the Dharma, renouncing suffering, had overcome that serious disease and brought him happiness in this life. Afterwards he become a great yogi.

We always have what we need

When we renounce attachment we're never without what we need. Renouncing attachment to friends, we have friends; renouncing attachment to a comfortable environment, we have a comfortable environment. Without making any effort from our own side, when we need something or somebody, it just naturally happens, due to the power of our practice of Dharma.

Kadampa Geshe Shawopa said,[54]

> We seek happiness in this and throughout all lives, and so, as a sign of this, neither crave for anything in your heart nor hoard anything.
> When you do not crave for gifts, this is the best gift.
> When your do not crave for praise, this is the best praise.
> When you do not crave for fame, this is the best fame.
> When your do not crave for retinues, this is the best retinue.

Not being attached to gain is the greatest gain. When we're attached to material pleasure, it's very hard to get. However, when we have renounced attachment to it, it seems to come naturally without need of much effort. The "greatest gain," however, isn't a lot of material possessions but enlightenment, ultimate happiness.

Not desiring reputation is the best reputation. For instance, although all the great pandits, like Milarepa, Lama Tsongkhapa and Shakyamuni Buddha, had completely renounced the desire for a good reputation, they still to this day have such amazing reputations that all sentient beings who just

[54] From *The Book of Kadam*, pp. 597–98.

hear their names prostrate and make offerings. We worldly people, on the other hand, spend much money and energy trying to get a good reputation. If we want a high position, like president or something, we have to spend millions and millions of dollars. It's very difficult to become successful.

The great Sakya Pandita Kunga Gyaltsen, who achieved the state of Manjushri, the Buddha of Wisdom, said that in order to obtain the happiness of this life we must work for the happiness of future lives by practicing Dharma and along the way the happiness of this life will come naturally. When we check up, this is quite obvious. If the worldly dharmas are the source of all our problems, then, of course, the moment we renounce them we'll achieve happiness. He said,

> If you wish to obtain the happiness of this life, practice the holy Dharma. Look at the difference in the perfections of holy beings and thieves.

We have already heard about the Kadampa lama, Geshe Ben Gungyal.[55] Before he started practicing Dharma he had a field big enough that he could harvest forty sacks of barley a year, giving him a comfortable living. But despite this rich harvest, he was never satisfied and felt he never had enough and was still too poor. So he used to rob by day, holding up people on the road, and thieve by night, sneaking into people's houses to steal their things. He had many weapons—knives, arrows and many other kinds—which he carried in his belt, bristling like thorns. Because of his evil lifestyle and annual harvest of forty sacks, people used to call him "forty sins."

Eventually he gave all that up, completely renouncing the eight worldly dharmas and living in the practice of Dharma. He lived in a hermitage with no material possessions and no fields. Before, when he had everything, it was never enough, but when he lived in the hermitage, renouncing the eight worldly dharmas, he received plenty of food and never wanted for means because of all the offerings people made. He would therefore say, "Before I practiced Dharma my mouth had trouble finding food but now food has trouble finding my mouth." What he meant was that before, his mouth was never satisfied with what it received, but once he had renounced the eight worldly dharmas he had more food than he could ever eat. This is what

---

[55] See also p. 119. This story is quoted in *Liberation in the Palm of Your Hand*, p. 297, as well.

Sakya Pandita means by the difference between holy beings and thieves. The holy being is always satisfied but the thief never has enough.

When Geshe Ben Gungyal was living in Penpo there was some trouble. Bandits and looters were everywhere taking things by force and everybody was busy trying to hide their possessions under the ground or in the mountains. People were running from the robbers, full of fear. Ben Gungyal, on the other hand, had no fear. The robes he wore and a clay water pot were his only possessions, so even when he encountered robbers they didn't bother him because he had nothing to steal. He walked in the streets in a very calm, relaxed way and was surprised that everybody around him was so afraid. He said, "This is the way worldly people hide their possessions; this is the way I hide my possessions." What he meant by "hiding his possessions" was renouncing the thought of the eight worldly dharmas, so there was no danger of people bothering him.

Thieves are never satisfied. Even if they get things by honest work, it's never enough, so they think they have to steal. But no matter how much they steal, it's still never enough. And stealing is negative karma and brings all sorts of other problems as well.

Holy beings are completely the opposite. Every action of their body, speech and mind is done purely to achieve enlightenment for the benefit of mother sentient beings, never for temporal needs. They have no use for temporal pleasures, so, without needing to steal anything, just by the power of pure Dharma practice, they easily receive whatever daily necessities they need.

Geshe Lama Konchog

Geshe Kharak Gomchung, said,

> It has never been heard of in the past, nor will it be heard of in the future, that true meditators die of hunger or cold. But meditators on the evil thought of the eight worldly dharmas will always have such problems. For them, this will always happen.

True meditators, those avoiding the evil thought of the eight worldly dharmas, will only experience peace; false meditators, we worldly beings who live only for the thought of the eight worldly dharmas, will only experience suffering. This is the experience of those great ascetic yogis.

We can see this in the story of Geshe Lama Konchog, who passed away in 2001.[56] His incredible life was the result of his Dharma practice and we can only strive to achieve the same thing.

When he and some friends were escaping from Lhasa, Chinese soldiers were on the roads, planes were flying overhead and the army was watching the borders, so it was very dangerous and difficult to escape. Geshe Lama Konchog did a protector puja on the road, causing clouds to gather and snow to fall, and even though the Chinese army vehicles were there in the road, covered by snow, the monks escaped by passing right next to the vehicles. Nobody bothered them.

After he left Tibet, Geshe Lama Konchog lived for many years in Tsum, high in the mountains in the northern Gorkha district of Nepal. Dupo Rinpoche had established a monastery and nunnery there. Tsum is an unbelievably beautiful, inspiring place near Tibet, exactly like it was a hundred years ago. Nothing has degenerated; everything is still pure. The people, their customs, their houses—everything is exactly as it was in olden times.

Geshe Lama Konchog's cave is near some caves used by the great yogi, Milarepa, and is close to the border. In that place there's nothing else to think about except Dharma. There's no business, nothing. This is not a place for the wandering mind, only for Dharma. It's unbelievable.

The way to the cave is so steep that when I went I had to clamber up using not only my legs but also my hands. The local people, however, are used to it and just walk normally. Geshe Lama Konchog's cave is totally amazing. His story is totally amazing. Exactly like the Buddha, Geshe Lama Konchog lived an ascetic life in this cave for six years. At such an altitude, perched on that steep cliff without tracks, there was nothing to disturb his meditation. He cut his connection with the people in that area in order to cut the eight worldly dharmas.

I heard that Geshe Lama Konchog was like the poorest beggar in the Tsum area. He wore very torn clothes, not enough even to cover his body. People didn't know he was living in the cave and when they saw this bedraggled person with very long hair, they were afraid and threw stones at him. The father of one family threw dirt all over Geshe Lama Konchog as he was walking along the road. Things like that happened because people saw only his external appearance and did not recognize that he was a great practitioner. I think the caretaker of the gompa at Kopan Monastery is the uncle

---

[56] For a more extensive version of this story, see *Teachings from the Medicine Buddha Retreat*, pp. 59–72.

or brother of that man and I heard that every time Geshe Lama Konchog saw him he said, "You're the one who threw dirt on me!" So for that person it's a little inauspicious.

One day nine strong men came to take away him away, so he went up to another cave for some time and then for two years meditated on a huge rocky mountain under a great tree without any shelter at all. His disciple, Geshe Tenzin Zopa, the former resident teacher at our center in Malaysia, said it was a Hayagriva mountain and tried to show me the tree when we were flying over it, but I missed it.

I think he lived without depending on food, using the chu-len technique. For a period of time you take nothing but the "essence," such as water or flower pills. How long you do the practice is up to the individual, but it's usually about seven days. If you have achieved "taking the essence," you can live on the pills after blessing them through the deity method. This allows you to be totally undistracted by things like looking for food and preparing and eating it, things that make you busy. It not only saves you a lot of time but it also brings far fewer physical hardships. You are less tired and have less chance of getting sick. You're free of the heavy, foggy mind and it's very easy to meditate; everything is very calm and clear, like calm, clear water. Your body becomes extremely light and when you walk, it feels like you're flying. There are many benefits. You never get wrinkles and gray hair turns black. Taking the essence has incredible benefits but you need very strong renunciation for your practice to succeed.

Practicing there for six years, he totally renounced the eight worldly dharmas. There's no doubt that when you sacrifice yourself that much to practice Dharma with that much renunciation, you'll definitely achieve realizations of lam-rim and tantra. The surprising thing is that even though Geshe Lama Konchog lived at Kopan for many years and told Lama Lhundrup and me many stories, we never heard any about how hard he practiced. But there in Tsum we found out what had happened and were really amazed. So, of course, Geshe Lama Konchog had to have had realizations.

After that, Geshe Lama Konchog did many years of practice in a few different caves and during that time did two thousand nyung-näs.

Every time his food ran out Geshe-la had to go to a nearby village to get more. Since this took a lot of time, one day he decided that he would never go to the village again, that when his tsampa had finished, that was it. The day he made that decision he had a dream of his root guru, His Holiness Trijang Rinpoche, who is also my root guru. His Holiness made *pak,* ate some very blissfully and gave the rest to Geshe-la. The next day, a man brought Geshe-la a huge load of tsampa and from that time on he never had to go out to get food. Geshe-la said that whenever his food was about to finish, somebody would always bring him more. That is the power of renouncing the eight worldly dharmas, of deciding not to go out for food.

Geshe Lama Konchog was somebody who practiced sutra and tantra and really sacrificed his life for others. When he was in his hermitage, as a puja for the long life of His Holiness Trijang Rinpoche, he read the whole *Kangyur*, more than a hundred volumes, by himself.

He came to Kopan a few times while Lama Yeshe was there. Once when he and I were alone in Lama's room he told me that he had completed Vajrayogini and *Guru Puja*. I heard him say that at least twice but I was a little confused about what he meant. One meaning is that you have finished reciting a certain number of mantras; the other is that you have completely realized the particular tantric practice you're talking about and are therefore enlightened. At the time I thought he was talking about the number of mantras but now I realize it was the other meaning.

From the stories about the benefit he could bring people, about the powerful effect he had on them, it's obvious that he had realized emptiness and bodhicitta. For example, living high in the mountains in Tsum, many people went crazy. When they got blessing strings, which have a special knot, from other, more famous lamas there, they rarely got better, but when they finally went to Geshe Lama Konchog, who gave them just a simple thread, nothing elaborate, nothing elegant, they recovered. This happened many times due to the power of his practice.

The many stories such as that show that he was great yogi with high tantric realizations, but just by looking at him you wouldn't have thought it. He really was a hidden yogi. There do exist beings like that who are enlightened but are still in an ordinary body.

Geshe Lama Konchog was also of incredible benefit to Kopan Monastery. He gave the nuns teachings on the preliminary practices and Vajrayogini commentaries. He bore many hardships for Kopan, helping with the fundraising for the buildings and teaching as well. He also taught and guided non-Tibetan students, not only at Kopan but also in Australia, Singapore, Hong Kong and Taiwan, giving initiations and teachings and doing pujas. He gave his life to me, to the FPMT centers and students and to sentient beings. Even though he had physical problems, he was very heroic in his work for others, whether doing pujas or giving teachings.

One time at Kopan it had been raining and the steps to the old gompa were slippery. There was one square step in front of the Tara statue that was under the bodhi tree. Geshe Lama Konchog slipped and fell very heavily down the steps banging his head on the cement. He felt very happy that it had happened. Why did he feel so happy? Because he immediately thought that he had experienced my life obstacles on himself. That's what he told me and that's what made him so happy. Even when things like that happened, that's the kind of attitude Geshe Lama Konchog normally had.

I'm not exactly sure when Geshe-la took the aspect of cancer, but it might have been a long time before he died. Even though hot weather didn't suit him much, since I had asked Geshe-la to go to Taiwan, Hong Kong and various other hot places to teach for a long time, he still went.

It seems that when he was dying Geshe Lama Konchog was able to recognize the twenty-five absorptions,[57] which we're supposed to meditate on when we do *sadhanas* in Highest Yoga Tantra practice. A few days before he passed away, Geshe-la told one of the Kopan geshes that the vision of the mirage and the smoke-like vision were happening. That means he was able to recognize the clear light and all those other things and on the basis of that able to apply the meditations of the Highest Yoga Tantra path.

Geshe-la remained in meditation for about a week.[58] Since he had already done the work by himself during his life, he didn't need to do *powa*, transference of consciousness, or anything like that. Powa is only for ordinary people.

I sent guidance about what to do with the body because we had done all that with Lama Yeshe. We didn't offer fire in an ordinary place where other people's bodies are burned but behind the hill at Kopan Monastery. Lama Lhundrup told me that when the holy body was offered to the fire, relics jumped out. It is said in the texts that relics come from the holy body of those who have the completion stage realization of clear light.

Geshe Lama Konchog's incarnation was found in Tsum and is now growing up in Kopan.[59] From his face, he seems to have a lot of merit and to be

[57] The signs that come to a dying person. A great meditator can stay in meditation through each absorption and be aware of what is happening. See *Death, Intermediate State and Rebirth in Tibetan Buddhism*.

[58] Great meditators will remain in meditation on the clear light, sitting upright for days or even weeks after their breathing has stopped, until they feel it is time for their mind to leave the body.

[59] For the story of finding Geshe Lama Konchog's reincarnation, see the documentary *The Unmistaken Child* (on DVD from Oscilloscope Productions, 2009).

somebody who is going to be very powerful, who will decide everything for himself. Even now, even though he is small, he wants to decide things for himself. I think he will be very dynamic. He is very special. When people ask him questions, he gives advice. In Singapore he gave advice to somebody who was sick, even telling them what time to do the practice. Because of the unbelievable merit collected in his past life, I think there is a great hope that this incarnation will really benefit the world, like the sun shining.

Geshe Lama Konchog did not reincarnate for his own benefit, for his own happiness, but to be of benefit to the world and his students, so that he could again guide his students.

Morality and vows

Thogme Zangpo said,

> Even though a person keeps moral conduct with effort, if he is bound by the rope of attachment to material possessions, he won't achieve the path of liberation. The rope that binds him to this samsaric prison is definitely in the hand of the evil thought.

We might try to lead a moral life and even take vows to refrain from negative actions, but if we're doing it "with effort" and our mind still naturally moves toward nonvirtue, if we're "tied by the rope of the eight worldly dharmas," such as attachment to comfort or reputation, it's extremely difficult not to slip back into nonvirtue.

For this reason, in order to follow the path to liberation, Guru Shakyamuni Buddha renounced the worldly life. His family was extremely rich—they had many incredible possessions, ruled a vast population and were renowned throughout India. As the future king he had the chance to live a life with every possible object of pleasure, to be with as many princesses as he desired, just like his father. However, he gave everything up—reputation, comfort, incredible luxury—throwing it away like rubbish, not because he was suffering from not having enough, but to be free from hindrances to the path of liberation in order to achieve nirvana. His renunciation was extremely strong, triggered by the danger that he would be tied by the rope of the eight worldly dharmas.

Following his example, at the beginning of their practice, while they're still in training, great yogis and meditators lead very simple lives. Before they have fully renounced the thought of the eight worldly dharmas, they find being surrounded by desirable objects to be a hindrance because of their uncontrolled mind. So living ascetic lives in solitary places means meditators face less distractions and can make quicker progress on the path.

After they have reached the level where their minds remain undisturbed no matter what objects they encounter, where nothing can become a hindrance to achieving enlightenment, then it doesn't matter how many worldly objects surround them. Even though they live in a king's palace with all his possessions, for them it's like they're in a cave. It wouldn't be like that for us. Unable to avoid the thought of the eight worldly dharmas, our mind would be boiling with pride and greed. We'd have no peace at all.

Thus the Buddha taught that the beginner's mind should be well content with very few possessions. As most work in the lay community is on behalf of the eight worldly dharmas, after ordination, monks and nuns are usually advised to live away from it, in a separate place such as a monastery. Traditionally set away from a city, such an environment is important before their minds get strong enough to cope. It's a place where they can more easily observe morality and avoid falling under the control of attachment to the comfort of this life. This is the meaning of "monastery" as the Buddha explained it in the sutra teachings.[60]

The purpose of taking vows such as the *pratimoksha* (individual liberation), bodhisattva and tantric vows[61] is to control greed and attachment. If we want to keep our vows purely, we need to work on our attachment to things, avoid the thought of the eight worldly dharmas and develop a good understanding of samsaric suffering. The vows of the person who doesn't try to avoid the thought of the eight worldly dharmas are like old torn clothes full of holes.

In the early stages of our development we still have attachment, so we try to keep moral conduct "with effort," as Thogme Zangpo said. Yet despite our good intentions, we can still find it hard to break our old habits and enter the path to liberation. It all depends on avoiding attachment. That is the root. Generally, when we have no strong mind renouncing this life and

[60] The Tibetan word for monastery is *dgon-pa* and has the connotation of a remote solitary place at least two miles (one *gyang-trag*, "range of hearing") away from any town or village; wilderness, hermitage, retreat.

[61] These are generally seen as the three levels of vows both lay and ordained people can take. The pratimoksha, or individual liberation, vows are restraints on physical and verbal actions; the bodhisattva vows are restraints on incorrect thought, especially self-cherishing; and the tantric vows are restraints on impure view. Although some commentators say the latter two can be taken without the pratimoksha vows, most, including Lama Tsongkhapa, state quite strongly they are a prerequisite.

little understanding of the nature of suffering, attachment arises easily, making it difficult for us to keep our vows.

Some students become monks or nuns when they go to the East but lose their ordination soon after returning home. This is very understandable. The powerful desire to meditate they had in the East gets lost at home because of the influence of the environment, which makes the thought of the eight worldly dharmas stronger in their minds.

Each set of vows moves our mind further along the path. The individual liberation vows are designed to guard us from wrong conduct. The bodhisattva vows help us avoid self-cherishing and transcend the mind that views things as "mine"—since we've dedicated everything we own to others, we cannot possess anything with self-cherishing.

The most subtle practice of all is tantra, in which we observe the tantric vows. Although a much more profound technique and a shortcut to enlightenment, it's also the most difficult to do. "Shortcut" doesn't mean easy. We can't hold the pure view that tantra requires unless we've transcended the sense of "me" and "mine," so tantric practice is founded on the bodhisattva vows, where the self-cherishing thought is overcome. This in turn grows from the basis of renouncing this life, the thought of the eight worldly dharmas. As long as our mind harbors the desire for the comfort of this life, it's extremely difficult for us to keep the more profound and subtle vows purely.

THE POWER OF RENOUNCING THE EIGHT WORLDLY DHARMAS

The wisdom of renouncing the eight worldly dharmas is inestimable; its power is such that we can never finish explaining its value. The more we recognize the Dharma, the more we recognize the infinite, transcendent knowledge of the buddhas. At the same time we discover for ourselves how powerful and precious this practice is. It is more precious than any jewel and there is no danger of its ever being lost or stolen. The more jewels we have, the greater the worry in our mind, the more we think about them—how to use them, protect them and so forth. But the more purely we practice renouncing the thought of the eight worldly dharmas, the more quickly wisdom arises and the sooner we escape from ignorance and the problems associated with worldly concern.

At the time of death, a person living in renunciation of temporal needs definitely avoids rebirth in the three lower realms, unlike somebody who still has attachment, even if that person has great psychic powers. In ancient times there was a Tibetan tantric practitioner who could kill a hundred people with merely a look. However, he had not developed renunciation and was reborn in the hell realms when he died. Anything that does not cut off attachment only keeps us in suffering and cannot guide us to liberation.

There are three powers in dependence upon which we can do miraculous things—the powers of medicine, mantra and the elements—but the practice of renunciation is the safest and strongest power there is for protecting the mind. Many, many past meditators protected themselves by this practice. And as we have seen with the example of Kharak Gomchung, it can even cure leprosy. Although his goal wasn't to be cured of leprosy, he was cured as a result of his strong determination to always avoid the thought of the eight worldly dharmas.

Renunciation of the eight worldly dharmas is more powerful than an atomic bomb. It might be possible to build a bomb powerful enough to destroy the whole planet and kill everybody on it, but it could not destroy their minds. People die anyway, this entire world system will end one day, but the mind continues, and with it the thought of the eight worldly dharmas. Even without this body and this world, our mind would find another body in another realm and we would meet other enemies. As long as we travel through the six realms behaving like a friend to the inner enemy, there'll be no end to the outer enemies we'll have to face.

The atomic bomb of renunciation, however, destroys the fundamental delusion that keeps us circling in samara, without depending on technology, chemicals or madness. Renouncing the eight worldly dharmas is the energy that allows us to enter the path and eventually carries us to enlightenment. It is the fuel for the rocket we need to give us a quick escape from ignorance and the deluded mind, a direct method of cutting the continuity of bad karma and bringing perfect happiness.

The power of an atomic bomb is tiny and its effect is only negative, whereas the benefits of renunciation are infinite. Shapeless and invisible, this mind has more power than the whole universe and can propel numberless sentient beings to enlightenment.

EQUALIZING THE EIGHT WORLDLY DHARMAS

As we cut attachment to the four desirable objects, our mind becomes clearer and we stop worrying about meeting the four undesirable objects.

Whatever happens due to changing circumstances, whether we meet the four desirable objects or the four undesirable ones, our mind remains calm, undisturbed, without any great ups and downs.

As a Dharma practitioner we should strive as much as we can to equalize the eight worldly dharmas, totally reversing our attitude toward these eight objects of attachment and aversion. Instead of liking the four desirable objects, we should train to dislike them, and instead of disliking the four undesirable objects, we should train to like them. Then we can start to achieve some sort of equilibrium, where nothing makes any difference to our mind. Comfort and discomfort will be experienced in the same way, as will a good and bad reputation, praise and criticism and so forth.

When we experience an object of desire, we don't allow our mind to become attached, stopping that sudden high of pleasure that it can bring. When we experience suffering or hardship, we don't allow our mind to become upset or depressed. Thus, we train to feel equal about whatever object we experience, pleasure or suffering, and in that way neither can disturb our mind.

When there is a pleasant sound such as music, we train to not be attached to it; when there is an unpleasant sound, we train not to have aversion to it. Either way there is no confusion, no disturbance to our mind, no going up and down depending on the object.

In the same way, we train our mind not to be attached when we receive a material object, such as a gift, and to let go and not feel unhappy when we don't. Neither circumstance bothers us at all; we live in equilibrium. Nor are we attached to praise or averse to criticism, knowing both are nothing more than sound hitting our ears. In that way, no matter which of the eight objects we experience, there is no confusion, no trouble. The renounced mind sees all the objects of its experience as equal, and nothing we encounter can cause negative emotional thoughts to arise.

With such a degree of equanimity, we have a very stable mind and a stable life. Our heart is filled with peace, satisfaction and happiness. Even if the only drink we ever have is water, we're totally satisfied. Even if all we ever eat is rice and *dal*,[62] we're totally satisfied.

Rice and dal is the staple Indian food of the poor, but Milarepa, as you probably know, ate only nettles. There was no salt, no chili, no oil—only

---

[62] Dal is a preparation of pulses (dried lentils, peas or beans) stripped of their outer husks and split and cooked into a stew or soup.

nettles. One day a thief came to Milarepa's cave and Milarepa cooked him nettle soup. When the thief asked for some salt and chili to spice the soup, Milarepa put a few more nettles in the pot and said, "This is the salt," and then a few more and said, "This is the chili." So there was nothing else, just nettles, yet Milarepa was totally satisfied. His heart was filled with great peace and happiness because his mind had let go of attachments and the emotional, dissatisfied mind.

The great saint Lingrepa said,

> In the samsaric superstition city
> Runs the zombie of the evil thought of the eight worldly dharmas.
> That is the most fearful cemetery;
> That is where the lama should equalize the points.[63]

This instruction has great meaning and shows us clearly how to practice Dharma. When he talks of charnel grounds and zombies, he doesn't mean external cemeteries or external zombies. (I learned the word "zombie" in the 1960s!) We worldly people fear that kind of cemetery but we're never frightened by the cemetery that is truly terrifying, the evil thought of the eight worldly dharmas. This inner cemetery is what we learn to fear when we practice Dharma and this fear gives us the determination to practice more strongly and gain realizations more quickly. If there were no internal cemetery, there'd be no external cemeteries.

Equalizing the points means equalizing the eight worldly dharmas. When the four pairs of opposites are equalized, nothing can disturb us and the sun of the happiness of Dharma can rise in our life. Equalizing the eight worldly dharmas is the fundamental Dharma practice; from that, all the others grow.

Therefore, equalizing the eight worldly dharmas was the fundamental practice of the great yogis such as Milarepa, Gampopa, Lama Tsongkhapa, Naropa, Tilopa and many others. They could use whatever they experienced—pleasure or suffering, gain or loss, good or bad reputation, praise or blame—to make their minds completely equal with the object.

Nothing shook their minds one tiny bit. In the most isolated mountains

---

[63] This is Rinpoche's translation. It is translated in *Liberation in Our Hands, Part Two*, p. 106, as: The zombie of the eight worldly dharmas wanders in samsara's city of thoughts. There's your terrifying cemetery. Guru, practice equanimity there. See also *Liberation in the Palm of Your Hand*, p. 297.

or the busiest city, they were always at peace. The definition of a yogi is, in fact, exactly this: a person who has equalized his or her mind, feeling neither attachment nor aversion to whatever is experienced. If the objects of the eight worldly dharmas had not been equal in their mind there's no way they could have been called yogis.

Dromtönpa, who also had abandoned all worldly activities, was once invited to a place called Rong to give money offerings to the monks during puja. Rong is a bit like Solu Khumbu, high in the mountains and a bit hot. They grow bananas and corn there. He called one of his disciples, Pelgye Wangchuk, and said to him, "You go this time. I can't. I'm here trying to give up this life."

Dromtönpa was not a monk but took the aspect of a lay person living in the five precepts for the benefit of sentient beings. In visualizations of the lam-rim lineage lamas he is visualized as a Tibetan nomad wearing a very warm blue *chuba* lined with an animal skin. He always wore very old, torn clothes. Sometimes he would throw the sleeves of his chuba over his shoulders and go off into the juniper forest and make a small shelter to meditate in by putting two or three poles together and covering them with animal hide, as Tibetan nomads do. Other Kadampa geshes have explained that Dromtönpa didn't need to lead an ascetic life for his own sake but did it solely for the sake of his disciples.

While walking through the forest he sometimes recited the verse from Nagarjuna's *Letter to a Friend*:

> Gain, loss, happiness, unhappiness, fame, notoriety, praise and blame: these eight worldly dharmas are not objects of my mind; they're all the same to me.[64]

He would also recite from *A Guide to a Bodhisattva's Way of Life*:

> I who am striving for freedom
> Do not need to be bound by material gain and honor.
> So why should I be angry
> With those who free me from this bondage?[65]

---

[64] *Letter to a Friend*, v. 29. Also quoted in *The Door to Satisfaction*, p. 36. There is a similar quote in *Liberation in the Palm of Your Hand*, p. 296.
[65] Ch. 6, v. 100.

While he was reciting it he would shake his head from side to side, indicating that he didn't need to be bound by receiving material things and respect. Similarly, Geshe Chengawa equalized the eight worldly dharmas by reciting this verse:

> Being happy when life is comfortable and unhappy when it is
>   uncomfortable:
> All activities for the happiness of this life should be abandoned as
>   poison.
> Virtue and nonvirtue are functions only of the mind.
> Cut off nonvirtuous motivations and those motivations that are nei-
>   ther virtuous nor nonvirtuous.

The latter refers to actions with indeterminate or variable motivation; these are termed "unpredictable" actions.

Just saying the words or having the wish for a stable life has no effect on destroying our attachment to worldly pleasures. We need to use whatever techniques work for us to actualize this. If we understand and use these techniques, the eight worldly dharmas can actually help us rather than become the cause of suffering; they can bring energy to our Dharma practice rather than rob us of it.

It might seem to you that I have placed too much emphasis on the suffering that the thought of the eight worldly dharmas brings us and not enough on its antidote, but the whole of the Dharma is its antidote. Every Dharma activity we do acts as an antidote to the thought of the eight worldly dharmas. All meditations on the graduated path to enlightenment help us diminish and destroy our attachment and thus help us destroy all our delusions.

Seeing problems as positive

There are many different ways of using the objects of the eight worldly dharmas, depending on the practitioner. Tantric practitioners use them in tantric practice, those following the bodhisattva path use them to generate bodhicitta and those trying to achieve the cessation of samsara use them to destroy their delusions.

For worldly people the confusion caused by suffering only brings more suffering and confusion, but as Dharma practitioners we have the opportunity of making suffering extremely beneficial by using it to cut confusion rather than to create it. In order to achieve enlightenment we have to experience both physical and mental difficulties, but bearing such difficulties is incredibly worthwhile because by doing so we reach a state where all suffering ceases forever. As we progress along the path to enlightenment, problems become fewer and fewer and therefore whatever we experience at this time only helps to bring about the end of the suffering that has no beginning.

We can learn to see a person who criticizes or harms us as incredibly precious and valuable.[66] Because that person truly helps us destroy our worldly concerns and self-cherishing thought, he is worth more than mountains of gold and diamonds. Worlds filled with gold and diamonds can't bring us real peace; only destroying the self-cherishing attitude can, which is exactly what somebody who harms us allows us to do. In that way, he is like a guru and we should treat him as more precious than our own life.

One of my teachers, the first teacher to teach me the debating subjects in India, was Geshe Rabten Rinpoche, who later lived in Switzerland and started a monastery there. If any person or lama ever criticized him he would invite that person over to his house and give him a special lunch of *momos* and take special care of him to thank him for his help.

One day when Gen Jampa Wangdu returned to his place he discovered that a robber had stolen a clock that somebody had offered him. He was immediately very happy that the robber now had a new clock. That sentient being had wanted something, had been able to get it and had therefore experienced a certain degree of happiness. This is what made Gen-la happy. Due to his realization of bodhicitta, he felt completely equal with others; to him, others' happiness was the same as his own.

Another example of training the mind to cut the thought of the eight worldly dharmas is the great Italian saint, St Francis of Assisi. Preferring criticism to praise, he asked his disciples to criticize him, something his disciples would never think of doing. He especially asked them to keep telling him he had done so many evil things that he would go to hell and so forth. His disciples, however, could see only the good in him and nothing at all to criticize. In that way, great meditators train themselves to like misfortune and, by transforming their minds, come to know great happiness.

When we are trying to control our mind we can start to recognize that

---

[66] This subject, seeing those who criticize us as precious, is covered in *The Door to Satisfaction*, pp. 112–15. It is also extensively covered in Rinpoche's *lo-jong* (mind training) discourses, including the book *Transforming Problems*.

bad conditions are times when we can really transform our mind. There are many ways of thinking about a problem. We can see criticism, for instance, as the result of some previous negative karma that we have created. Then we can feel that there is nothing to be upset about because actually the result of that negative karma is finishing and we won't have to experience it in the future. Thinking like this changes our mind. We worry less and are happy to be finishing that particular negative karma.

We can also train ourselves to feel that the problem is the result of negative karma that we have created in the past by harming another being and therefore determine that in future we are going to be careful not to let that happen again, to not submit to this evil thought, our one enemy, and to try to subdue it as much as possible.

The actual problem is not the situation itself; it's our clinging to the four desirable objects. We have to realize the shortcomings of these four desirable objects and abandon clinging to them. This is the basic psychology. If we use this method, undesirable situations will no longer disturb us.

When somebody praises us or when we hear that we have a good reputation, we can reflect on its shortcomings. A wise meditator knows that there's nothing beneficial in having a good reputation because we become attached to it and pride follows. We start to believe that we're really important and famous and many other delusions arise because of that.

On the other hand, there's nothing bad about criticism. It's very good to be criticized because it stops delusions such as attachment or pride from arising. Criticism points out faults that we're currently unaware of, allowing us to confront and correct them. Meditators usually say that they're not happy when they're being praised and much prefer to be criticized.

In the same way, rather than upsetting us, not receiving a birthday present from a friend can cause us to confront and avert our attachment. We can think how fantastic it is that that person didn't give us anything. If she had, attachment would arise, we'd become more conditioned to receiving presents, more under the control of the thought of the eight worldly dharmas, more unable to not create negative karma and more likely to eventually be reborn in the suffering lower realms. By not bringing us a present our friend saved us from all that. She really, truly is our dearest and best Dharma helper.

Reflecting like this—seeing that meeting unfavorable conditions is not, in fact, a problem—is the complete opposite of how attachment sees the situation. Before, under the control of attachment, we were incredibly angry with the person who "harmed" us but now, thinking the complete opposite, that uncomfortable mind—that schizophrenic, nervous, unhappy mind—instantly disappears and we have a good feeling for that person.

The best way to train our mind in equalizing the eight worldly dharmas is to expect to be criticized, expect to be disrespected, rather than the opposite. That's the psychology. Then, no matter what actually happens, we're ready and there's no shock. It cannot harm our mind.

The happiness we seem to get from the four desirable objects is false. It disturbs our mind and interferes with our search for true happiness. Understanding this becomes a great protection, and seeing how meeting unfavorable conditions is a time when we can truly grow, we can develop a mind that actually likes problems. By overcoming our dislike for the four undesirable objects we can complete all the realizations, cease all the obscurations and eventually attain enlightenment.

In this way, no matter what happens, we're able to maintain a continual Dharma practice. Nothing can interfere with it. Even if we're just starting our practice and don't yet accept reincarnation, by controlling attachment our mind can always remain undisturbed. Perhaps we don't even consider ourselves to be a Buddhist, but if we use this practice when conditions change—when we lose friends, find friends, whatever—our mind will remain peaceful, in balance, undisturbed. Just as a rider's peaceful nature calms her horse, so the elements of our body will also be undisturbed and we will enjoy much better health, with little risk of high blood pressure or a heart attack.

As the great bodhisattva Shantideva said, we can use any problems we have in life to generate compassion for others. People who have AIDS or cancer feel very strongly for others who have the same disease. Because they're experiencing the same problem themselves, they're able to recognize how unbearable it is for others and therefore strong compassion naturally arises. In that way, the suffering we feel is very useful.

Just as a broom sweeps away dirt, illness and other problems are the broom that sweeps away past negative karmas and obscurations. If we have a guru from whom we've received teachings, we should think that the problems we experience are his blessing to purify our negative karma.

Attachment is created by the mind and does not truly exist

We can also think that any problems we experience are a manifestation of emptiness.

Our body and mind are causative, impermanent phenomena, yet we instinctively see them as independent and permanent. Because of that we mistake transient samsaric pleasures as real happiness and the impure body as pure, causing attachment to arise. Our wrong conception that the eight worldly dharmas bring happiness is rooted in our sense that we and they truly exist, that everything is real and exists from its own side.

Our own mind creates life's problems. Our mind creates them, labels them and then believes they are real. We can see this very clearly when we thoroughly investigate it. Both attachment to the four desirable objects and worry and fear about meeting the four undesirable objects are superstitions created by our mind.

If practicing Dharma seems difficult to us, if we seem to have no time to practice, it is precisely because the obstacles we face seem to be real and permanent. But neither the obstacles nor the eight worldly dharmas truly exist. If they did there would be no way we could transform them. In fact, *nobody* would ever have been able to transform the mind of attachment into the mind of Dharma and nobody would ever have renounced this life. Nobody would have time to practice Dharma. But lack of time is not an intrinsic product of time itself; it is a concept of our own mind.

If we could realize the nature of the I—that it does not truly exist—then there would be no way for attachment to the four desirable objects to arise, nor would there be any way for aversion to the four undesirable objects to arise. Seeing how things actually exist, comfort and discomfort and the other worldly pairs can be seen for what they are and our mind can remain untroubled, no matter what it experiences.

Understanding emptiness is the best way of taking care of ourselves because it cuts the root of suffering. And there is no question that it leads to bodhicitta and enlightenment. What better practice is there than this? What else do we need?

MEDITATIONS

Meditation on letting go of clinging to the body

The thought of the eight worldly dharmas arises particularly strongly when we're in a relationship with another person. At that time our mind is extremely confused, totally under the control of the eight worldly dharmas. There is too much clinging to the body and, because of that, many problems arise.

A good way of controlling such attachment is to meditate on the body of the person to whom you're attached. This is called "mindfulness of the body" and comes from the sutra teachings. If the person is in front of you, the meditation is very easy to do; you don't have to visualize. However, even if the person is in another country, you can examine his or her body.

At the beginning, visualize that person's body and consider whether it's as beautiful or handsome as your mind makes it seem or whether your mind has in some way exaggerated its qualities. If you're honest, you will see that your attachment has exaggerated the beauty of that body. Secondly, you believe in absolute beauty. After your mind has imputed this exaggerated beauty onto the body, it believes that that beauty is real and absolute. This is how it appears to your mind. Then your mind creates more and more reasons, more and more commentaries on why this body is absolutely beautiful—because of the hair, because of the nose and so forth—and you completely believe it. You really think that that beauty is intrinsically there.

There is a body there but does it really exist as it appears to you? It exists like *this* but to you it appears like *that*. Then you believe in that unreal appearance and attachment develops. Your mind becomes very confused, very unpeaceful. Check up. Actually, in reality, is there a real, absolute— and beautiful or handsome—body as you see it?

Break the body down. Check inside beneath the skin: the skeleton and so forth. From the head down to the feet, check inside. Now you are seeing the reality, the essence that is inside, the skeleton. The head is a skull of bone with big holes for the eyes and a long one for the mouth. The neck is bones piled up, one on top of the other. There are very tiny bones and big ones, there are the backbone and the ribs, the long bones wrapped around the front. Then the thighs and the legs and the feet. Lots of holes, lots of different sized bones. Visualize and meditate on the whole skeleton as clearly as you can. You cannot find the absolute existence of the beautiful body. Not inside one single bone can you find it.

Then, after the skeleton, visualize the organs. Start with the brain. It's a little bit like a football, with lots of squiggles on it like a map. Is the brain the real, intrinsic, beautiful body? Then work through the other organs, the heart, the lungs, the kidney, the liver and so forth, right down to the feet. Is there a real, intrinsic beautiful body there? You cannot find it. There's nothing to cling to.

You might argue that there *is* something there from the body's side, some real beauty. There is definitely something there. But check up. There is no real beauty, not in the skeleton, not in the flesh or the organs, not in the blood.

Maybe it's the skin. The only thing left is the skin. That's what you see when you look at the body, so maybe the real beauty is from the side of the skin. Therefore, take off the skin, peel it off the rest of the body and put it some other place. Separated from the rest of the body, what does it look like? Is *that* the real beauty that you so strongly believe in? Check. All that skin is kind of like a skirt left there in a pile on the ground. On the skin there is no object to cling to. So now, that absolute beauty is completely lost. The real, absolute beautiful object, where it is? It's nowhere.

Before, when it was all collected together—bones, flesh, organs and everything all wrapped in skin—there seemed to be some beauty there but when you take it apart you can't find that beauty anywhere.

So then even the beautiful-looking skin is just a formation of atoms. Spread those atoms all over the place, like sand grains. Visualize that they're scattered everywhere. Then where is that real, absolute, existent beauty? Check. You cannot find it. It's just skin—a collection of atoms that have come together. Put them together in another way and they will make other shapes—vases, pots, bricks and so forth—but here they make skin. That's all.

Concentrate on that. When your mind is confused and you're about to go crazy because your attachment isn't getting what it wants, this meditation really is the best medicine. Right away, as you meditate on this, your incredibly painful attachment goes away. Your mind becomes peaceful and relaxed. This is such an effective meditation.

Meditating on the lack of true existence of the object

A more advanced technique to attack the thought of the eight worldly dharmas is to check the nature of the object of desire to see that it is not self-existent, not intrinsically attractive. If you can see the emptiness of the self-existence of the object, there is no way for attachment to arise, because while you have that understanding of emptiness your view has changed. You see the object as it actually exists, not as your attachment believes it to exist. You see that the beauty was only a projection of attachment and does not exist anywhere. To check like this, you need the skill to analyze in this way, to be able to distinguish between what doesn't exist—the wrong conception of a self-existent object and a self-existent beauty—and what does exist—the object that is completely devoid of self-existence. In short, you need a degree of wisdom that understands emptiness to use this method.

Say you are attached to music. You can meditate on the beauty of the music you like in the same way. As you're listening to the beautiful music, ask yourself if it really exists as you think it exists. If not, how does it exist? Checking like this is also useful to diminish and eliminate attachment and to realize the true nature of the sound. For instance, if a person is playing a guitar, does the sound exist on the guitar—on its body or neck, on one of the strings, on all of the strings—or on the person playing? Does it exist on the person's hands or fingers? Such analysis is very useful.

Another method you can use when there is the danger of attachment arising is to think like this. The beautiful music or pleasing words are like an echo bouncing back from a cliff. If somebody makes a noise in front of a cliff, because of the sound waves and the shape of the cliff, that sound comes back as an echo. It happens due to all these conditions coming together. Actually, there is no echo that exists by itself, that exists independently, without depending on the rock, the person making the noise and the elements, the wind, the air. An echo that exists separately without relating to any of these conditions is meaningless. Because it is meaningless, there is nothing to be attached to. And so it is the same thing with pleasing sounds such as music or praise; the sounds are like the echo.

And if you hear words that make you feel that you are wonderful, like praise, check where that wonderfulness comes from. For instance, the other person tells you, "You're very wise and intelligent." You believe the words he says actually exist and you believe your feelings about them actually exist. But investigate. Check *where* they exist. They don't exist on you, on him, anywhere. This wrong belief brings confusion to your mind. Think how the words to which you're so attached are simply a creation of the tongue, the palate, the movement of air—nothing more. "You're very wise" is merely sound, so what is the point of being attached to it? Isn't that funny? There's nothing other than the movement of air hitting your eardrums but you get so attached to it.

9. Practicing Pure Dharma

THE TEN INNERMOST JEWELS[67]

BECAUSE WE DON'T understand that renouncing this life and practicing Dharma are synonyms, we fail to see how there's a gap between what we think of as our Dharma practice and the life we lead. No matter how advanced our practice—even if we practice *dzogchen* or the completion stage of Highest Yoga Tantra—normally, our mind is *here* while the Dharma is *there*. We try to follow the Mahayana teachings but we don't become Mahayanists or gain much benefit from what we do. Everything remains the cause for us to stay in samsara, not the cause for us to be one with the Dharma. Without renouncing the eight worldly dharmas, it's unlikely we can even close the door to rebirth in the lower realms. Therefore we must definitely equalize the eight worldly dharmas in order to practice the holy Dharma.

There's a practice called "the ten innermost jewels," also called the ten innermost "possessions," or "treasures." This teaching is the Kadampa geshes' advice on how to renounce the thought of the eight worldly dharmas. If we follow it, we will be able to practice Dharma purely and will experience real peace of mind.

The great ascetic meditators who practice pure Dharma equalize the eight worldly dharmas in this way, differentiating between neither the four desirable nor the four undesirable objects. Their attitude is so different from ours that it is very useful to understand just how they're able to bring total stability and tranquility into their lives, even though we might be a very long way from being able to follow in their footsteps. Even an understanding of what

---

[67] See the appendix of this book for Lama Zopa Rinpoche's practice on these.

the ten innermost jewels are can make a big difference to how we perceive what we encounter in life.

I am going to briefly describe the ten innermost jewels as taught by the great lama Pabongka Dechen Nyingpo, who said that this is the very best practice for renouncing the evil thought of the eight worldly dharmas.[68]

The ten innermost jewels comprise the four entrustments, the three vajras and achieving the three ranks:

1. Entrust the depths of the attitude to the Dharma
2. Entrust the depths of the Dharma to the beggar
3. Entrust the depths of the beggar to death
4. Entrust the depths of death to the cave
5. The uncaptured vajra
6. The shameless vajra
7. The transcendent wisdom vajra
8. Expulsion from the rank of human beings
9. Achieving the rank of the dog
10. Achieving the rank of the divine beings

1. Entrust the depths of the attitude to the Dharma

Relying on the first of the four entrustments, or reliances, is to entrust the depths of our attitude to the Dharma. This means we rely on the Dharma, not just superficially but in our innermost mind. It is like when we go to Nepal and see all those amazing places but our real motivation is to meet up with our girlfriend or boyfriend. Even though we do a lot of other things, that is our main aim, our main consideration; that is what is innermost in our mind. That is why we came to Nepal. In the same way, no matter what we do, in our innermost mind, our main consideration should be relying on Dharma.

At this time, we have this perfect human rebirth, with its eight freedoms and ten richnesses, we have met the guru who has shown us the Dharma and who leads us on the path to enlightenment. This perfect human rebirth is highly meaningful, difficult to find again and does not last. Death is defi-

---

[68] There is also an explanation of the ten innermost jewels in the *Tibetan Tradition of Mental Development*, pp. 42–45; in *Liberation in our Hands, Part 2*, p. 106, n. 29, and p. 108, where they are called the "ten jewels of ultimate commitment"; in *The Principal Teachings of Buddhism*, pp. 66–69; and in *The Life of Shabkar*, pp. 309–10, where they are called the "ten cardinal treasures of the past saints."

nitely going to happen and the actual time of death is uncertain. And at the time of death, nothing worldly can benefit us even one tiny bit—our own body, our material possessions, the people around us, our reputation. The only thing that can benefit us is our Dharma; there is nothing else. And not only at death time, but beyond. Therefore, the practice we do in this life is extremely important.

We should think like this: "Only Dharma benefits me at the time of death, nothing else. Therefore, I must practice Dharma. I must make a complete determination, like this. This is the only thing that never gives me any harm, never causes even the slightest suffering. This is what brings me benefit and happiness in this and all future lives. This is the only thing that benefits at death, that most critical time; everything else is without essence. Therefore, I must practice; I must practice Dharma." Make a strong determination like this. Our main aim, our main plan, our main concern is to practice Dharma.

When a politician gives a speech, he says many things but we can easily figure out his real intention, what's in the depths of his heart. It's to gain power, perhaps even to control all the people on earth, to rule the world or even destroy it. That's his main aim. Our aim, however, is to entrust ourselves to the Dharma. Thus we need to be very certain that nothing but the Dharma will benefit us in this life, at death time and in our future lives.

Therefore we *must* practice Dharma and only Dharma, because to work for this life alone is of no benefit at all. It is utterly meaningless, can only bring us harm and cause much worry at the time of death and we have to experience the result of this nonvirtuous action in future lives in the lower realms of the transmigratory beings. Therefore, we *must* practice Dharma and only Dharma.

2. Entrust the depths of the Dharma to the beggar

The second of the ten innermost jewels is to entrust the depths of the Dharma to the beggar. With the first one—entrusting our innermost mind to the Dharma—our mind completely takes refuge in the Dharma, and we no longer take refuge in our husband, wife, parents, possessions or any other worldly thing because we see that none of this can help at the time of death. But we worry that if we do entrust our innermost mind to the Dharma without taking care of material concerns, we will surely become a beggar, without the means to live, let alone practice Dharma.

This is a natural fear, because we're turning our mind away from our beginningless habit of doing this life's work. Without involving ourselves in getting the money for clothes, food and a comfortable environment, surely we're impoverishing ourselves. Then, how will we ever practice Dharma? The answer is this: when we entrust the depths of the Dharma to the beggar, we simply don't care if we become a beggar. The only important thing is to practice the holy Dharma, and we determine to do that despite the external conditions. Compared to living in luxury with a miserly, self-centered mind, being a beggar is much better, so even if it means begging, even if it means having only the most ordinary food and the poorest clothes, we will only practice Dharma. Nothing matters except Dharma, and if we have to experience hardships and austerities and wear torn, ugly rags and eat poor food, then that is perfectly all right.

When we work for only this life, no matter what good things we do, all that effort is completely wasted; there's not one single beneficial result. On the other hand, all the hardships we experience practicing Dharma are highly meaningful; they always bring the result of happiness. The hardships themselves are purification.

In Tibet, the nights and early mornings were very, very cold but the monks would have to debate in the open air for a long time, wearing only thin robes, no matter how low the temperatures got. Thousands of monks did this. In the bitter cold, they would chant the meditations and prayers composed by the lamas who founded the monastery and then debate for hours on end until the skin on their hands and feet would crack from the freezing conditions. Conversely, sometimes there would be so many monks in the prayer hall that it became unbelievably hot and crowded, with nowhere for even their feet to relax. They'd be squeezed together like this for hours and hours, experiencing such hardship in order to practice Dharma, to study and listen to lam-rim teachings explained by high lineage lamas. All this helped them purify the negative karma that they had collected in the past times to be born in the cold and hot hells.

It is similar when we have to experience hardship: heat, cold, back pain and so forth. Putting up with hardship in this way is the best way to purify our accumulated negative karma.

When it becomes difficult to keep the precept of not eating after midday, we should try to remember karma and the benefits of keeping precepts. Remember the happiness of future lives; remember the kind mother sentient beings and how we are one person but they are numberless. However much hunger and thirst we feel, however hard it is, this is real purification, purifying the negative karma created in the past to be born as a hungry ghost.

Practicing Dharma brings great peace, great happiness, great stability, great clarity and freedom from the worldly fears of separating from objects of attachment—children, other loved ones, friends and material possessions, to which we cling so much. It makes us very happy. And because we have practiced pure Dharma in this life, there's no need to talk about the results in our future lives. We can easily find a perfect human body again and easily achieve enlightenment.

Entrusting the depths of the Dharma to the beggar doesn't mean literally becoming a beggar—immediately throwing away all our clothes, tearing our house down and then, after burning all our money, hanging around the city or going to the mountain alone to practice Dharma with the birds, or maybe even the monkeys, if they'll let us practice Dharma with them!

I'm sure many people have practiced this kind of Dharma. In the early days, when Lama Yeshe and I were teaching in Nepal, many of the young people were hippies. To us they seemed like primitive Tibetans: they didn't take much care of their body, accepted whatever they got—food, clothes and so forth—and just let their hair grow as long as possible, not worrying if it got dirty. They slept in sleeping bags, sometimes in the mountains, sometimes in the forest with the monkeys, sometimes in the street. Even if it was twelve o'clock and everybody was running around, busy working, they were still sleeping. Whereas other people had definite homes, the hippies were not like that; they were happy to stay wherever they were, in a tent or a guest house.

From their external appearance they seemed very much like the ascetic meditators who followed the Kadampa geshes' advice. Having nothing to hold on to, lacking interest in material possessions and wanting to lead a quiet life without much worry, there were definite similarities on the surface.

The big difference was in the mind. What was missing was renunciation of the eight worldly dharmas. If the hippies could have had that mind renouncing the eight worldly dharmas, renouncing the desire for this life, then they really could have become pure Dharma practitioners. The external circumstances were there but they also needed that inner transformation.

As we have seen, the actual thing to renounce is not the objects of the senses but the confused mind, the evil thought. That is the thing that interferes with our work to achieve nirvana and enlightenment. That is the creator of our problems; that is what we should renounce.

In ancient India there were many bodhisattva kings, and apart from certain times of degeneration when there were irreligious kings, most of the time since the Buddhadharma reached Tibet the kings there were embodiments of Chenrezig. They didn't give up their possessions but they renounced the thought of the eight worldly dharmas and offered extensive benefit to sentient beings. Each one has an amazing life story, saying things that can't be comprehended by ordinary people's minds. Then in the present time there is His Holiness the Dalai Lama.

Therefore, we should make the determination that, in order to control the thought of the eight worldly dharmas, we will stop the interference, the distractions that are within our mind, to continue to practice pure Dharma. These are the techniques that the Kadampa geshes advise.

3. Entrust the depths of the beggar to death

With the third of the ten innermost jewels, entrusting the depths of the beggar to death, we determine that nothing will stop us from having great meaning in this life. Even dying for the Dharma while practicing austerities is far better than experiencing all the riches in the world, collecting much negative karma and then dying.

Perhaps we have reconciled ourselves to living like a beggar, but fears arise. We see that, if we follow this path and become a beggar, our entire life will be preoccupied with staying alive and there'll be no way to complete our life's work. We will surely either die of starvation or exposure. This fear comes from the thought of the eight worldly dharmas. We should counter it with the determination that no matter what, this is the path we will follow. Even if we do die practicing the Dharma, still our life will have been truly worthwhile.

Everybody has to die, rich people and beggars. In the end it is the same. Rich people who work very hard all the time have to die and so do beggars who do nothing. All that incredibly hard work the rich put into acquiring their riches is done solely with the thought of the eight worldly dharmas and is therefore only ever nonvirtue, with suffering its only possible result.

It might help if we could take our material possessions with us into our future life: wherever we were reborn—the god realm, the hungry ghost realm, the animal realm or some primitive place—maybe we could use all those possessions. But the only thing we can take with us is all the negative karma that we've accumulated trying to get those possessions and haven't purified. If we die with a miserly mind, if we aren't practicing Dharma, then that clinging mind will make it impossible for us to be born in the realms of the happy transmigrators.

And thus we determine that we will practice Dharma no matter how difficult it is, even if we have to die as a result of the austerities we practice. At least we won't have accumulated all that negative karma, and even if we die suddenly, it will be all right. The austerities we experience for the practice of Dharma—the heat, the freezing early mornings where we shake with cold, the pain when we meditate, the long hours of sitting—all become purification; we purify the past negative karma we've accumulated.

By practicing Dharma, our life has great meaning and the manner of our death is of no consequence. Therefore, we make the strong determination never to renounce the holy Dharma.

The advice from the Kadampa geshes is that we should not cheat ourselves by having fear and doubt about what might happen if we follow the Dharma. "If I don't have any possessions or friends or helpers around me all the time, what will happen if I get sick, what will happen when I become old and can't walk or move any more? Even when I die, I'll need somebody to serve me to make sure my corpse is treated well and not left in a room somewhere, rotting, smelling and full of worms. I'll definitely need somebody to burn my corpse or arrange it in a nice box and carve the year of my death on a piece of stone."

When fears and doubts like this arise, we're clinging to the pleasures of this life. The answer is to think that anyway, there's no certainty that we'll live long enough to get old. Death can come at any moment. Therefore we need to make this determination to practice Dharma no matter what the external circumstances are. Think, "If I die from austerities while practicing Dharma, who cares what happens to my corpse? Even if nobody looks after it and it's left on the street or in a cave in the mountains, putrid or desiccated, it doesn't matter. Without being attached to the pleasures of this life, this body, I am going to practice pure Dharma."

If we die of cold while doing it, that's fine; if we die of heat, that's also fine. Whatever happens, we won't renounce the Dharma. To make such a determination we really need to understand the great advantages of practicing Dharma. The more we understand, the stronger our determination will become. Then, whether starvation or exposure to cold face us, we won't even think of renouncing the Dharma. Our determination will be that strong.

I once read a book about the experiences of a lady who died and her consciousness was able to see her body. She explained everything that happened after she died. All her relatives came to the house, crying and worrying so much. But she felt that she had not finished her work, whatever that was, and she reentered her body. She concluded from her experience that there is definitely life after death. Not only that—her experience made her realize that she had wasted her whole life by working for only this life and not making preparations for her future lives. She felt very upset about this. I found it very interesting. She was basically just talking about lam-rim without knowing it. I found what she said very useful, very effective, even for my mind, which doesn't have even the scent of Dharma. I think that there must be many people who have had similar experiences.

In fact, we don't have to worry about dying of cold or starvation. Even if we become a beggar through renouncing the thought of the eight worldly dharmas, there's no need to be scared because Shakyamuni Buddha himself dedicated the merits so that his followers, those who live in pure Dharma practice, will never be bereft of the means of living. In the *Compassionate White Lotus Sutra* he said that when he was generating bodhicitta in a previous life he prayed for the sake of sentient beings:

> If the followers of my teachings, the Buddhadharma, who wear even four inches of robe don't get food, then my having achieved buddhahood has betrayed sentient beings and may I not receive enlightenment.

He also predicted that there would be such an incredible famine on earth that people would have to sell all their jewels for food, but even at that time pure Dharma practitioners would never go hungry. Even though the rest of the people on earth had fields only the size of a fingernail in which to grow their crops, he promised that his followers who lived in renunciation and were pure Dharma practitioners would never be devoid of the means of living.

As we have seen, Geshe Kharak Gomchung said that no true meditator could ever die of hunger or cold. It hasn't happened in the past and it won't happen in the future, because the mind of dissatisfaction has been renounced. If we're really pure Dharma practitioners, renunciation of this life carries the power of practice. Geshe Lama Konchog is a good example of this.[69]

[69] See Geshe Lama Konchog's story, p. 148 ff. See also *Cave in the Snow* about the hardships

Actually, there is not one single story from anywhere—India, Tibet or anywhere else—about a pure Dharma practitioner dying of starvation or cold or other hardships. If you ask many of the learned geshes in the monasteries about their life, you will find amazing stories. What they went through, bearing the difficulties of cold, heat, very little food—sometimes even no solid food to eat, just tsampa mixed with tea in a bowl. Many of the monks didn't even have butter tea. For lunch and dinner, they always ate the same thing and spent the whole time studying Buddhadharma, taking teachings, studying, thinking, debating. This is just the monks in the monastery. I'm not even talking about the great meditators in the caves.[70]

Because of this, after a few years their knowledge of Dharma developed and in later life they had no difficulties obtaining what they needed to live, even for their immediate needs. Sometimes they received so much food they would get bored having such a large quantity around.

It is not like that for somebody who only practices Dharma on the surface. That person has many difficulties and there are many stories of people who have died like this.

If we practice Dharma purely we should have no fear of dying. We should think that if we die clinging to the pleasure of this life, we're throwing ourselves into the lower realms, whereas if we practice the holy Dharma without the thought of the eight worldly dharmas, then even if we have to live in a cave in complete solitude, we'll have happiness now, when we die and in future lives. So we should determine always to practice Dharma, even if we don't have one single helper, even if we die alone leaving a corpse like a dead dog, full of worms.

4. Entrust the depths of death to the cave

Meditators who make the decision to entrust the depths of death to the cave practice Dharma without fear of death by living in solitary places, such as dry, barren caves—not the nice, moist ones we have in the mountains of Nepal.

There are many sorts of meditators. There's the meditator who can generate realizations of the graduated path living in a monastery or a city rather than a cave and there's the meditator who lives in a cave but has not

---

faced by Ven Tenzin Palmo, a Western meditator who lived in a cave in the Himalayas for twelve years.
[70] See Geshe Rabten's autobiography, *The Life of a Tibetan Monk*.

renounced worldly concerns, whose body is living in an isolated place but whose mind is busy with the eight worldly dharmas. So, who is in retreat? The person in the cave with the attached mind, way up there in the Himalaya mountains, or the person whose mind is living away from the eight worldly dharmas, right in the center of New York City? Actually, the person in New York, working, communicating with others, is the one in retreat because he is retreating away from the eight worldly dharmas.

However we live, the most important thing is the mind living in solitude, the mind living in the cave of the mind, whether the body is in isolation or not. Having renounced all meaningless worldly affairs, we can complete the stages of the path and achieve the omniscient mind. In that way we can attain full enlightenment in this lifetime without having to wait for another life.

At the very end of *The Three Principal Aspects of the Path*, Lama Tsongkhapa said,

> In this way you realize exactly
> The vital points of the three principal aspects of the path.
> Resort to seeking solitude, generate the power of effort,
> And quickly accomplish your final goal, my child.[71]

The solitude he refers to is solitude of the mind rather than that of the body. Real isolation is realized when we have cut off clinging to this life. In general, we also have to be isolated from the self-cherishing thought and self-grasping, the ignorance that believes the I to be truly existent. If that's our mindset, then no matter where we live—at the beach, in the busiest city, in the most luxurious hotel—we're living in an isolated place. That place is our hermitage.

Gen Jampa Wangdu used to encourage me when I slept too much because I was so lazy. As I mentioned before, he lived in a cave beneath what was not so much a rock as a big stone. It was not luxurious like my place at Lawudo. I lived in comparative luxury, with everything there to help practice the eight worldly dharmas, to cherish them and make them more powerful,

---

[71] Translated by Lama Zopa Rinpoche as found on the LYWA website (LamaYeshe.com), *"Three Principal Aspects of the Path."* See also *FPMT Essential Buddhist Prayers, Vol. 1*, Lama Yeshe's *Essence of Tibetan Buddhism*, Lama Zopa Rinpoche's *Virtue and Reality* and Geshe Sonam Rinchen's *The Three Principal Aspects of the Path*.

which is why it had so many decorations. His cave was a Kadampa geshe's cave, for somebody who had renounced this life, with no decorations, just bare rock and so low you couldn't even stand up or stretch your body. To sleep, there was no spring mattress; he simply put leaves on the floor and sat on them.

One day a Tibetan nun who lived in Nepal, whose family was very wealthy, came to visit. I think they were related; she was his aunt or something. She knew he was a great meditator and so, wanting to receive lam-rim teachings from him, brought him an offering of a big round of butter, like the big cheeses they sell in Kathmandu, which is very useful for monks to make Tibetan tea with. After offering the butter she sat on the bare ground and asked him to give teachings. He said, "I don't know any teaching, I can't teach, I don't know anything," and then said, "What I do know is how to make prostrations, that's all I know. I can teach you that. If you want teachings, go and see some other lamas. Also, I don't need the butter, so please take it away."

I don't know if the nun got angry or not because he refused to teach her, but afterwards I think she had nothing to say, so she left. He didn't care that her family was wealthy or that she was a relative.

Except for what is necessary, like robes if they're monks, those ascetic meditators keep nothing, no possessions, decorations or anything. When they become well known and many people start coming to make offerings, they move to another place, another cave or even another country, where they're unknown. Then the people there find out about them and start bringing offerings, so again they escape to another place, from one mountain to another. Many don't accept offerings at all or, if they take them, get rid of them right away by offering them to the monasteries or their gurus.

The great yogi Milarepa prayed,

> If I am able to die at this hermitage without my relatives knowing
> my happiness, without my enemies knowing my suffering, then
> I, the yogi, have had my wish fulfilled. If I am able to die in this
> hermitage without friends knowing my old age and without my
> sister knowing my sickness, then I, the yogi, have had my wish
> fulfilled. May this prayer that I have made with no one around to
> hear be successful for the benefit of all the sentient beings.

There are many prayers like this.

5. The uncaptured vajra

After the four entrustments, the next three in the ten innermost jewels are the three vajras. The first one is the practice of the uncaptured vajra, seeking the conviction to leave behind any discouragement. This is based on a determination that nobody can change or disturb our decision in any way. No matter who tries to persuade us to not practice pure Dharma—our parents, our dearest friends—we remain adamant. Because of the diamond-hard quality of that determination it is called "vajra," and "uncaptured" suggests something utterly unchangeable.

A cat hunts a mouse, but no matter how good a hunter the cat is, the mouse still escapes. In the same way, we have renounced this life and the eight worldly dharmas, and no matter how much people ask us to delay our practice, to not do it now but leave it for another time, we don't listen. Without fear that we might lose their love, we don't change our mind but make the firm decision, "I must, I must practice, I must practice pure Dharma."

So in that sense, like the mouse, we're able to avoid being captured by worldly people and distracted from practicing Dharma. We're already relying on the four entrustments—of the Dharma, the beggar, death and the cave—which are to do with our own attitude toward practicing Dharma—but there's still a danger that our relationships with others will interfere with our Dharma practice. Perhaps we're planning to go into retreat but our parents are unhappy and try to convince us that we're not ready for it, that there's no hurry. "What's the point of torturing yourself like that, going to those isolated places? You'll get sick in that terrible cave! You'll die! Who will help you?"

And if that doesn't work, "That's not a good idea. You don't know what you're doing. It would be better if you stayed home and worked and made your life comfortable. Have a lot of children! Then you'll have a nice big family, with many relatives, with many brothers and sisters. We'll give you a property, a really nice house. We'll give you land so that you can do anything you want. You can makes lots of money and enjoy your life. You can travel anywhere you want. What's the point of going to that primitive place where you'll probably get TB or cancer? You might get diarrhea! It's much better that you stay here. Then in future, when you've finished your work, *then* you can practice Dharma if you want. If that's what you want, you can do it then. But aren't you foolish, even thinking about leaving such a comfortable, luxurious place where there's such a wonderful variety of food and everything is so clean, where you can get everything you want? How can you even consider going to that primitive place where there's nothing and just stay in a hut. There's not even a supermarket. Not even a bar!"

Anyway, I'm joking. But we can have doubts when we decide to practice Dharma. We think going to an isolated place for retreat will help, but we also see the difficulties and think we might be fooling ourselves. Those doubts make us delay our Dharma practice, and our friends and family encourage those doubts by telling us how good our worldly life could be.

So this uncaptured vajra mind is the strong determination to practice Dharma no matter what, to not let the mind come under the control of the thought of the eight worldly dharmas for even a second. If the most positive thing we can do is go to a place of solitude for retreat, then with the utmost conviction we decide to do just that. No matter how much others try to persuade us to do otherwise, we have the strength of mind to do only what is most beneficial.

You might have heard about the life of the great bodhisattva Atisha. He was born as a prince in India. His family ruled a great population and had incredible power. Their palace had twenty-five rooms with golden roofs. But all he wanted to do was leave and lead an ascetic life.

Wanting him to take over from his father and become king, his parents tried to dissuade him from this many times, extolling the joys of having the rank of a king and being married. They gathered all the beautiful girls in the country and threw him a huge party. They tried very hard but nothing could change his mind. It was really like a vajra. He told his parents, "For me, wearing expensive brocades and wearing rags are the same; eating delicious food and eating dog meat are identical; so are drinking nectar and drinking blood and pus; and there's no difference between having a princess or a daughter of Mara." This is the practice of the uncaptured vajra.

The great Milarepa advised his disciple Rechungpa,

> Son, if you want to practice the holy Dharma and have devotion arise from the depths of your heart, do not look back on this life. Follow my truth. Relatives are Mara, who delay you, who prevent you from practicing the holy Dharma. Don't believe what they say. Cut off attachment to them. Food and possessions are the spies of Mara. Objects of desire bind you like Mara's noose, therefore definitely cut off attachment.

I have already talked about how relatives say nice things to us and we start to believe them and thus get trapped. But Milarepa goes on to say that food and possessions are Mara's spies, in that the more familiar we get with them the worse it gets.

Generally with a spy, the friendlier we get with him, the more he understands us and the more he can exploit us. He pretends to be friendly, he pretends he's not cheating us, and we start to trust him completely. He seems sincere, a really good friend. He takes us to restaurants, gives us food and drinks, flatters us and offers us any help we need. Slowly he finds out more things about us and discovers our weaknesses. He shows us a good time and sooner or later offers us drugs. Maybe we're reluctant to try them but because we don't want to lose his friendship we do. We trust him and at first it is OK, but after a while he gets us to take more and more and before we know it we're hooked and completely under his control. This is what he's wanted all along. Our "friend" has completely cheated us and we end up in prison. This is like Mara's noose, where we get more and more entangled in attachment.

It's the same with alcohol and tobacco. The first time we try them they seem nothing special but then the more we have them, the more familiar we get with them, the worse it gets. We find it extremely difficult to stop. Because of our attachment, these objects bind us like a noose. Entangled in objects of desire, our dissatisfied mind just gets stronger and stronger and we spend all our time trying to get more of whatever it is. Then we find we have no time to retreat or practice Dharma.

Maybe we're not attached to another person's body, but if we're attached to objects we get from that person we get attached to her in another way. We start to rely on people who give us things, such as benefactors who offer us material support. Concerned about receiving things, praise and the like, our behavior deteriorates and we break the moral code we're trying to live by, causing our mind to become scattered and making our Dharma practice even harder to do.

We find ourselves trapped by attachment to the objects that other people offer and therefore powerless not to follow them. We're afraid to go against their wishes because we need what they give us, and so our conviction and our practice deteriorate and we end up doing nonvirtuous things, completely involved in worldly work again.

I once met a monk who planned to do a retreat on calm abiding through chu-len. Although he was trying his best to live as an ascetic, his rich brother tried to convince him that he was so close to his final geshe examinations that he'd be crazy not to get his degree first and offered to be his benefactor and make offerings to the monastery on his behalf. At his brother's insistence, the monk finally agreed and came out of retreat to take his exams. He obtained the title of geshe, became busier and busier and was never able to complete the practice of calm abiding. This is just one example of how easy it is for us to get completely trapped in the hands of other people because we haven't achieved this practice of the uncaptured vajra.

This is the essence of Milarepa's advice to his disciple: avoid becoming ensnared in Mara's noose. Even with a good motivation, we'll encounter many obstacles, others will give us many reasons why we must delay our practice, why we can't go to a solitary place just yet to meditate.

We love our family and our friends so much, they're there in our heart, but even if our eyes fill with tears, even if we worry about them, we should have this vajra resolve, this indestructible, unchangeable vajra thought to never be separated from the holy Dharma, to always be in a solitary place, without attachment, to practice Dharma purely. Don't forget, as we have seen, being in a "solitary place" doesn't necessarily mean being physically isolated. No matter how much our relatives cry or scream at us, whether they follow us begging us not to go, we should never change our mind but keep it as indestructible as a vajra. This what "uncaptured vajra" means.

6. The shameless vajra

The second vajra is living within the shameless vajra. The uncaptured vajra is the preliminary to this one. We not only have the determination to go to an isolated place and practice, despite the pleas of our family and friends, now we are actually doing it, but, having renounced this life and become a beggar, filthy and hungry, with no clothes to wear, we might worry about what others think of us.

When people see us on the street they complain about how lazy and foolish we look, criticizing us for our looks, our lifestyle, what we think. They complain about us and joke that we have four limbs or call us lazy because we wander around jobless. While everybody else has to work for a living, we just sit around, begging, lazy and crazy.

Other people, on the other hand, might think we're an amazing yogi. We stay in a cave wearing only rags and don't need a luxurious house, family, friends or possessions—we must have become some kind of divine god!

We need to be especially careful of people we like and respect, such as family and friends. Even with them, we should be indifferent to and "shameless" of the praise or abuse they give us. Following what they say can be a big hindrance to our Dharma practice.

The Kadampa advice is to not worry about this at all. Whether people criticize us for our filthy appearance or praise us because we look like great ascetic practitioners, whether we are a devil or a yogi in their eyes, it doesn't make any difference to us. We know that to follow their ideas would be a shortcoming of the eight worldly dharmas, that doing so would be doing the work of this life and creating negative karma. In that way, we lose the fear of criticism.

When we are certain that the way we have chosen is good, we should not care about reputation and praise or notoriety and abuse. Knowing that concern for reputation is a major hindrance to our Dharma practice and determining to concentrate on practicing pure Dharma without considering others' opinions, we are shameless. This is living within the shameless vajra.

7. The transcendent wisdom vajra

The next vajra is living within the transcendent wisdom vajra. This means we resolve never to break the promise we have made to practice pure Dharma by renouncing this life. Completely turning away from all that is essenceless and meaningless, we make the firm, unshakable, indestructible determination to make our life equal with the holy Dharma.

"May my life be equal to my practice, like Milarepa's was" is recognized as a very important prayer in Tibetan Buddhism. This means that if we live ten years, we practice Dharma for ten years, not that life is longer and Dharma practice is shorter. We make the determination to practice until death.

To be able to do that, we need unchangeable, unshakable resolve. We cannot practice properly if we're easily overcome by delusions and therefore, despite our efforts, our life becomes unequal, with less time for Dharma and more time for meaningless activities that only *seem* important. That is why it is most essential that we make the strong determination never to break our promise to completely renounce the meaningless work of this life and have the unchangeable determination to make our life equal with the practice of the holy Dharma.

8. Expulsion from the rank of human beings

Of the last three aspects of the ten innermost jewels, the first is expulsion from the rank of human beings. When we renounce this life, we no longer fit into the ways of worldly people. Nothing of the perfections of this life interests us. Whereas everybody else, from pauper to millionaire, works solely for the perfections of this life, our thinking is the complete opposite of this. Everything we think or do is only for the happiness beyond this life and to obtain happiness for other sentient beings. In that way we are completely out of tune with the rest of the world—we are outcasts—and others simply can't understand how we think or what we do. That is what being "expelled from the rank of human beings" means. If our actions of body, speech and mind were in accord with those of worldly people, then whatever we did wouldn't be holy Dharma.

According to society, the criterion for being crazy is being out of line with how normal people think, so from that point of view we're completely crazy. But we see how normal people destroy their chance at true happiness by chasing worldly perfections, so to us they're crazy. They all try so hard to acquire as many possessions and have as good a reputation as possible; they all love to be praised and hate to be criticized. Their lives are devoted to such pursuits.

We, as Dharma practitioners who have renounced this life, no longer seek the happiness of this life, so we're indifferent to the four desirable and four undesirable objects. Therefore our attitude is the complete opposite to that of the rest of the world.

Many Western Dharma students returning to the West after a one-month course at Kopan find it rather difficult to practice. At first they try as best they can, confronting the thought of the eight worldly dharmas, but soon their energy wanes and their old habits return. They start back at their old jobs but feel they don't have any connection to the people around them. They feel that the world they inhabit is completely different from the world everybody else inhabits because their attitude is so different. This is what is meant by being expelled from the ranks of the human beings. It really means being out of step with worldly beings who are concerned only for this life.

9. Achieving the rank of the dog

After achieving expulsion from the ranks of the human beings, the next achievement is reaching the rank of the dog. Everybody complains about the dog; he has such a bad reputation. They say he is harmful but for him this is not like criticism. He has no concept of reputation, and whether his owners scold or praise him, he's still faithful to them and still tries to protect them from intruders. They keep him out in the cold, don't give him any shelter from the weather, feed him poor quality food, but whatever happens, no matter how many difficulties he has to suffer, he bears it, obediently staying with his family.

Of course, this is a Tibetan dog we're talking about. In the West, dogs tend to have nice homes and good food and their owners might even give them warm clothes when they're cold. Westerners have a lot of concern for their animals and that's extremely good. However, for Tibetan dogs, whatever limited or poor quality food they're given, they just stay there and accept it. They bear whatever difficulties there are.

This is the same as the Dharma practitioner (although of course, dogs work only for the happiness of this life and so everything they do is meaningless). If we want to practice Dharma but have a weak mind, we will always have difficulty. We might think that we need money, a comfortable room and all our meals prepared for us before we can start to meditate. Or we might start but soon run out of money and have to live on apples and sandwiches. Or perhaps our place is very uncomfortable and run down, full of spider webs, without heating and with only the cold floor to sleep on. At that stage, we totally forget about Dharma. We completely give up. But if we were to wait until everything were comfortable and easy and our situation were stable, we might never begin to practice Dharma.

If we can't stand hunger, thirst, cold, heat, discomfort, lack of sleep and so forth, then even if we try to practice Dharma, these concerns will always get in the way and we'll encounter many hindrances. As long as comfort is a consideration we'll find it difficult to do any Dharma practice and impossible to realize the steps of the path to enlightenment.

We need to understand the infinite advantages of experiencing hardships while practicing Dharma, that all this becomes great purification. We should remember that Shakyamuni Buddha and the great yogis like Milarepa spent years living in austerity and achieved enlightenment through enduring great hardship. They didn't live comfortably with delicious food and the best clothes. If we have less, we should remember this—it is very beneficial for our mind when we have difficulty practicing Dharma.

Renouncing concern for food, clothing, shelter, reputation and so forth, we experience the happiness of practicing Dharma. Whatever food or clothing we get, we just accept; whatever difficulties arise—hunger, thirst, heat, cold—we bear them all in order to practice Dharma.

Geshe Chengawa gave some advice on the four opposite attitudes, something that is relevant to reaching the rank of a dog. He said that worldly people cherish the Buddha more than sentient beings, happiness more than suffering, people who help them more than people who harm them and themselves more than others. For a Dharma practitioner who wishes to achieve enlightenment, it is the complete reverse. A Dharma practitioner should cherish sentient beings more than the Buddha,[72] suffering more than happiness, people who harm more than people who help and others more than themselves. The main point of this is that we should cherish suffering more than happiness.

This is what "reaching the rank of the dog" means. However difficult a dog's life is—even if some days he doesn't get any food—he still hangs around, wanting to protect the family. Similarly, whatever hardship arises, we must continue to practice Dharma, without changing our mind.

10. Achieving the rank of the divine beings

The last of the ten innermost jewels is achieving the rank of the divine beings. It means basically that through all the previous practices we have reached the goal and completed our practice. We have achieved the state of buddhahood, the highest state amongst all beings. In Hindu culture, worldly gods such as Brahma and Indra are considered higher than any human and, therefore, higher than the arhats, but in fact the worldly gods aren't free from samsara whereas the arhats are, so in reality arhats are higher than worldly gods. A buddha is higher still.

I have explained the ten innermost jewels because if we wish to practice pure Dharma and renounce the thought of eight worldly dharmas, we need the Kadampa geshes' advice very, very much. As a foundation, this is extremely important. Even if we can't practice like this, it is very useful to understand it, especially when we get confused or are too lazy to practice Dharma.

The whole point of the Kadampa geshes' advice on the ten innermost jewels is to equalize the eight worldly dharmas, the four desirable objects and the four undesirable ones. This is the basic method we need to stop the difficulties of our life and cut our confusion. A Dharma practitioner

---

[72] Cherishing sentient beings more than the Buddha is part of the bodhisattva's training. The Buddha should be revered because he gave us the tools to attain enlightenment but it is only through working for other sentient beings that we gain every realization. Therefore it is a mistake to cherish the Buddha but ignore others.

wishing to realize the graduated path to enlightenment values this teaching in the way that a worldly person values money.

This practice is more than a verbal or physical one; it is mind practice. The whole thing is determination. The essence is to bring our mind to the point where we can make a firm decision to practice Dharma purely. This practice of the ten innermost jewels is especially needed if we've taken vows. Whether they're the vows of the fully ordained monk or nun, the thirty-six novice vows, the bodhisattva vows or the tantric vows, we need practices such as the ten innermost jewels that keep our renunciation of the eight worldly dharmas firm.

PURE DHARMA NOT MOUTH DHARMA

When great bodhisattvas give instructions they're not just saying the words. It's not like a parrot or a tape recorder. A parrot can repeat what it hears but has no understanding of the meaning, so it's just talking nonsense; a tape recorder has no consciousness, so it doesn't understand either. When, on the other hand, great bodhisattvas give instructions, their words are not dry and empty; they come from their full understanding of the nature of samsaric suffering. They talk from experience. They have discovered the profit, the infinite benefit, of renouncing this life and, living in the practice, they instruct their followers accordingly.

If we don't know how to practice, we might think that we're renouncing this life but our actions won't be Dharma and we'll get into trouble, like those Western students who threw away all their possessions and went to India to be like Milarepa but didn't throw away their mind clinging to this life. We need some understanding.

Maybe you think I'm making Dharma complicated and difficult, that I should explain things to make your life easy and comfortable. Maybe you think I explain things like the eight worldly dharmas to scare you. However, this is the actual meaning of the Dharma and without going through it there's simply no way to practice Dharma.

No matter how much we say we're practicing Dharma, if we practice without understanding, there's no way for our actions to become pure Dharma. No matter what advanced practices we do, no matter how much we meditate or talk about Dharma, no matter how famous we might be at yoga or meditation, no matter how much power we have, without understanding renunciation and living in the practice, there's no way for anything we do to become pure Dharma.

Therefore it's necessary that the Dharma that we're trying to practice doesn't become just mouth Dharma but pure Dharma, even if we meditate only once a day. If we want to create virtuous actions, to create the cause of liberation, to make every action pure, it's necessary to remember what Dharma means by remembering the border between Dharma and non-Dharma. Then, even if we do only one small action a day, it can become pure Dharma. If we do that action free of the evil thought of the eight worldly dharmas, we've planted the real seed of liberation, the actual seed that can bring enlightenment; if we don't, we're in danger of planting the wrong seed.

We need to be very careful in what we do. We need to make sure that whatever we do is not simply mouth Dharma. Pure Dharma is extremely profound. Its meaning is like a deep well—extremely difficult to see its depths and even more difficult to realize. The Dharma that is done with the thought renouncing this life is more profound than profound. It is such a special method; it is *the* method to release us from suffering and lead us to true happiness.

Renouncing pleasure brings the best pleasure

Renouncing attachment to worldly pleasure brings the best pleasure. Renouncing attachment to receiving material things is the best receiving and brings the best continual receiving of material things; renouncing attachment to praise is the best praise and brings the greatest praise; renouncing attachment to reputation is the best reputation and brings the greatest reputation.

All the great yogis of the past, such as Guru Shakyamuni Buddha, renounced all four desirable objects, but that does not mean that the Buddha never enjoyed pleasure, never had a good reputation or was never praised. He had infinite pleasure, infinite happiness all the time, unceasingly; it never stopped. If we could compare the combined pleasure of all the worldly samsaric beings that have ever existed and the Buddha's pleasure, there'd be no comparison. Theirs would be so limited. And, not seeking praise, the Buddha received the best praise because of his qualities; he had praise in the past, has praise in the present and will continue to have praise in the future. For enlightened beings, there's no sound that's not the sweetest, no taste that's not the best. Our clothes might feel rough or smooth on our bodies but for enlightened beings there's no such thing as rough feeling or bad smell. The Buddha and all other enlightened beings continually enjoy the most sublime, unceasing happiness. For them, everything is infinite bliss, everything is in the nature of infinite happiness. All this comes from the practice of renunciation. Remember what Shakyamuni Buddha said:

> If you wish all happiness, renounce all attachment. If you renounce all attachment, you will achieve the supreme happiness.

This quote is short but it's extremely profound. It sums up all the teachings on the eight worldly dharmas: by renouncing, we receive. If we avoid all samsaric desires, we'll achieve the most supreme happiness. As long as we follow samsaric desire we can never find satisfaction.

The reason we have never been truly satisfied so far is because we haven't tried to avoid samsaric desires. To do that we need wisdom. When we achieve satisfaction with wisdom we are far happier than anyone who tries to attain satisfaction by fulfilling samsaric desires. We can never find satisfaction while we're under the control of craving and attachment. That's the way it works.

As we have seen, there might be some pleasure in scratching an itch but it's far better not to have the itch in the first place. The pleasure is just a temporary relief of suffering. If we're attached to the pleasure derived from scratching, doing it once is never enough. We need to do it three or more times, the pleasure diminishes the more we do it, and sooner or later we create a wound. Instead of more and more pleasure, which is what we're hoping for, it turns to suffering. It can't last; it must change into suffering. *That* is the nature of samsaric pleasure.

When jaundiced, we might see white snow mountains as yellow and even believe that they're yellow, but when we recover we see that, in fact, they were white all along. In the same way, when attached, we believe that we can be happy by obtaining objects of desire. We really believe that. But noble beings who have transcended that wrong view and renounced attachment to samsaric pleasure understand that samsaric pleasure is in the nature of suffering.

We need to think on examples like this and many more, and we need to be very wary whenever we meet an object of desire. If we can see that samsaric pleasure is in the nature of suffering, our Dharma wisdom will continue to grow and whatever actions we do will be the cause of future happiness.

We can't discover this through words alone; we have to experience it in our practice. Don't think I want you to deny yourself any happiness or that what I'm talking about is impossible. Even people who have studied this in the past still need to go over it again and again because it takes time to really understand.

We have to be very patient with ourselves. If we can learn the fundamental points by heart, we have a tool to check whatever comes up in our mind and our practice becomes much more effective. We have to go over the main points of our practice repeatedly, using them constantly like background to whatever we do.

Of course, if we can completely counter the thought of the eight worldly dharmas at all times, that is without question *the* perfect method for happiness in not only this life but in all future lives as well. But it doesn't happen immediately, like a snap of the fingers. It takes time for our mind to turn around. We have to train, but as we do it gets easier and easier.

The more we integrate lam-rim subjects such as the eight worldly dharmas into our daily life, the more we can see how true they are; our understanding of their meaning gets deeper and deeper. At the very beginning, I'm sure it probably seems like a kind of fantasy nonsense, like baby talk. When we first come across this subject we can't figure it out; it doesn't make much sense at all. But the nature of wisdom is such that if we constantly keep at it, we will definitely make progress and our wisdom will grow. This is the nature of mind.

We can practice like Atisha's disciple, the Kadampa yogi Geshe Ben Gungyal, did. He kept a collection of black and white stones. Whenever the thought of the eight worldly dharmas arose he'd put down a black stone and whenever he had a virtuous thought he'd put down a white one. He'd do this throughout the entire day and last thing at night would check to see how many stones of either color there were. At the beginning there were no white stones at all, only black ones. Gradually, however, there were a few white stones and then a few more. Eventually, after a long time, he found nothing but white stones. So it's all a matter of training; we can't expect it to happen quickly. It all depends on continual energy, determination and practice.

Even though at present we can't live our whole life in the Dharma, completely renouncing the thought of the eight worldly dharmas like those ascetic meditators did, it is extremely important to be mindful and try our best to make each action virtuous.

Otherwise we might mistakenly believe that our seemingly religious actions are Dharma, which is very dangerous. We have such a short life that if we can't create virtue even when doing good actions, it's very upsetting. It's like owning a shop and thinking we're making a lot of money, but when, at the end of the day, we look closely at what we've taken we find that all the notes we've been given are counterfeit. Everything we thought was real is not and we have totally wasted all our time and energy. But even if we were a millionaire and discovered that all our money was counterfeit and utterly worthless, that would be nothing compared to working for the thought of the eight worldly dharmas, thinking that we're working for happiness whereas in actuality all we're working for is rebirth in the lower realms. Mountains of counterfeit money can't cause us to be reborn in the lower realms, can't disturb the happiness of future lives, but nonvirtuous actions done out of the thought of the eight worldly dharmas can. Therefore it's extremely important that we make even the smallest virtuous action as perfect as possible.

The most powerful remedy is meditation on impermanence and death. Remembering how the time of death is indefinite, reflect how following the evil thought of the eight worldly dharmas causes us to do nonvirtuous actions that lead us to rebirth in the lower realms and makes us suffer, even in this life.

By remembering this and generating a positive motivation, our mind won't become one with the thought of the eight worldly dharmas—and the best positive motivation we can generate is bodhicitta. Whenever we do something for another being, no matter how small that action is, we should do it with bodhicitta, thinking we are doing it in order to achieve enlightenment for the benefit of all sentient beings. Even if it's just giving a tiny scrap of food to a dog, the benefits of doing that with bodhicitta on the basis of renouncing the thought of the eight worldly dharmas are infinite, uncountable, unimaginable.

Knowing the distinction between Dharma and non-Dharma gives us the choice. Once we have that wisdom, we can make all our actions Dharma whenever we want.

Appendix
The Ten Innermost Jewels of the Kadampa Geshes.[73]

These are the ten innermost jewels of the Kadampas. By merely keeping them in the heart, the fortress of delusion collapses, the ship of evil negative karma disintegrates and one will reach the very blissful ground of remedy. Therefore, if one has these ten innermost jewels, one will achieve liberation and enlightenment quickly and without hardships; and, by the way, one will attain the happiness of this life and the happiness of all future lives.

I request the possessor of the mighty one, the kind gurus, the direct and indirect gurus, please bless me to give up this life, as in the holy biographies of the previous holy beings.

By seeing sickness, old age and death, the unequaled son of Tsetsang (Prince Siddhartha)[74] felt great sadness and then abandoned his reign of the kingdom. At the end of six years, having lived the austere life of an ascetic, on the banks of the great river Naranjana,[75] he became fully enlightened. Like that, as in the life stories of previous holy beings who reflected on impermanence and death, felt great sorrow, gave up this life, practiced in solitary places and achieved enlightenment in one life; in this way, reflect on the nature of the uncertain nature of death: why shouldn't I give up the activities of this life—home, field, house, relatives, food and wealth—all of which do not allow pure Dharma practice to arise?

Except for the needs of survival—the three robes, begging bowl and so

---

[73] *FPMT Retreat Prayer Book*, pp. 171–73. *Lama Chöpa Jorchö*, pp. 197 & 199.
[74] Both names for the being who would become Shakyamuni Buddha, the historical Buddha.
[75] The river (now called the Lilajan) that flows past Bodhgaya, the small town in the north of India where the Buddha became enlightened.

forth—I won't keep gold or jewels or anything extra, not even one piece, for myself. What is definite to occur for me is death. At that time, wealth, family, friends (cats and dogs, too) will not benefit me. Furthermore, there is the suffering of separation from them. By reflecting in this way, I should give up seeking the means of this life.

I should entrust the depths of my attitudes to the Dharma.

I should entrust the depths of the Dharma to the beggar.

I should entrust the depths of the beggar to death.

I should entrust the depths of death to the cave.

I should proceed well with the uncaptured vajra. *(By proceeding with vajra mind, not changing from renouncing this life, I practice Dharma without being captured by the beloved ones.)*

I should definitely leave behind the vajra without shyness. *(Leave behind worldly concern: whatever people say about me, good or bad, I won't change my mind when I go out into the world with renunciation for this life. This mind is the vajra without shyness.)*

The transcendent wisdom vajra should accompany me. *(I should equalize Dharma and my life together without transgressing the commitment to renouncing this life I live in.)*

I should attempt to be out of line with the human beings. *(I should be out of line with worldly human beings who are attached to this life.)* I should keep a lowly position, wearing ragged clothes.

I should reach to the line of dogs and achieve to the line of devas. *(Accept the loss of food, clothing and reputation. No matter how much hunger, thirst, hardship happens, I will bear it to practice Dharma. When one gives up all the works of the mundane world and completes one's practice in solitary places, one achieves the supramundane deva of the devas, which is enlightenment in this life.)*

In short, impermanence and death will come soon. Now is the time to give up this life. Due to the compassion of the guru and my own virtue, may I be able to give up the work of this life.

If one recites these words verbally and reflects on their meaning, one will be able to give up quickly the works of this life completely.

Colophon

This self-liberated speech, imbued with the blessings of the yogi Khedrup Nyiden Shabkar Tsogdruk, was lightly edited by the humble, ignorant beggar without Dharma [Thubten Zopa]. It was written with the thought that if I and those who are like me, when reciting the "Reviewing the Stages of the Path" prayer in the *Guru Puja*, were to recite these words after the verse that starts "Realizing how this body of liberties and endowments," it would benefit by inspiring Dharma in the mindstream. By this, may all migrating beings be liberated from their grasping at the eight dharmas and quickly attain the highest, complete enlightenment. It would also be good to recite it when teaching the lam-rim to others.

Translator's colophon added June 2004
This text was written by the highly attained lama Shabkar Tsogdruk Rangdrol and translated by Lama Thubten Zopa Rinpoche with the assistance of Venerable Tsenla on the 23rd day of the first month of the year of the Earth Rabbit, March 10, 1999, at Kachoe Dechen Ling, Aptos, CA, USA; dictated to Ven. Lhundup Ningje. May all beings benefit. Lightly edited by Kendall Magnussen, FPMT Education Services, July 2004.

Glossary

(Skt = Sanskrit; Tib = Tibetan)

aggregates (Skt: skandha). The association of body and mind; a person comprises five aggregates: form, feeling, recognition, compositional factors and consciousness.

anger. A disturbing thought that exaggerates the negative qualities of an object and wishes to harm it; one of the six root delusions.

arhat (Skt). Literally, foe destroyer. A person who has destroyed his or her inner enemy, the delusions, and attained liberation from cyclic existence.

arya (Skt). A being who has directly realized emptiness.

Aryadeva. The third-century Indian master and disciple of Nagarjuna.

Asanga. The fourth-century Indian master who received directly from Maitreya Buddha the extensive, or method, lineage of Shakyamuni Buddha's teachings; guru and brother of Vasubandhu.

asura (Skt). demigod.

Atisha Dipamkara Shrijñana (982–1054). The renowned Indian master who went to Tibet in 1042 to help in the revival of Buddhism and established the Kadam tradition. His text *Lamp for the Path* was the first lam-rim text.

attachment. A disturbing thought that exaggerates the positive qualities of an object and wishes to possess it; one of the six root delusions.

Avalokiteshvara (Skt). See *Chenrezig.*

bardo (Tib). The intermediate state; the state between death and rebirth, lasting anywhere from a moment to forty-nine days.

Ben Gungyal, Geshe (Tsültrim Gyalwa). A student of Kadampa Geshe Gönpawa, he was a robber and a thief before he renounced his life of crime, got ordained and became a great yogi.

bhumi (Skt). Literally, stage, or ground. Bodhisattvas must traverse ten bhumis on their journey to enlightenment, the first being reached with the direct perception of emptiness.

bodhicitta (Skt). The altruistic determination to achieve full enlightenment in order to free all sentient beings from suffering and bring them to enlightenment.

bodhisattva (Skt). One who possesses bodhicitta.

bodhisattva vows (Skt). The vows taken when one enters the bodhisattva path.

Boudhanath. A village just outside Kathmandu that is built around the Boudhanath Stupa, a famous Buddhist pilgrimage site.

Brahma. A powerful Hindu deity in the god realm.

buddha, a (Skt). A fully enlightened being. One who has purified all obscurations of the mind and perfected all good qualities. See also *enlightenment, Shakyamuni Buddha.*

Buddha, the (Skt). The historical Buddha, Shakymuni. See also *enlightenment, Shakyamuni Buddha.*

Buddhadharma (Skt). See *Dharma.*

buddhahood. The state of being a buddha

calm abiding. (Skt: shamatha; Tib: shi-nä). A state of concentration in which the mind is able to abide steadily, without effort and for as long as desired, on an object of meditation.

capable being (lower, middle or higher) See *three levels of practice.*

causative phenomena. Things that come about in dependence upon causes and conditions; includes all objects experienced by the senses, as well as the mind itself; impermanent phenomena.

chakras (Skt). Literally, wheels. Formed by the branching of channels at various points along the central channel, the six main chakras are at the brow, crown, throat, heart, navel and sex organ.

Chakrasamvara (Skt). Heruka Chakrasamvara. A male meditational deity of Highest Yoga Tantra, whose tantra especially emphasizes clear light.

Chandragomin. A famous seventh-century Indian lay practitioner who challenged Chandrakirti to a debate that lasted many years. His writings include *Twenty Verses on the Bodhisattva Vows* and *Letter to a Disciple.*

chang (Tib). Beer made from fermented grain, often barley.

Chengawa, Geshe (Chengawa Tsultrim Bar, 1038–1103). Patriarch of the Kadam Instruction lineage and one of Dromtönpa's three main disciples.

Chenrezig (Tib; Skt: Avalokiteshvara). The Buddha of Compassion. The male meditational deity that embodies the compassion of all the buddhas. The Dalai Lamas are said to be emanations of this deity.

chuba (Tib). Lay Tibetan's coat, with long sleeves and wrap-around front.

chu-len (Tib). Literally, "taking the essence." Chu-len pills are made of essential ingredients; taking a few each day, accomplished meditators can remain secluded in retreat for months or years without having to depend upon normal food.

circumambulation. The practice of purifying negative karma and accumulating merit by walking clockwise around a holy object such as a stupa or statue.

compassion. The sincere wish that others be free from suffering and its causes.

completion stage. The more advanced of the two stages of Highest Yoga Tantra.

daka (Skt). The male equivalent of a dakini.

dakini (Skt). Literally, sky-goer; a female being with tantric realizations of the generation or completion stages.

Dalai Lama, His Holiness (Gyalwa Tenzin Gyatso, b. 1935). Revered spiritual leader of the Tibetan people and tireless worker for world peace; winner of the 1989 Nobel Peace Prize and the 2012 Templeton Prize; a guru of Lama Zopa Rinpoche.

deity (Tib: yidam). An emanation of the enlightened mind used as an object of meditation in tantric practices.

delusions. The disturbing, negative thoughts, or minds, that are the cause of suffering. The three root delusions are ignorance, anger and attachment.

dependent arising. The way that the self and phenomena exist conventionally as relative and interdependent. They come into existence in dependence upon (1) causes and conditions, (2) their parts and, most subtly, (3) the mind imputing, or labeling, them.

desire realm. One of the three realms of samsara, comprising the hell beings, hungry ghosts, animals, humans, asuras and the six lower classes of suras; beings in this realm are preoccupied with desire for objects of the six senses.

deva (Skt). A god dwelling in a state with much comfort and pleasure in the desire, form or formless realms.

Dharamsala. A village in the north-west of India, in Himachal Pradesh. The residence of His Holiness the Dalai Lama and the Tibetan Government-in-Exile.

Dharma (Skt; Tib: chö). In general, spiritual practice; specifically, the teachings of Buddha, which protect from suffering and lead to liberation and full enlightenment.

Dharmakirti. A seventh-century Indian scholar and one of the founders of Buddhist philosophic logic.

Dharma protectors. Beings, some worldly and others enlightened, who protect Dharma teachings and practitioners.

disturbing thoughts. See *delusions.*

Domo Geshe Rinpoche (1866–1936) was a famous ascetic meditator in his early life who later established monastic communities in the Tibet-Nepal border area and in Darjeeling. He was the guru of Lama Govinda, who wrote *The Way of the White Clouds.* His next incarnation (1937–2001) was a friend of Lama Yeshe and Lama Zopa Rinpoche. The current incarnation is studying at Sera Je Monastery.

dorje (Tib; Skt: vajra). See *vajra.*

Drepung Monastery. The largest of the three major Gelugpa monasteries; founded near Lhasa by one of Lama Tsongkhapa's disciples. Now reestablished in exile in south India.

Drogön Tsangpa Gyare (1161–1211), a reincarnation of Naropa and a main disciple of Lingrepa, founded the Drukpa Kagyü lineage of Tibetan Buddhism and established monasteries, including several in Bhutan.

Dromtönpa (Dromtön Gyalwai Jungné, 1005–64). Lama Atisha's heart disciple and chief translator in Tibet; propagator of the Kadampa tradition, founder of Reting Monastery.

dzogchen (Tib). Literally, "Great Perfection," the practice to attain the mind's natural, primordial state, the central teaching of the Nyingma tradition.

eight freedoms. The eight states from which a perfect human rebirth is free. See *perfect human rebirth.*

Eight Mahayana Precepts. One-day vows to abandon killing; stealing; lying; sexual contact; taking intoxicants; sitting on high seats or beds; eating at the wrong time; and singing, dancing and wearing perfumes and jewelry.

eight worldly dharmas (Tib: jig-ten kyi chö-gyä). The worldly concerns that generally motivate the actions of ordinary beings: being happy when given gifts and unhappy when not given them; wanting to be happy and not wanting to be unhappy; wanting praise and not wanting criticism; wanting a good reputation and not wanting a bad reputation. See also note 16, page 16.

emptiness (Skt: shunyata). The absence, or lack, of true existence. Ultimately, every phenomenon is empty of existing truly, or from its own side, or independently. (See *merely labeled.*)

enlightenment. Full awakening; buddhahood; omniscience. The ultimate goal of Mahayana Buddhist practice, attained when all faults have been removed from the mind and all realizations completed; a state characterized by the perfection of compassion, wisdom and power.

evil-gone realms. See *lower realms.*

faith. There are three kinds: believing, or pure-hearted, faith; lucid, or understanding, faith—faith based on logical conviction; and yearning, or aspirational, faith.

five precepts. The vows against killing, stealing, lying, sexual misconduct and using intoxicants taken by lay Buddhist practitioners.

five uninterrupted negative karmas. Killing one's father, mother or an arhat; maliciously drawing blood from Buddha; causing a schism within the Sangha.

form realm. The second of samsara's three realms, with seventeen classes of gods.

formless realm. The highest of samsara's three realms, with four classes of gods involved in formless meditations.

four kayas. The bodies a buddha achieves at enlightenment—the truth body (*dharmakaya*) and the form body (*rupakaya*)—each divided into two aspects respectively: nature body (*svabhavikakaya*) and wisdom body (*jñanakaya*); and enjoyment body (*sambhogakaya*) and emanation body (*nirmanakaya*).

four noble truths. The subject of Shakyamuni Buddha's first teaching, or first turning of the wheel of Dharma: true suffering, true cause of suffering, true cessation of suffering and true path.

Gampopa (Sönam Rinchen) (1079–1153). The "sun-like" disciple of Milarepa, guru of the first Karmapa and author of *The Jewel Ornament of Liberation*, was also called Dagpo Lhaje (the physician from Dagpo).

Ganden Monastery. The first of the three great Gelugpa monastic universities near Lhasa, founded in 1409 by Lama Tsongkhapa. It was badly damaged in the 1960s and has now been reestablished in exile in south India.

Ganden Tripa (Tib). The title of the head of the Gelug tradition of Tibetan Buddhism. The representative of Lama Tsongkhapa, who sits on Lama Tsongkhapa's throne at Ganden Monastery.

Gelug (Tib). One of the four traditions of Tibetan Buddhism, it was founded by Lama Tsongkhapa in the early fifteenth century and has been propagated by such illustrious masters as the successive Dalai Lamas and Panchen Lamas.

Gelugpa (Tib). A follower of the Gelug tradition.

gen (Tib). Literally, elder. A title of respect.

generation stage. The first of the two stages of Highest Yoga Tantra.

geshe (Tib). Literally, spiritual friend. The title conferred on those who have completed extensive studies and examinations at Gelugpa monastic universities.

Geshe Lama Konchog. (1927–2001). A great meditator who spent over 20 years (6 in strict austerity with chu-len practice) in retreat in Tsum, a valley in Nepal, before becoming one of the main teachers at Kopan monastery.

getsul (Tib). A novice Buddhist monk.

god. See *deva*.

Gomo Rinpoche (1921–85). A lay lama, guru of both Lama Yeshe and Lama Zopa Rinpoche, who taught at many FPMT centers, especially in Italy; passed away and reincarnated in Canada.

gompa (Tib). Usually refers to the main meditation hall, or temple, within a monastery.

Gönpawa (Wangchuk Gyaltsen, 1016–82). A prominent student of both Atisha and Dromtönpa and abbot of Reting Monastery for five years. See *The Book of Kadam*, p. 658, note 525.

graduated path to enlightenment. See *lam-rim*.

Great Treatise on the Stages of the Path to Enlightenment. See *Lam-rim Chen-mo*.

guru (Skt; Tib: lama). Literally, heavy, as in heavy with Dharma knowledge. A spiritual teacher, master.

guru devotion. The sutra or tantra practice of seeing the guru as a buddha then devoting to him with thought and action.

Guru Puja (Skt; Tib: Lama Chöpa). A special Highest Yoga Tantra guru yoga practice composed by Panchen Losang Chökyi Gyaltsen.

hearer (Skt: shravaka). Follower of the Hinayana who strives for nirvana on the basis of listening to teachings from a teacher.

hell. The samsaric realm with the greatest suffering. There are eight hot hells, eight cold hells and four surrounding hells.

heresy. A general term for negative thoughts toward the guru and fundamental tenets of Buddhism such as the law of karma; the opposite of devotion.

Heruka (Skt). See *Chakrasamvara*.

Highest Yoga Tantra (Skt: anuttara yoga tantra). The fourth and supreme of the four classes of tantra. It mainly emphasizes internal activities. The others are Kriya (Action) Tantra, Charya (Performance) Tantra and Yoga (Union) Tantra.

Hinayana (Skt). Literally, the Lesser Vehicle. The path of the arhats, the goal of which is nirvana, or personal liberation from samsara.

hungry ghost (Skt: preta) One of the six classes of samsaric beings, pretas experience the greatest sufferings of hunger and thirst.

ignorance. A mental factor that obscures the mind from seeing the way in which things exist in reality. There are basically two types of ignorance, ignorance of karma and the ignorance that holds the concept of true existence, the fundamental delusion from which all other delusions arise.

illusory body. A subtle body generated through practice of the completion stage of Highest Yoga Tantra; the cause of the rupakaya.

impermanence. The gross and subtle levels of the transience of phenomena.

imprints. The seeds, or potentials, left on the mind by positive or negative actions of body, speech and mind.

individual liberation. The liberation achieved by the hearer or solitary realizer within the Hinayana tradition, as compared to enlightenment achieved by a practitioner of the Mahayana tradition.

individual liberation vows. See *pratimoksha vows.*

Indra. A powerful Hindu deity in the god realm.

inherent existence. See *true existence.*

initiation. Or empowerment. The transmission of the practice of a particular deity from a tantric master to a disciple, which permits the disciple to engage in that practice.

inner fire. See *tum-mo.*

Jampa Wangdu, Gen (d. 1984). An ascetic meditator who was a close friend of Lama Yeshe and a guru of Lama Zopa Rinpoche.

Kadampa geshe. A practitioner of the Buddhist tradition that originated in Tibet in the eleventh century with the teachings of Lama Atisha. Kadampa geshes are renowned for their practice of thought transformation.

Kagyü (Tib). One of the four traditions of Tibetan Buddhism, having its source in such illustrious lamas as Marpa, Milarepa, Gampopa and Gyalwa Karmapa.

kaka. Slang for feces.

Kalachakra (Skt). Literally, Cycle of Time. A male meditational deity of Highest Yoga Tantra. The Kalachakra Tantra contains instructions in medicine, astronomy and so forth.

Kangyur (Tib). The part of the Tibetan Canon that contains the sutras and tantras; literally, "translation of the (Buddha's) word." It contains 108 volumes.

karma (Skt). Literally, action. The working of cause and effect, whereby positive actions produce happiness and negative actions produce suffering.

khatag (Tib). A white cotton scarf used by Tibetans for greetings and for offering to holy objects.

Kharak Gomchung Wangchuk Lodrö (ca eleventh century). One of the principal disciples of the Kadam teacher Gönpawa, who was a student of both Atisha and Dromtönpa. See *The Book of Kadam*, page 661, note 547.

Kirti Tsenshab Rinpoche (1926–2006). A highly attained and learned ascetic yogi who lived in Dharamsala, India, and was one of Lama Zopa Rinpoche's gurus.

Kopan Monastery. The monastery near Boudhanath in the Kathmandu valley, Nepal, founded by Lama Yeshe and Lama Zopa Rinpoche.

Kriya Tantra. Literally "Action Tantra," the first of the four classes of tantra in Tibetan Buddhism.

kundalini yoga (Skt). A Non-Buddhist practice (yoga) that utilizes the nadis and chakras.

Kyabje (Tib). Literally, lord of refuge. A title of respect.

lama (Tib). See *guru*.

Lama Chöpa. See *Guru Puja*.

Lama Lhundrup Rigsel, Khensur Rinpoche (1941–2011) arrived at Kopan Monastery to teach the young monks at Lama Yeshe's request in 1973. He was acting abbot from 1984 to 2001, when he was officially appointed abbot and remained in that position until two months before he passed away in September 2011.

Lama Tsongkhapa Guru Yoga. A guru yoga practice related to Lama Tsongkhapa that is performed daily in Gelugpa monasteries.

Lama Yeshe (1935–1984). Born and educated in Tibet, he fled to India, where he met his chief disciple, Lama Zopa Rinpoche. They began teaching Westerners at Kopan Monastery in 1969 and founded the Foundation for the Preservation of the Mahayana Tradition (FPMT) in 1975.

lam-rim (Tib). The graduated path (to enlightenment), a step-by-step presentation of Shakyamuni Buddha's teachings first formulated by Atisha in Tibet and considered by Tibetans to be the crucial basis of any Dharma practice.

Lam-rim Chen-mo (Tib). The Great Treatise on the Stages of the Path to Enlightenment. Lama Tsongkhapa's most important work, a commentary on Atisha's *Lamp for the Path*, the fundamental lam-rim text.

Lawudo. The cave in the Solu Khumbu region of Nepal where the Lawudo Lama meditated for more than twenty years. Lama Zopa Rinpoche is recognized as the reincarnation of the Lawudo Lama.

liberation (Skt: nirvana; Tib: thar-pa). The state of complete freedom from samsara; the goal of a practitioner seeking his or her own freedom from suffering.

lineage lama. A spiritual teacher who is in the line of direct guru-disciple transmission of teachings, from Buddha to the teachers of the present day.

Lingrepa (1128–88). A great lay practitioner and guru of Tsangpa Gyare Yeshe Dorje, founder of the Drukpa Kagyü lineage of Tibetan Buddhism.

Ling Rinpoche, His Holiness (1903–83). Senior Tutor of the 14TH Dalai Lama and one of Lama Zopa Rinpoche's gurus. He was also the ninety-seventh Ganden Tripa.

lo-jong. See *thought transformation.*

loving kindness. The wish for others to have happiness and its causes.

lower realms. The three realms of cyclic existence with the most suffering: the hell, hungry ghost and animals realms.

Madhyamaka (Skt). The Middle Way School, a philosophical system founded by Nagarjuna, based on the *Perfection of Wisdom Sutras* of Shakyamuni Buddha, and considered to be the supreme presentation of Buddha's teachings on emptiness. One of the two main Mahayana schools of Buddhist tenets.

mahamudra (Skt; Tib: chag-chen). The great seal. A profound system of meditation upon the mind and the ultimate nature of reality.

Mahayana (Skt). Literally, Great Vehicle. The path of the bodhisattvas, those seeking enlightenment in order to enlighten all other beings.

Maitreya Buddha (Skt; Tib: Jampa). The Loving One. The next buddha and fifth, after Shakyamuni, of the thousand buddhas of this present world age.

mala (Skt; Tib: threng-wa). A rosary of beads for counting mantras.

mandala (Skt). The purified environment of a tantric deity; the diagram or painting representing this.

mandala offering. The symbolic offering of the entire purified universe.

Manjushri (Skt; Tib: Jampel Yang). Generally, the Buddha of Wisdom, Manjushri is also seen as a bodhisattva in the retinue of the historical Buddha.

mantra (Skt). Literally, mind protection. Sanskrit syllables usually recited in conjunction with the practice of a particular meditational deity and embodying the qualities of that deity.

Mara. The chief embodiment of the maras.

maras (Skt). Internal interferences, such as those from delusion and karma, or external interferences, such as those from spirits or devas.

Marpa (1012–1096). A great Tibetan Buddhist translator; a founding figure of the Kagyü tradition and root guru of Milarepa.

meditation. Familiarization of the mind with a virtuous object. There are two main types of meditation: analytical and placement.

merely labeled. The subtlest meaning of dependent arising; every phenomenon exists relatively, or conventionally, as a mere label, merely imputed by the mind.

merit. The positive energy accumulated in the mind as a result of virtuous actions of body, speech and mind. The principal cause of happiness.

method. All aspects of the path to enlightenment other than those related to emptiness, principally associated with the development of loving kindness, compassion and bodhicitta.

Middle Way. See *Madhyamaka.*

Milarepa (1040–1123). A great Tibetan yogi and poet famed for his impeccable relationship with his guru, Marpa, his asceticism and his songs of realization. A founding figure of the Kagyü tradition.

mind. Synonymous with consciousness. Defined as "that which is clear and knowing"; a formless entity that has the ability to perceive objects.

mind training. See *thought transformation.*

momo (Tib). A fried or steamed dumpling, usually filled with meat; a favorite food of Tibetans.

mudra (Skt). Literally, seal. Symbolic hand gestures used in images of Buddha or in tantric rituals.

nadis (Skt). The energy channels that flow through a body.

naga (Skt). Snake-like beings of the animal realm who live in or near bodies of water; commonly associated with fertility of the land but can also function as protectors of religion.

Nagarjuna. The great second-century Indian philosopher and tantric adept who propounded the Madhyamaka philosophy of emptiness.

Nalanda. A Mahayana Buddhist monastic university founded early in the first millennium in north India, not far from Bodhgaya, which served as a major source of the Buddhist teachings that spread to Tibet. Destroyed in the twelfth century.

narak (Skt). Hell, either an overall term for the hell realm, or a specific term, as in the hot hells or cold hells.

Naropa (1016–1100). The Indian mahasiddha, a disciple of Tilopa and guru of Marpa and Maitripa, who transmitted many tantric lineages, including that of the renowned Six Yogas of Naropa.

negative karma. See *nonvirtue.*

ngagpa (Tib). A lay tantric practitioner, a yogi often associated with rites and ascetic practices.

Ngawang Dhargyey, Geshe (1921–95). A tutor to many Gelug *tulkus* and resident teacher at the Library of Tibetan Works and Archives in Dharamsala, India, before leaving to establish his own centers in New Zealand, where he passed away.

Ngawang Lekshe. Lama Zopa Rinpoche's first alphabet teacher.

nirmanakaya (Skt). Emanation body; the form in which a buddha appears to ordinary beings.

nirvana (Skt). See *liberation.*

nonvirtue. Negative karma; that which results in suffering.

Nyingma (Tib). The oldest of the four traditions of Tibetan Buddhism, it traces its teachings back to Padmasambhava, or Guru Rinpoche.

nyung-nä (Tib). A two-day Thousand-Arm Chenrezig retreat that involves fasting, prostrations and silence.

obscurations. The negative imprints left on the mind by negative delusion and karma, which obscure the mind. The disturbing-thought obscurations (Tib: *nyön-drib*) obstruct attainment of liberation and the more subtle obscurations to omniscience (*she-drib*) obstruct attainment of enlightenment.

omniscient mind. See *enlightenment.*

oral transmission (Tib: lung). The verbal transmission of a teaching, meditation practice or mantra from guru to disciple, the guru having received the transmission in an unbroken lineage from the original source.

Pabongka Dechen Nyingpo (1871–1941). One of the great lamas of the twentieth century, the hugely influential author of *Liberation in the Palm of Your Hand,* a commentary on Tsongkhapa's seminal *Lam-rim Chen-mo.* He was also the root guru of HH the 14TH Dalai Lama's senior and junior tutors, Kyabje Ling Rinpoche and Kyabje Trijang Rinpoche respectively.

Padmasambhava. The eighth-century Indian tantric master mainly responsible for the establishment of Buddhism in Tibet, revered by all Tibetan Buddhists, but especially by the Nyingmapas.

pak (Tib). Tsampa mixed with butter tea.

pandit (Skt). A great scholar and philosopher.

paramitas (Skt). See *perfections.*

Paramitayana (Skt). Literally, Perfection Vehicle. Also called Sutrayana. The bodhisattva vehicle; the Mahayana sutra teachings; one of the two forms of Mahayana, the other being Tantrayana (or Vajrayana or Mantrayana).

Penpo. A county in Tibet just east of Lhasa.

perfect human rebirth. The rare human state, qualified by eight freedoms and ten richnesses, which is the ideal condition for practicing Dharma and attaining enlightenment. The eight freedoms are freedom from rebirth 1) in the hells, 2) as a hungry ghost, 3) as an animal, 4) as a long-life god, 5) as a barbarian in an irreligious country, 6) deaf, 7) as a heretic, or 8) during a time when the Buddha has not descended. The ten richnesses are 1) birth as a human being, 2) birth in the center of a religious country, 3) birth with perfect organs, 4) not having created the five uninterrupted negative karmas, 5) belief in the practice of Dharma, 6) birth when the Buddha has descended, 7) birth after the Buddha has turned the Wheel of Dharma, 8) the existence of realized teachings, 9) following the path of the Buddha's teachings, and 10) receiving the kindness and compassion of others. Taken from *The Wish-fulfilling Golden Sun.* See also Rinpoche's forthcoming book on the perfect human rebirth and *Liberation in the Palm of Your Hand,* pp. 271–87.

perfections (Skt: paramitas). The practices of a bodhisattva. On the basis of bodhicitta, a bodhisattva practices the six paramitas: generosity, morality, patience, enthusiastic perseverance, concentration and wisdom.

pervasive compounding suffering. The most subtle of the three types of suffering, it refers to the nature of the five aggregates, which are contaminated by delusion and karma.

Potowa, Geshe (Potowa Rinchen Sel, 1031–1105). Entered Reting Monastery in 1058 and became its abbot for a short time; one of the three great disciples of Dromtönpa, patriarch of the Kadampa Treatise lineage.

powa (Tib). The practice whereby the consciousness is forcibly ejected from the body into a pure land just before the moment of death.

Prajnaparamita (Skt; Eng: Perfection of Wisdom). The second teaching, or turning of the wheel, of Shakyamuni Buddha, in which the wisdom of emptiness and the path of the bodhisattva are explained.

Pramanavarttika or *Pramanavarttikakarika (Skt; Tib: Tshad ma rnam 'grel gyi tsig le'ur byas pa).* Dharmakirti's *Commentary on (Dignaga's) Compendium of Valid Cognition.*

Prasangika Madhyamaka (Skt). The Middle Way Consequence School; considered to be the highest of all Buddhist philosophical tenets.

pratimoksha (Skt). The vows of individual liberation taken by monks, nuns and lay people.

preliminaries. The practices that prepare the mind for successful tantric meditation by removing hindrances and accumulating merit.

preta (Skt). See *hungry ghost.*

prostrations. Paying respect to the guru-deity with body, speech and mind; one of the tantric preliminaries.

protector. A worldly or enlightened being who protects Buddhism and its practitioners.

puja (Skt). Literally, offering; a religious ceremony.

pure realm. A pure land of a buddha where there is no suffering; after birth in a pure land, the practitioner receives teachings directly from the buddha of that pure land, actualizes the rest of the path and then becomes enlightened.

purification. The removal, or cleansing, of negative karma and its imprints from the mind.

Rabten Rinpoche, Geshe (1920–86). The learned Gelugpa lama who was a religious assistant to His Holiness the Dalai Lama before moving to Switzerland in 1975; a guru of Lama Yeshe and Lama Zopa Rinpoche.

Rechungpa (*Dorje Drakpa,* 1083–1161). The "moon-like" disciple of Milarepa.

refuge. The heartfelt reliance upon Buddha, Dharma and Sangha for guidance on the path to enlightenment.

relics. Small, pearl-like pills that manifest spontaneously from holy objects such as statues, stupas or the cremated bodies of great practitioners.

renunciation. The state of mind not having the slightest attraction to samsaric pleasures for even a second and having the strong wish for liberation.

Reting (Radreng) Monastery. The monastery north-east of Lhasa founded by Dromtönpa and, over the years, home to many Kadampa geshes.

Rinpoche (Tib). Literally, precious one. Generally, a title given to a lama who has intentionally taken rebirth in a human body to continue helping others. A respectful title used for one's own lama.

sadhana (Skt). Literally, method of accomplishment. Meditational and mantra practices associated with a particular deity, often performed as a daily practice.

sadhu (Skt). A wandering Hindu yogi.

Sakya (Tib). One of the four principal traditions of Tibetan Buddhism, it was founded in the eleventh century by Drokmi Shakya Yeshe (933–1047).

Sakya Pandita. The title of Kunga Gyaltsen (1182–1251), a master of the Sakya tradition, who spread Tibetan Buddhism in Mongolia and China.

samsara (Skt; Tib: khor-wa). Cyclic existence; the six realms: the lower realms of the hell beings, hungry ghosts and animals, and the upper realms of the humans, demigods and gods; the recurring cycle of death and rebirth within one or other of the six realms. It also refers to the contaminated aggregates of a sentient being.

Sangha (Skt). The third object of refuge; absolute Sangha are those who have directly realized emptiness; relative Sangha are ordained monks and nuns.

self cherishing. The self-centered attitude of considering one's own happiness to be more important that that of others; the main obstacle to the realization of bodhicitta.

sentient being. Any unenlightened being; any being whose mind is not completely free of ignorance.

Sera Monastery. One of the three great Gelugpa monasteries near Lhasa; founded in the early fifteenth century by Jamchen Chöje, a disciple of Lama Tsongkhapa; now also established in exile in south India. It has two colleges, Sera Je, with which Lama Zopa Rinpoche is connected, and Sera Me.

seven-limb practice. The seven limbs are prostrating, making offerings, confessing, rejoicing, requesting to turn the Dharma wheel, requesting the teachers to remain in the world and dedicating.

Shakyamuni Buddha (563–483 BCE). The founder of the present Buddhadharma. Fourth of the one thousand founding buddhas of this present world age, he was born a prince of the Shakya clan in North India and taught the sutra and tantra paths to liberation and full enlightenment.

shamatha (Skt; Tib: shi-nä). See *calm abiding.*

Shantideva (685–763). The great Indian bodhisattva who wrote *A Guide to the Bodhisattva's Way of Life,* one of the essential Mahayana texts.

Sharawa, Geshe (1070–1141). Ordained by Geshe Potowa and guru of Geshe Chekawa.

Shawopa (Shawopa Pema Janchup, or *Shawo Gangpa,* 1067–1131). An important student of both Potowa and Phuchungwa, two of the three Kadam brothers. See *The Book of Kadam,* p. 662, note 558.

Sherpa. A native of the Everest region of Nepal. Two famous Sherpas are Sherpa Tenzin, the first person to climb Everest, and Lama Zopa Rinpoche.

shi-nä (Tib). See *calm abiding.*

shunyata. See *emptiness.*

Siddhartha, Prince. The prince of the Shakya clan who became Shakyamuni Buddha, the historical Buddha.

siddhis (Skt). realizations, usually used in reference to psychic powers (both mundane and supramundane) acquired as a by-product of the spiritual path.

single-pointed concentration. The ability to focus effortlessly and for as long as wishes on an object of meditation.

six realms. The general way that Buddhism divides the whole of cyclic existence, there being three suffering realms (hell, hungry ghost and animal) and three fortunate realms (human, demi-god and god).

Six Yogas of Naropa. A set of completion stage tantric practices: inner fire meditation, the yoga of the illusory body, the yoga of clear light, transference of consciousness, transference into another body and the yoga of the intermediate state.

Solu Khumbu. The area in north-eastern Nepal, bordering Tibet, where Lama Zopa Rinpoche was born; populated by the Sherpas.

spirits. Beings not usually visible to ordinary people; can belong to the hungry ghost or god realms; can be beneficent as well as harmful.

stupa (Skt). A reliquary symbolic of the Buddha's mind.

subtle obscurations. See *obscurations.*

sur practice (Tib). A tantric practice where tsampa is burned and offered to the spirits.

sura (Skt). Another term for deva or god.

sutra (Skt). The open discourses of Shakyamuni Buddha; a scriptural text and the teachings and practices it contains.

taking the essence. See *chu-len.*

tantra (Skt). The secret teachings of the Buddha; a scriptural text and the teachings and practices it contains. Tantric practices generally involve identification of oneself with a fully enlightened deity in order to transform one's own impure states of body, speech and mind into the pure states of that enlightened being. See also *Vajrayana.*

tantric vows. Vows taken by tantric practitioners.

Tara (Skt; Tib: Drölma). A female meditational deity who embodies the enlightened activity of all the buddhas; often referred to as the mother of the buddhas of the past, present and future.

ten nonvirtues. The three nonvirtues of body are killing, stealing and sexual misconduct; the four nonvirtues of speech are lying, slander, harsh speech and gossip; the three nonvirtues of mind are covetousness, ill will and wrong views.

ten richnesses. The ten qualities that characterize a perfect human rebirth. See *perfect human rebirth.*

Tengyur (Tib; Skt: shastra). The commentaries on the Buddha's sutras by the Indian great masters.

thangka (Tib). Painted or appliquéd depictions of deities, mandalas, buddhas and so forth, usually set in a framework of colorful brocade.

Thogme Zangpo (Gyalse Ngulchu Thogme, approx. 1297–1371). A great scholar and bodhisattva, he wrote *The Thirty-seven Practices of a Bodhisattva* and a famous commentary on Shantideva's *Guide.*

thought transformation (Tib: lo-jong). A powerful approach to the development of bodhicitta, in which the mind is trained to use all situations, both happy and unhappy, as a means to destroy self-cherishing and self-grasping.

Three Baskets. See *Tripitaka.*

three doors. Body, speech and mind.

three great meanings. The happiness of future lives, liberation and enlightenment.

three higher trainings. The higher trainings in morality, concentration and wisdom.

Three Jewels. Another term for the Triple Gem.

three kayas. Dharmakaya, sambhogakaya and nirmanakaya. See also *four kayas.*

three levels of practice. Also known as the three scopes, the three levels of lower, medium and higher capable being, based on the motivations of trying to attain a better future rebirth, liberation or enlightenment.

three poisons. Ignorance, attachment and anger.

three principal aspects of the path. The essential points of the lam-rim: renunciation of samsara, bodhicitta and right view, or emptiness.

Tilopa (988–1069). Indian mahasiddha and guru of Naropa; source of many lineages of tantric teachings.

transmigratory beings. Sentient being, beings who transmigrate from one realm to another, locked in cyclic existence.

Trijang Rinpoche, His Holiness (1901–81). Junior Tutor of the His Holiness the 14th Dalai Lama and the root guru of Lama Yeshe and Lama Zopa Rinpoche. He edited *Liberation in the Palm of Your Hand.*

Tripitaka (Skt). Literally, "three baskets," the way the Buddha's teachings are traditionally divided: the *Vinaya* (monastic discipline and ethics), *Sutra* (the Buddha's discourses) and *Abhidharma* (logic and philosophy).

Triple Gem. The objects of Buddhist refuge: Buddha, Dharma and Sangha.

true existence. The type of concrete, real existence from its own side that everything appears to possess; in fact, everything is empty of true existence.

tsampa (Tib). Roasted barley flour, a Tibetan staple food.

tsa-tsa (Tib). A print of a buddha's image made in clay or plaster from a carved mold.

Tsongkhapa, Lama (1357–1419). The revered teacher and accomplished practitioner who founded the Gelug order of Tibetan Buddhism. An emanation of Manjushri, the Buddha of Wisdom.

Tsum. A region in western Nepal, where Geshe Lama Konchog (and his reincarnation) were born.

tum-mo (Tib). A completion stage tantric meditation technique, the first of the Six Yogas of Naropa, in which all the winds are brought into the central channel to generate the clear light.

twenty-five absorptions. The various visions that a person sees as he is dying, due to the winds (subtle energies) absorbing into the central channel.

Vaibhashika (Skt). The Great Exposition School, one of the two principal Hinayana schools of Buddhist tenets.

vajra (Skt; Tib: dorje). Literally, "adamantine," often translated as "thunderbolt" but usually left untranslated, the vajra is the four- or five-spoke implement used in tantric practice.

vajra and bell. Implements used during tantric rituals: the vajra, held in the right hand, symbolizes bliss and the bell, held in the left, emptiness.

Vajrasattva (Skt; Tib: Dorje Sempa). A male tantric deity used especially for purification.

Vajrayana (Skt). Also known as Tantrayana, Mantrayana or Secret Mantra. The quickest vehicle of Buddhism, capable of leading to the attainment of full enlightenment within one lifetime.

Vajrayogini (Skt; Tib: Dorje Näljorma). A semi-wrathful female deity in the Chakrasamvara cycle.

Vinaya (Skt.); The Buddha's teachings on ethical discipline (morality), monastic conduct and so forth; one of the three baskets.

virtue. Positive karma; that which results in happiness.

virtuous friend (Tib: ge-wai she-nyen). See *guru*.

voidness. See emptiness.

winds. Energy-winds. Subtle energies that flow in the channels in the body, which enable the body to function and which are associated with different levels of mind.

wisdom. All aspects of the path to enlightenment associated with the development of the realization of emptiness.

wish-granting jewel. A jewel that brings its possessor everything that he or she desires.

Yamantaka. A wrathful tantric deity.

yidam. See *deity*.

yoga (Skt). Literally, to yoke. The spiritual discipline to which one yokes oneself in order to achieve enlightenment.

Yoga Tantra (Skt). The third of the four classes of Buddhist tantra.

yogi (Skt). A highly realized meditator.

Bibliography

Atisha and Dromtönpa. *The Book of the Kadam*. Translated by Thupten Jinpa. Boston: Wisdom Publications, 2008.

Buddha Shakyamuni. *The Vajra Cutter Sutra (aka The Diamond Cutter Sutra)*. Translated by George Churinoff. Portland: FPMT, 2002. (See www.fpmt.org.)

Dalai Lama, The Seventh. *Nyung Nä: The Means of Achievement of the Eleven-Face Great Compassionate One*. Translated by Lama Zopa Rinpoche and George Churinoff. Portland: FPMT, 2005.

Dhargyey, Geshe Ngawang, *Tibetan Tradition of Mental Development*. Dharamsala, India: Library of Tibetan Works and Archives, 1974, 1985.

FPMT. *Essential Buddhist Prayers: An FPMT Prayer Book, Volume 1, Basic Prayers and Practices*. Portland: FPMT, 2006.

———. *FPMT Retreat Prayer Book: Prayers and Practices for Retreat*. Portland: FPMT, 2009.

Gampopa. *The Jewel Ornament of Liberation*. Translated by Khenpo Konchog Gyaltsen Rinpoche. Ithaca: Snow Lion Publications, 1998.

Gyatso, Tenzin, the Fourteenth Dalai Lama. *Path to Bliss: A Practical Guide to the Stages of Meditation*. Translated by Thupten Jinpa. Ithaca: Snow Lion Publications, 1991. (Based on Panchen Losang Chökyi Gyältsen's *Path to Bliss Leading to Omniscience*.)

Jinpa, Thupten (trans). *Mind Training: The Great Collection*. Boston: Wisdom Publications, 2006.

Mackenzie, Vicki. *Cave in the Snow*. London: Bloomsbury, 1998.

Lati Rinbochay and Jeffrey Hopkins. *Death, Intermediate State and Rebirth in Tibetan Buddhism*. Ithaca: Snow Lion Publications, 1985.

Milarepa. *The Hundred Thousand Songs of Milarepa*. Translated by Garma C. C. Chang. Boston: Shambhala Publications, 1999.

Nagarjuna. *Nagarjuna's Letter to a Friend*. Translated by Padmakara Translation Group. Ithaca: Snow Lion Publications, 2005.

———. *Nagarjuna's Letter*. Translated by Geshe Lobsang Tharchin and Artemus B.

Engle. Dharamsala: Library of Tibetan Works and Archives, 1979, 1995.

———. *Buddhist Advice for Living and Liberation: Nagarjuna's Precious Garland.* Translated by Jeffrey Hopkins. Ithaca: Snow Lion Publications, 1998.

Pabongka Rinpoche, *Liberation in the Palm of Your Hand.* Translated by Michael Richards. Boston: Wisdom Publications, 1991, 2006. (Page numbers refer to the latter edition.)

———. *Liberation in Our Hands* (three parts). Translated by Geshe Lobsang Tharchin and Artemus B. Engle. Howell: Mahayana Sutra and Tantra Press, 1990, 1994, 2001.

——— (Dechen Nyingpo) and Lama Zopa Rinpoche. *Heart Advice for Retreat,* Portland: FPMT, 2007.

Panchen Losang Chökyi Gyältsen and Jamphäl Lhundrub. *Lama Chöpa Jorchö.* Compiled and edited by Lama Zopa Rinpoche. Portland: FPMT, 2011.

Patrul Rinpoche. *The Words of My Perfect Teacher.* Translated by Padmakara Translation Group. Boston: Shambhala Publications, 1998.

Rabten, Geshe. *The Life of a Tibetan Monk.* Translated by B. Alan Wallace. Le Mont Pèlerin: Editions Rabten, 2000.

Rinchen, Geshe Sonam. *Atisha's Lamp for the Path to Enlightenment.* Translated by Ruth Sonam. Ithaca: Snow Lion Publications, 1997.

———. *The Three Principal Aspects of the Path.* Translated by Ruth Sonam. Ithaca: Snow Lion Publications, 1999.

Shabkar Tsogdruk Rangdrol. *The Life of Shabkar: The Autobiography of a Tibetan Yogin.* Translated by Matthieu Ricard (and others). Ithaca: Snow Lion Publications, 2001.

Shantideva. *A Guide to the Bodhisattva's Way of Life.* Translated by Stephen Batchelor. Dharamsala: Library of Tibetan Works and Archives, 1979, 1992.

Tsongkhapa, *The Great Treatise on the Stages of the Path to Enlightenment (Lam Rim Chen Mo)* (three volumes). Translated by the Lamrim Chenmo Translation Committee. Ithaca: Snow Lion Publications, 2000, 2004, 2002.

———. *The Three Principal Aspects of the Path.* Translated by Lama Zopa Rinpoche. Boston: Lama Yeshe Wisdom Archive, 2006. (See www.lamayeshe.com.)

———. *The Principal Teachings of Buddhism.* Translated by Geshe Lobsang Tharchin. Howell: Mahayana Sutra & Tantra Press, 1988.

Wangmo, Jamyang. *The Lawudo Lama.* Boston: Wisdom Publications, 2005.

Yeshe, Lama Thubten, *The Essence of Tibetan Buddhism.* Boston: Lama Yeshe Wisdom Archive, 2001.

Zopa Rinpoche, Lama. *Aroma Charity for Spirits (Sur Offering).* Portland: FPMT, 2006.

———. *Bodhisattva Attitude: How to Dedicate Your Life to Others.* Boston: Lama Yeshe Wisdom Archive, 2012.

———. *The Door to Satisfaction: The Heart Advice of a Tibetan Buddhist Master.* Boston: Wisdom Publications, 2001.

———. *Heart of the Path: Seeing the Guru as Buddha.* Boston: Lama Yeshe Wisdom Archive, 2009.

———. *Teachings from the Medicine Buddha Retreat.* Boston: Lama Yeshe Wisdom Archive, 2009.

———. *Transforming Problems Into Happiness.* Boston: Wisdom Publications, 2001.

———. *Virtue and Reality.* Boston: Lama Yeshe Wisdom Archive, 1998, 2008.

———. *The Wish-fulfilling Golden Sun.* Boston: Lama Yeshe Wisdom Archive, 1976. (See www.lamayeshe.com.)

——— and Kathleen McDonald. *Wholesome Fear: Transforming Your Anxiety about Impermanence and Death.* Boston: Wisdom Publications, 2010.

Index

LAMA YESHE WISDOM ARCHIVE

The LAMA YESHE WISDOM ARCHIVE (LYWA) is the collected works of Lama Thubten Yeshe and Lama Thubten Zopa Rinpoche. Lama Zopa Rinpoche, its spiritual director, founded the ARCHIVE in 1996.

Lama Yeshe and Lama Zopa Rinpoche began teaching at Kopan Monastery, Nepal, in 1970. Since then, their teachings have been recorded and transcribed. At present we have well over 12,000 hours of digital audio and some 90,000 pages of raw transcript. Many recordings, mostly teachings by Lama Zopa Rinpoche, remain to be transcribed, and as Rinpoche continues to teach, the number of recordings in the ARCHIVE increases accordingly. Most of our transcripts have been neither checked nor edited.

Here at the LYWA we are making every effort to organize the transcription of that which has not yet been transcribed, edit that which has not yet been edited, and generally do the many other tasks detailed below.

The work of the LAMA YESHE WISDOM ARCHIVE falls into two categories: archiving and dissemination.

Archiving requires managing the recordings of teachings by Lama Yeshe and Lama Zopa Rinpoche that have already been collected, collecting recordings of teachings given but not yet sent to the ARCHIVE, and collecting recordings of Lama Zopa's on-going teachings, talks, advice and so forth as he travels the world for the benefit of all. Incoming media are then catalogued and stored safely while being kept accessible for further work.

We organize the transcription of audio, add the transcripts to the already existent database of teachings, manage this database, have transcripts checked, and make transcripts available to editors or others doing research on or practicing these teachings.

Other archiving activities include working with video and photographs of the Lamas and digitizing ARCHIVE materials.

Dissemination involves making the Lamas' teachings available through various avenues including books for free distribution and sale, eBooks on a wide range of readers, lightly edited transcripts, a monthly e-letter (see below), DVDs and online video, articles in *Mandala* and other magazines and on our website. Irrespective of the medium we choose, the teachings require a significant amount of work to prepare them for distribution.

This is just a summary of what we do. The ARCHIVE was established with virtually no seed funding and has developed solely through the kindness of many people, some of whom we have mentioned at the front of this book and most of the others on our website. We sincerely thank them all.

Our further development similarly depends upon the generosity of those who see the benefit and necessity of this work, and we would be extremely grateful for your help. Thus we hereby appeal to you for your kind support. If you would like to make a contribution to help us with any of the above tasks or to sponsor books for free distribution, please contact us:

LAMA YESHE WISDOM ARCHIVE
PO Box 636, Lincoln, MA 01773, USA
Telephone (781) 259-4466
info@LamaYeshe.com
www.LamaYeshe.com

The LAMA YESHE WISDOM ARCHIVE is a 501(c)(3) tax-deductible, non-profit corporation dedicated to the welfare of all sentient beings and totally dependent upon your donations for its continued existence. Thank you so much for your support. You may contribute by mailing a check, bank draft or money order to our Lincoln address; by making a donation on our secure website; by mailing us your credit card number or phoning it in; or by transferring funds directly to our bank—ask us for details.

LAMA YESHE WISDOM ARCHIVE MEMBERSHIP

In order to raise the money we need to employ editors to make available the thousands of hours of teachings mentioned above, we have established a membership plan. Membership costs US$1,000 and its main benefit is that you will be helping make the Lamas' incredible teachings available to a worldwide audience. More direct and tangible benefits to you personally include free Lama Yeshe and Lama Zopa Rinpoche books from the ARCHIVE and Wisdom Publications, a year's subscription to *Mandala* and a year of monthly pujas by the monks and nuns at Kopan Monastery with your personal dedication. Please see www.LamaYeshe.com for more information.

MONTHLY E-LETTER

Each month we send out a free e-letter containing our latest news and a previously unpublished teaching by Lama Yeshe or Lama Zopa Rinpoche. To see more than one hundred back-issues or to subscribe with your email address, please go to our website.

The Foundation for the Preservation of the Mahayana Tradition

The Foundation for the Preservation of the Mahayana Tradition (FPMT) is an international organization of Buddhist meditation study and retreat centers, both urban and rural, monasteries, publishing houses, healing centers and other related activities founded in 1975 by Lama Thubten Yeshe and Lama Thubten Zopa Rinpoche. At present, there are more than 160 FPMT centers, projects and services in over forty countries worldwide.

The FPMT has been established to facilitate the study and practice of Mahayana Buddhism in general and the Tibetan Gelug tradition, founded in the fifteenth century by the great scholar, yogi and saint, Lama Je Tsongkhapa, in particular.

Every quarter, the Foundation publishes a wonderful news journal, *Mandala*, from its International Office in the United States of America. To subscribe or view back issues, please go to the *Mandala* website, www.mandalamagazine.org, or contact:

FPMT
1632 SE 11th Avenue, Portland, OR 97214
Telephone (503) 808-1588; Fax (503) 808-1589
info@fpmt.org
www.fpmt.org

The FPMT website also offers teachings by His Holiness the Dalai Lama, Lama Yeshe, Lama Zopa Rinpoche and many other highly respected teachers in the tradition, details about the FPMT's educational programs, an online learning center, a complete listing of FPMT centers all over the world and in your area, a link to the excellent FPMT Store, and links to FPMT centers—where you will find details of their programs—and other interesting Buddhist and Tibetan pages.

FPMT Online Learning Center

In 2009, FPMT Education Services launched the FPMT Online Learning Center to make FPMT education programs and materials more accessible to students worldwide. While continuing to expand, the Online Learning Center currently offers the following courses:

- Meditation 101
- Buddhism in a Nutshell
- Heart Advice for Death and Dying
- Discovering Buddhism
- Basic Program
- Living in the Path

Living in the Path is particularly unique in that it takes teachings by Lama Zopa Rinpoche and presents them in theme-related modules that include teaching transcripts, video extracts, meditations, mindfulness practices, karma yoga, and questions to assist students in integrating the material. Current modules include: *Motivation for Life, Taking the Essence, What Buddhists Believe, Guru is Buddha, Introduction to Atisha's text, The Happiness of Dharma, Bringing Emptiness to Life, The Secret of the Mind, Diamond Cutter Meditation,* and *Refuge & Bodhichitta.*

All of our online programs provide audio and/or video teachings of the subjects, guided meditations, readings, and other support materials. Online forums for each program provide students the opportunity to discuss the subject matter and to ask questions of forum elders. Additionally, many retreats led by Lama Zopa Rinpoche are available in full via audio and/or video format.

Education Services is committed to creating a dynamic virtual learning environment and adding more FPMT programming and materials for you to enjoy via the Online Learning Center.

Visit us at: onlinelearning.fpmt.org

OTHER TEACHINGS OF LAMA YESHE AND LAMA ZOPA RINPOCHE CURRENTLY AVAILABLE

BOOKS PUBLISHED BY WISDOM PUBLICATIONS

Wisdom Energy, by Lama Yeshe and Lama Zopa Rinpoche
Introduction to Tantra, by Lama Yeshe
Transforming Problems, by Lama Zopa Rinpoche
The Door to Satisfaction, by Lama Zopa Rinpoche
Becoming Vajrasattva: The Tantric Path of Purification, by Lama Yeshe
The Bliss of Inner Fire, by Lama Yeshe
Becoming the Compassion Buddha, by Lama Yeshe
Ultimate Healing, by Lama Zopa Rinpoche
Dear Lama Zopa, by Lama Zopa Rinpoche
How to Be Happy, by Lama Zopa Rinpoche
Wholesome Fear, by Lama Zopa Rinpoche with Kathleen McDonald
When the Chocolate Runs Out, by Lama Yeshe

ABOUT LAMA YESHE:

Reincarnation: The Boy Lama, by Vicki Mackenzie

ABOUT LAMA ZOPA RINPOCHE:

The Lawudo Lama, by Jamyang Wangmo

You can get more information about and order the above titles at wisdompubs.org or call toll free in the USA on 1-800-272-4050.

TRANSCRIPTS, PRACTICES AND OTHER MATERIALS

See the LYWA and FPMT websites for transcripts of teachings by Lama Yeshe and Lama Zopa Rinpoche and other practices written or compiled by Lama Zopa Rinpoche.

What to do with Dharma teachings

The Buddhadharma is the true source of happiness for all sentient beings. Books like this show you how to put the teachings into practice and integrate them into your life, whereby you get the happiness you seek. Therefore, anything containing Dharma teachings, the names of your teachers or holy images is more precious than other material objects and should be treated with respect. To avoid creating the karma of not meeting the Dharma again in future lives, please do not put books (or other holy objects) on the floor or underneath other stuff, step over or sit upon them, or use them for mundane purposes such as propping up wobbly chairs or tables. They should be kept in a clean, high place, separate from worldly writings, and wrapped in cloth when being carried around. These are but a few considerations.

Should you need to get rid of Dharma materials, they should not be thrown in the rubbish but burned in a special way. Briefly: do not incinerate such materials with other trash, but alone, and as they burn, recite the mantra OM AH HUM. As the smoke rises, visualize that it pervades all of space, carrying the essence of the Dharma to all sentient beings in the six samsaric realms, purifying their minds, alleviating their suffering, and bringing them all happiness, up to and including enlightenment. Some people might find this practice a bit unusual, but it is given according to tradition. Thank you very much.

DEDICATION

Through the merit created by preparing, reading, thinking about and sharing this book with others, may all teachers of the Dharma live long and healthy lives, may the Dharma spread throughout the infinite reaches of space, and may all sentient beings quickly attain enlightenment.

In whichever realm, country, area or place this book may be, may there be no war, drought, famine, disease, injury, disharmony or unhappiness, may there be only great prosperity, may everything needed be easily obtained, and may all be guided by only perfectly qualified Dharma teachers, enjoy the happiness of Dharma, have love and compassion for all sentient beings, and only benefit and never harm each other.

LAMA THUBTEN ZOPA RINPOCHE was born in Thangme, Nepal, in 1945. At the age of three he was recognized as the reincarnation of the Lawudo Lama, who had lived nearby at Lawudo, within sight of Rinpoche's Thangme home. Rinpoche's own description of his early years may be found in his book, *The Door to Satisfaction*. At the age of ten, Rinpoche went to Tibet and studied and meditated at Domo Geshe Rinpoche's monastery near Pagri, until the Chinese occupation of Tibet in 1959 forced him to forsake Tibet for the safety of Bhutan. Rinpoche then went to the Tibetan refugee camp at Buxa Duar, West Bengal, India, where he met Lama Yeshe, who became his closest teacher. The Lamas went to Nepal in 1967, and over the next few years built Kopan and Lawudo Monasteries. In 1971 Lama Zopa Rinpoche gave the first of his famous annual lam-rim retreat courses, which continue at Kopan to this day. In 1974, with Lama Yeshe, Rinpoche began traveling the world to teach and establish centers of Dharma. When Lama Yeshe passed away in 1984, Rinpoche took over as spiritual head of the FPMT, which has continued to flourish under his peerless leadership. More details of Rinpoche's life and work may be found in *The Lawudo Lama* and on the LYWA and FPMT websites. Rinpoche's published teachings include *Wisdom Energy* (with Lama Yeshe), *Transforming Problems, Virtue and Reality, Ultimate Healing, Heart of the Path* and *How Things Exist*.

GORDON MCDOUGALL first met Tibetan Buddhism in Hong Kong in 1986 and was the director of Cham-Tse Ling, the FPMT center there, for two years. Since then he has been involved with various FPMT centers and projects. In 2001 he became the spiritual program coordinator of Jamyang Buddhist Centre, London, where he worked with the resident teacher, Geshe Tashi Tsering, to develop the Foundation of Buddhist Thought, the two-year campus and correspondence course that is part of the FPMT core education program. He administered the course and worked at Jamyang for seven years, editing the six FBT books, first as study books for the course and then as "stand-alone" books for Wisdom Publications. He has also led lam-rim courses in Europe and India and was involved with the creation of the Discovering Buddhism program. After moving to Bath he became a full time editor with the LAMA YESHE WISDOM ARCHIVE in 2008, managing the Publishing the FPMT Lineage project and editing the books in this series.